Worship
and Grace

Worship and Grace

Dave Bilbrough

New Wine Press

New Wine Ministries
PO Box 17
Chichester
West Sussex
United Kingdom
PO19 2AW

Scripture quotations are taken from the following versions of the Bible:

NIV – The Holy Bible, New International Version. Copyright © 1973, 1978, 1984 by International Bible Society. Used by permission of Hodder and Stoughton Limited.

NKJV – The Holy Bible, New King James Version. Copyright © 1982 by Thomas Nelson Inc.

The Message. Copyright © 1993, 1994, 1995, 1996, 2000, 2001, 2002 by Eugene H. Peterson.

TLB – The Living Bible. Copyright © 1978 Tyndale House Publishers.

ISBN 1-903725-68-2

Typeset by CRB Associates, Reepham, Norfolk
Cover design by CCD, www.ccdgroup.co.uk
Printed in Malta

Acknowledgements

This book would not have been possible without the many people who, knowingly or unknowingly, have influenced and shaped not only my thinking but my life. Particular thanks go to Tony Horsfall for his friendship and insights, and Maurice Smith who has taught me so much about grace.

Thanks also to...

- Adrian and Pauline Hawkes, Mike and Chris Walters, Roger Stedman, and Gerald and Anona Coates.
- Jan Doidge, my secretary who always works so hard and conscientiously.
- My team and band: Steve Criddle, Simon Nelson, Lizzie Deane, Danny Cope, Ron Knights and Matt Hay.
- Tim Pettingale for suggesting and believing in this project.

- my two sons, Jon and Dan (who is also my drummer), and Ros my new daughter-in-law, all of whom I am very proud.
- and of course to Pat, the love of my life, who is my constant support and encouragement.

"Grace isn't a little prayer you chant before receiving a meal. It's a way to live."
(Jackie Windspear)

We all need God's grace working actively in our lives

One morning, someone prayed the following prayer:

> *"So far today God, I have done alright.*
> *I haven't gossiped; I haven't lost my temper;*
> *I haven't been greedy, nasty, grumpy, selfish*
> *or overindulgent . . . "*

> *" . . . I'm really glad about that Lord, but in a*
> *few minutes I am going to get out of bed. And*
> *from then on I am going to need a lot more*
> *help!"*

Most of us understand that we need God's grace working actively in our lives. It makes no difference if we have an active role in ministry in the church such as worship leading, teaching, preaching, caring for people pastorally, or whether we are holding down a nine-to-five job, we all need to function out of God's grace.

Simply put, "law" means that we have got to do something for God, but "grace" means that God does something for us. We need to be sure that our vision is fixed constantly on the God who does things for us. The problem is, we often just don't see God in that way because our vision is flawed. We don't see Him as clearly as we ought to. I hope the following story serves as an illustration:

Most people who know me, know that I am an ardent West Ham supporter. In their hey day they were *the team* to watch. The squad included such luminaries as Bobby Moore, Geoff Hurst and Martin Peters, without whom England would never have won the '66 world cup! Supporting the Hammers is something of a tradition in my family. First of all my Granddad supported West Ham, then my Dad, and as soon as I was old enough to stand up straight I was taken along to Upton Park to see the glorious team in action.

Most of my school mates were enthusiastic supporters too. All they could talk about was West Ham. As for me, I would go down to Upton Park and stand on the terraces, but I really couldn't see very much. Occasionally I would see the ball come flying past me. At other times I would see a claret and blue shirt flash by. I would cheer along with everybody else, but if you asked me what I thought of West Ham, I would have to say I wasn't that impressed.

Then, when I was nine or ten, sitting in my class at school, my teacher called over to me, "Bilbrough, I have been looking at you and I think that you're either an exceedingly dim child or you can't read what has been written on the blackboard. I am going to send you to the optician."

I duly went and at the end of my eye examination the optician said to me, "I am sorry, but you are going to need a set of National Health glasses." Can you remember what National Health glasses looked like? In my day they were even worse than they are now. They were very round and very unfashionable with springy wire frames! I don't know why, but girls always seemed to have a pink plaster on the left lens to hold it in! I remember putting these glasses on and feeling incredibly embarrassed because those were the days when "short back and sides" haircuts were in fashion and when I put them on the end of the arms curled round my ears making them stick right out. I looked like the Milky Bar kid!

However, although I felt incredibly embarrassed, I suddenly I realised that I could *see* with a vision that I didn't know I possessed!

Before I had those glasses I would literally look in the mirror and see a fuzzy face that I thought was me. I would cross roads and cars would swerve out of the way to avoid me. I thought that's what happened to everyone. Of course, the next time I went to watch West Ham play I was transformed. Now I could see what a great team they were. I became a die-hard fan, not because my family and friends were fans, but because I could now see for myself how good they were.

The point of the story is, if we are to grow in maturity as believers and in our personal worship of God we too need to see for ourselves *who Christ is*, and see that His nature towards us is unreserved, undiluted, complete and utter grace upon grace upon grace. Our vision of who God is must be utterly transformed.

If it's not, then the longer we function in ministry, or try to walk out our calling, or try to use our gifts for God's glory, the harder it will become. Rather than simply *being* and enjoying God's grace and favour upon our lives, we will be task-focused "do-ers", going round in circles, striving for achievement and trying to fulfil what we believe are God's expectations of us. Without a vision of grace we are performance-orientated workers, labouring on a treadmill we believe is the path to earning God's favour.

> **"We throw open our doors to God and discover at the same moment that he has already thrown open his door to us. We find ourselves standing where we always hoped we might stand – out in the wide open spaces of God's grace and glory, standing tall and shouting our praise."**
> (Romans 5:2)

But trying by our own efforts to bring God's blessing into our lives is self-defeating and exhausting. We can strain and struggle, but we will never able to pull down from heaven what God is willing to give us freely. The good news that Jesus came to bring is that God loves us unreservedly. He knows full well that no matter how hard we try to be "good Christians", we will never be "good enough". How can we possibly judge what is *good enough* anyway? Thankfully, this question has been answered in the person of

Jesus – the only One who was ever good enough and who met God's expectations for His life fully. It is through Jesus alone that we have free access into all the blessings God has in store for us.

Jesus came to reverse the trend of every world system and every religion; to turn on its head the ideology of the religious people of His day. Jesus came to change our whole perspective. He came to live the perfect life. He completed His mission so that for us in the future, the emphasis would never again be on the treadmill of working to please God, but upon Christ Himself who accomplished, fulfilled and achieved all that was necessary to win for us peace with the Father.

Carrying God on our shoulders

As a musician, every now and then I have the wonderful privilege of travelling overseas. In particular, some of the countries of the Far East have been a real joy to visit. I appreciate the culture and food, however occasionally I am reminded of the differences between the spiritual landscapes of the Eastern and Western worlds. In the Far East there are certain religious days on the calendar that are set apart as public holidays to worship idols. These "gods" are worshipped by many people and a sight you will often see is a god in the form of an idol being carried through the streets on someone's shoulders.

In Isaiah 45:20–21 God declares,

> *"Ignorant are those who carry about idols*
> *of wood,*
> *who pray to gods that cannot save ...*
> *there is no God apart from me,*
> *a righteous God and a Saviour."*

And again in Isaiah 46:7 speaking of a manmade idol He says,

> *"They lift it to their shoulders and carry it;*
> *they set it up in its place, and there it*
> *stands.*
> *From that spot it cannot move.*
> *Though one cries out to it, it does not answer;*
> *it cannot save him from his troubles."*

But God reveals His heart towards us, and how He desires to carry us, in Isaiah 46:4:

> *"... I am he who will sustain you.*
> *I have made you and I will carry you;*
> *I will sustain you and I will rescue you."*

God makes it abundantly clear to us that we are not to carry idols around with us, either literally or metaphorically! He wants to carry our burdens for us and He wants to set us free. I want you to ask yourself, are you trying to carry God, or are you allowing God to carry you?

Carry Me

You take me by the hand
And though there are times I don't understand
Your love will never fail
And my heart belongs to you
Even when the rain clouds break
And the cold wind blows all around me
I will not be put to shame
Lord my hope is in your name
You will carry me on your shoulders
And lead me home

Carry me over troubled waters
Carry me over stormy seas
When the skies are dark and heavy
By your grace You'll carry me
Though the way can seem uncertain
Because the time of change has come
You will carry me on your shoulders
And lead me home[1]

[1] *Carry Me*, written by Dave Bilbrough. Copyright 2000, Kingsway/
Thank You Music, from the album *Personal Worship*.

As we live out our Christian lives it is all too easy to become weighed down by our responsibilities. For me, it could be the responsibility of leading worship, finding appropriate songs, and being sensitive to the Holy Spirit's leading. For others it will be a whole variety of other tasks and commitments. But in all that we do, are we allowing "things" to weigh us down and crush the life and joy out of us, or are we allowing to God to hold us up and carry us? Religion is very hard work; it is effort, strife and struggling. God's grace cuts right across such thinking and has the ability to liberate us to function as He intended us to.

> **"Find a quiet, secluded place so you won't be tempted to role-play before God. Just be there as simply and honestly as you can manage. The focus will shift from you to God, and you will begin to sense his grace."**
> (Matthew 6:6)

I grew up in the sixties when weekend television was a real event. As a kid, the highlight of my Friday night was a show called *Crackerjack*.

Some readers may be old enough to remember it! They did lots of crazy games with kids and the consolation prize was always a Crackerjack pencil!

Saturday night was reserved for the police drama, *Dixon of Dock Green*. It was the first real TV programme about police work. Now there are scores of them, but I liked this show because PC Dixon always gave a little epilogue at the end of the show summarising what had happened and telling you how crime didn't pay! PC Dixon always looked far too old to be an active policeman and in today's world his fatherly chats to camera would have hardly persuaded the local hoodie graffiti artists to lay down their spray cans and take up a neighbourhood road sweeping scheme! But, it had a charm of its own.

Sunday night however, was the best TV night of all. We always had the *Sunday Night at the London Palladium* variety show, during which all the latest pop bands, comedians and magicians would come and do a turn. Amongst them would often be a guy doing a plate spinning act. He would start at the back of the auditorium and gradually work his way further and further towards the front, setting a long line of plates spinning on sticks and trying to keep them all going without any falling off and smashing.

We used to call this entertainment before the
Eurovision Song Contest came along!

If our focus is only upon what we do for God,
rather than who we are in Him, then we will be
little better than spiritual plate spinners! We will
run around desperately trying to keep all our
plates (responsibilities) spinning, especially those
that are looking very wobbly and are about to
come crashing down. We may get into such a
position due to a genuine zeal and a desire to
serve God, but in our enthusiasm we often get
carried away with things that God has not called
us to do. Not only is "plate spinning" not a good
way to manage your life, but it actually hinders
that which God really wants: for us to be still in
His presence and allow Him to guide and direct us.
We need constantly to review where we are at in
life and make sure that we are functioning under
God's grace and not under law.

I love a nice cup of coffee first thing in the
morning. In fact the highlight of the morning for
me is when I wake up and make that first cup of
coffee. I love the smell of it, I love drinking it, and
I love then to go and make myself another one.
Bovril, however, is an acquired taste. For the
uninitiated "Bovril" is a very British drink made
out of beef stock and served piping hot. Some

people love it. It's designed to warm you up after a hearty stroll on a winter's day out in the country,

> "Grace is available for each of us every day –
> our spiritual daily bread – but we've got to
> remember to ask for it with a grateful heart
> and not worry about whether there will
> be enough for tomorrow."
> (Sarah Ban Breathnach)

or an afternoon on the football terraces. In fact, by 1994 enough Bovril had been sold to make over 90 million mugs of the hot drink – that's enough for every person attending a Football League match to have one at the beginning, one at half-time, one at the end and another cup when they got home! It must be popular, but have you ever tried mixing coffee and Bovril? I doubt it. It would taste horrible. It's awful when things that don't mix are put together and they become neither one thing nor the other. Yet, ever so subtly in our Christian lives we mix up law and grace in our walk with God – and they don't mix well! We fall into the achievement trap so easily. That's why we need to keep reminding ourselves:

it's not what we can do for God, but what God *has done* for us.

I have been a songwriter for more than thirty years now. For me, there is nothing better than composing a new song to the Lord, but I suffer from falling into the performance trap just as much as anyone. Ever so subtly I can slip into writing something to God and thinking that it will somehow gain me a bit of extra favour and acceptance with Him. And of course, it won't! The thing that helps keep me fresh is when I am reminded why I do what I do. When someone asks me, "Why are you still writing songs?" I come to that place again where I realise that the core of my motivation is actually God's outrageous, unconditional love for me. It's what He has done for me that stirs me to do something for Him, and not the other way around.

I remember one day where Pat, my wife, was heading into London to do some teaching and I took the opportunity to work on a song I had been writing. It was a song about spiritual warfare – a proactive declaration of the victory of Christ over the enemy. When I felt that the song was finished I was quite pleased with it and thought I would record a rough version of it to commit the

idea to tape. For some reason the tape recorder
was playing up and wouldn't work properly.
I fiddled around with it for a long time, but still it
wasn't behaving itself! Then, when I did start to
record, I wasn't giving a good performance of the
song – I got a word wrong here, a line wrong
there, played a wrong chord on my guitar! And so
it went on. By the time Pat returned home she was
on receiving end of all my frustrations. "What
have you been doing with my tape recorder?" I
demanded, and then it hit me. Here I was trying to
write a song about spiritual warfare but acting in
an incredibly un-spiritual way!

I remember feeling guilty about my attitude
and later that evening we went out for a meal
with friends where I chilled out a bit. It's great to
have friends around you to help you to receive the
love of God. Later I sat quietly on my own in my
little room at home and told the Lord, "I'm really
sorry Lord. What a dope I am! I try to be so
spiritual and I blow it. Here I am Lord, coming
back to you just as I am. Whether I ever write
another song is not the issue. It's all about You
and me, right here." The warmth and acceptance
that flooded over me right then was precious and
tender. All of us need to come back again and
again to that place of surrender to our Father,

to realise that we can do nothing to earn His love and favour. Amazingly, what happened next was that a new song began to flow out of me. It virtually wrote itself, a song that was eventually recorded on an album and turned out to be a far better song than the original had been. It's awesome to witness God's grace in action, to allow the river of His grace wash over us.

John the apostle said, *"God is love."* He didn't say God *has* lots of love, as if it was some commodity: God has plenty of love to throw around! Rather God is love, He is the embodiment of it. We know true love when we simply recognise God for who He is.

> **"The grace of Christ is the only good ground for life."**
> (Hebrews 13:9)

The thing about grace is, it doesn't matter how long we have been walking with God or how mature we are as believers, our need of it never diminishes. We need to continually draw from the Father's vast reservoir of love, grace and acceptance, and God really wants us to be able to receive from Him. Often we forget that. We don't see it.

Sometimes when I travel overseas, I will arrive at the airport and check through with my guitar and baggage, and then I will be wandering around trying to connect with a person who has been sent to meet me off the plane. Invariably, they know what I look like, but I don't know what they look like and it can lead to some humorous misunderstandings! I will be standing there, holding my guitar, making eye contact with anyone who looks as though they are approaching me, trying to figure out if this is "them". There might even be a nod and a smile from someone, and just as I'm about to open my mouth to greet them, they look past me and greet someone standing behind me! On occasion, I have had people meet me who were a bit unsure if it was "really" me, who have slowly walked by me whistling one of my tunes to make sure!

But one incident stands out from the rest. There I was at the airport waiting for my contact when a guy came up to me and said cheerfully, "It's Dave isn't it?"

"Yes," I responded, smiling.

"Great," he said. "Come with me." And so I did. We jumped into his car and drove off from the airport. We were chatting away making small talk when about two miles down the road I suddenly realised that I had left with the wrong guy! It was a case of mistaken identity. He had no idea who I was, and I had no idea who he was! He was there to meet a different Dave!

Sometimes we mistake God's identity and it brings us into an uncomfortable place. The vision we have of Christ and His grace for us affects how we live our lives. If we have a flawed understanding of who Jesus is, it's very like getting into the wrong car and driving away with a stranger! We are not heading in the direction we thought we were and we certainly won't arrive at the destination we expect.

Our vision of God and His grace towards us has a profound affect on how we worship. If we mistakenly see God as someone whom we must try hard to please and who puts burdens upon us, then our worship will not be full-blooded and wholehearted. We will tend to hold back a little bit for ourselves. God wants to wash over us with His grace so that we know in the core of our beings that we are truly loved and that His favour is towards us. Then our worship will be free and unhindered and we will be able to give ourselves fully to Jesus. I love the story of Jesus' baptism.

He has been in the wilderness for forty days and comes down to the River Jordan to be baptised. The Holy Spirit descends on Jesus and the voice of the Father is heard to say, *"This is my beloved Son in whom I am well pleased."*

Jesus hadn't performed a miracle or proclaimed anything about the kingdom of God. He hadn't done anything at all that would manifest the authority of who He was, or that could be seen as earning Him favour with God the Father in any way. But the Father said, "I am well pleased with you." And God says the same today to all those who are born anew in Christ. He looks down on you and says, "I'm well pleased with you son/ daughter." He wants to embrace us; let us know that our identity and acceptance is encompassed in Christ dwelling in us by His Spirit; it's nothing to do with anything we might accomplish.

> **"GOD, a God of mercy and grace, endlessly patient – so much love, so deeply true."**
> (Exodus 34:6)

A few years back I was getting ready to go on stage and give a concert. The event was billed as,

"Dave Bilbrough and band in concert", there were several hundred people gathered in the audience, and a buzz of excitement seemed to be going around the hall. It looked as if it was going to be a great night. We were going to perform a set of around two hours, so I thought it would be advisable to visit the bathroom five minutes before I was due on stage. As I stood in the Gents, a chap standing next to me, who seemed a friendly kind of guy, smiled and said to me, "Dave Bilbrough?"

"Yes," I smiled back.

"Is he any good?" the man asked.

"Err, yes, he's OK," I replied, a little perplexed.

"So you've seen him before then?" he continued.

"Yes," I replied truthfully. "I've seen him a few times!"

Five minutes later I would be standing on the stage doing this concert. I don't know who was more confused! It reminds me of another time when I was in Germany. I was being put up by the church I was visiting and the pastor arranged for me to stay at the house of a guy who looked exactly like me! I would be sitting on the sofa talking to him and thinking, "This is like talking to myself!" Was it me or was it him? I was confused. I guess that's how celebrities feel when they visit themselves at the world famous tourist attraction, Madame Tussauds in London. Frequently during the conversation I had to get up and have a good stare at myself in the bathroom mirror to remind myself who I was!

This is exactly what we have to do as Christians. C. S. Lewis said, "People need reminding just as much as teaching." So often we lose sight of who we are in Christ; what God has invested in us; what is our position in Him and the love that flows constantly towards us. Our identity in Christ must always precede our Christian service.

Why is acknowledging our identity so important? Because it doesn't matter who we are, how anointed we might be, how gifted we are, the moment we seek to flow in the power of the Spirit and function in the gifts God has given us we will receive knock-backs. I have led worship at some large events and heard speakers who commanded the attention of the people with incredible authority and anointing, yet as soon as they finished speaking were in a very vulnerable place. After a great flow of anointing it is as if the enemy attacks from all sides to try to bring us down. It can happen in all kinds of ways. Someone makes an insensitive remark to you, or they make an inappropriate joke. Things come at you like fiery darts and catch you unawares. It is all to do with the enemy's desire to rob you of your true standing in Christ and cause you to doubt your identity. That's why our identity must always be stronger than our function.

Look at the life of Jesus. He was secure in who He was. He could be speaking to thousands of people one day and then be on His own, praying in a secluded place the next, or avoiding being apprehended by the authorities. What He was doing at any particular moment wasn't of any great concern to Him because He was secure in identity and in His relationship with the Father.

> **"I do not at all understand the mystery of grace – only that it meets us where we are but does not leave us where it found us."**
> (Ann Lamott)

In the early days of the Charismatic renewal I would often travel with a friend of mine called Maurice Smith. Maurice was a highly anointed, gifted preacher, but he was also very prophetic too. The thing about prophetic people is that they can sometimes be a bit unpredictable, especially if you happen to be working with them as a worship leader! Sometimes Maurice would speak for an hour and I would just accompany him during the ministry time and maybe sing one song. Another time he would speak for five minutes and then announce to me, "That's it, I've got nothing else to share. Over to you Dave" and I would end up having to fill the remaining hour and a half! I never knew what would happen next. As a result I found myself in all kinds of scrapes and situations.

On one such occasion Maurice and I were down in the West Country and on our way to a house church meeting. As we arrived, we were welcomed at the door by a man who greeted us with the following: "There are about fifty people here from all over the region who have come to hear you. We are all so looking forward to this, but I need to let you know that my wife has been taken ill with severe back pains. We want you to carry on with the meeting as you would normally, but the doctor has called for an ambulance to come and take my wife to hospital." Looking at one another we asked the man if he was really sure we should have the meeting, but he was insistent that both he and his wife wanted it to go ahead, so in we went.

We began our meeting and were well into it when the doorbell rang and sure enough it was the ambulance, come to collect the man's wife who at present was lying on her bed. We put the meeting on pause while the ambulance crew trooped through the house and prepared to bring her downstairs on a stretcher. It was at this point that Maurice turned to me and issued the immortal words, "Dave, it would be really good if you would lead us all in a song as Mrs Jones comes through on the stretcher. We want to send her on her way with faith in her heart!"

Anyone who has led worship before will know that there are moments when your mind goes totally blank. This was one of those moments for me. There are only two solutions I know of when my mind goes blank. One is to get everyone to stand up and hope that something will pop into your mind as they are getting ready to sing. The other is to pray an angel appears beside you and whispers the title of the perfect song in your ear. Needless to say, I got everyone to stand up!

Another tactic I employ when blankness of mind strikes is to begin to gently strum my guitar. I hope that it will stir some faith and activity among the congregation and that something

might begin to emerge and happen. Everyone
stood. I strummed meaningfully. And then I
launched into the only song I could think of as
this lady was carried to the ambulance on her
stretcher: "Jesus take me as I am, I can come no
other way"!

We all hopefully learn from our mistakes don't
we, but the truth is, we can only come to God as
we are. Often we try to be too sophisticated, to do
all the right things, read all the right books, get
all the latest teaching CDs, go to all the right
conferences and seminars. We are concerned with
doing, and being seen to be doing, the right thing.
But all God wants us to do is come into His
presence and let His love transform us.

It reminds me about the doctor who greeted one
of his patients on the street:

"Hi Ken, I haven't seen you lately."

"No," replies Ken, "I've been ill!"

Although a joke, it speaks a truth to us.
Sometimes in our relationship with our Creator
we can carry forward that same mentality – you
know, thinking we can only to come to Him when
we've really got ourselves together. Forsaking an
encounter with the only One who can really can
bring healing to us, we try to pull ourselves up by
our own bootstraps using every method and every

technique available in preference to His simple invitation.

Even when we feel there is more life in an old Duracell battery than ourselves, Jesus invites us by saying, "Come to me and learn the unforced rhythms of my grace." Yet, we still try to find another way. By grace He welcomes us into His presence. That's profound! This is our reason for worship.

> **"Walk with me and work with me – watch how I do it. Learn the unforced rhythms of grace. I won't lay anything heavy or ill-fitting on you."**
> (Matthew 11:29)

One of the great secrets of the spiritual life is being in step with God; being aware of what He is doing and falling in line with Him. We don't need to achieve in order to be successful in God's economy. We simply need to plug into what God has already done for us. As we lay hold of His grace for our lives, His acceptance, His love, then He will make our lives effective and we will become a living, walking testimony of His grace.

Are you working for God or resting in God?
So often I find in my own life that when I am
trying to work for God, God is at rest! It is so
easy to get out of step with the Spirit. I have
found that whenever I am simply resting in God,
in the blessing of His provision of grace for me,
that in that place God begins working. He was
waiting for me to be still so that He could begin
working through me by His Spirit. Yes, God
wants us to cooperate with Him; yes, He wants
us to work in partnership with Him; yes, He
wants us to obey the things He says to us – but
it is an easy burden. His yoke of grace is so easy
to bear.

The apostle Paul began each of his New
Testament letters with the words, *"grace and peace
to you"* and then would follow it with words of
encouragement to the gathered believers. The one
exception to his positive affirmation was when he
was writing to the Galatian Christians who had
lost sight of the grace of God in their lives! They
had started out with the realisation that apart from
Christ they could do nothing, but very quickly
they lost the plot and found themselves
entrenched in a works-orientated way of living.
Paul acted swiftly to correct this error by writing
his famous epistle. After a short initial greeting he

quickly gets to the core of the issue by rebuking them for deserting the grace of Christ for a *"different gospel"*. What made him angry was their forsaking of the pure Good News to return to the old way of thinking of law-based religion. True peace can only be found in our lives when we experience God's grace in action. The peace and grace that Paul coupled together so frequently speak of wholeness.

There are three important things about grace that I want us to reflect on:

■ God's grace brings healing

God's grace brings healing for our past sins. For all those things we've done, and continue to do at times, that are wrong, God can bring healing as we repent.

I used to love to play football. To me there was nothing better than finishing a match covered in mud. I guess it's a man thing. And then what a great feeling to step under that shower and feel all that mud being washed away. God's grace and forgiveness is like that; it washes away our sins, our failures and inadequacies. God's grace is a relentless stream gushing towards us and we can experience it continually if we will only step under the shower and allow Him to change us.

God's grace means freedom from trying to make the grade

Being a self-employed person as I am, I like to pay for most things using my Visa card. One of the reasons I like it is because each month I receive a statement summarising all my expenditure and it's easy to put that record through my accounts. But I also like it because my particular card earns me points every month. The more I spend, the more points I get. I realised recently that I have enough points to get me to Australia and back! Thankfully God does not deal with us in the same way as credit card companies. He doesn't watch to see how much time we are spending with Him and credit our heavenly account accordingly. We don't need to point score with Him. Yes, God wants us to be more Christlike and full of the Holy Spirit, but He blesses us on the basis of His grace towards us and His grace alone.

If you were to spend a significant amount of time with me you would soon realise that as well as being fairly impractical when it comes to putting up shelves and fixing things (although I'm a dab hand at changing light bulbs!), I have a particular aversion to board (bored!) games. Some people at Christmas time are just filled with joy and anticipation at the thought of shaking the dice and hearing it bounce in that hollow kind of way on the foldable board. I am filled with trepidation because I never seem to master the rules or keep my concentration up for long enough to make any significant impact on the game. Monopoly is a particular favourite of many of my friends. Huge amounts of time and energy are invested in placing small plastic houses on familiar London streets including Mayfair and Old Kent Road. Monopoly money is exchanged freely and the winner always seems to have a huge wedge of notes and a big smile. I must confess to getting more than a little jealous of their endurance and their growing collection of "luka" enabling them to buy some of the most prestigious areas of Britain's capital city. Imagine, however, the triumphant winner visiting his local car showroom and attempting to buy the latest Jaguar sports car, a convertible coupe 4.2 litre edition, with the spoils of his victory. The salesperson would look at him with astonishment because, of course, the currency that our winner had collected would not be valid outside of the Monopoly game.

In the same way it would be foolish to say that our works are not important – they are – but in order to gain God's approval they count for nothing. The currency of the kingdom is pure grace!

The Message gives a beautiful translation of Matthew 11:28–29 that I often hear quoted:

> *"Are you tired? Worn out? Burned out on religion? Come to me. Get away with me and you'll recover your life. I'll show you how to take a real rest. Walk with me and work with me – watch how I do it. Learn the unforced rhythms of grace. I won't lay anything heavy or ill-fitting on you."*

There is an incredible lightness to God's grace. He wants us to live in it and to love it. There are some church meetings I've been at that have had such an atmosphere of heaviness about them that I was convinced the people must have left in a worse state than when they arrived. The conviction of the Holy Spirit is one thing, but a graceless heaviness is another thing entirely. Conviction leads to repentance and repentance to the source of life which is Christ Himself. That which is not true Holy Spirit conviction only leaves us feeling weighed down with guilt.

Grace is the antidote for low self-esteem

"Where are you from?" asked the Turkish sales assistant. "If I'm asked that question one more time I'll knock that persons block off" I thought, but never said, smiling patiently. "How about a leather jacket? A watch? A shave?" This bombardment was beginning to get to me. My emotional thermostat was beginning to rise. Here I was in the middle of a Turkish Bazaar trying to find some souvenir of our family vacation to take home that wasn't just a fake brand name – imitation Armani, Gucci and Rolex watches abounded – but a product of the "real" Turkey. Then we found it, opposite the Turkish baths. Across the road from the white stained mosque, on the corner of the small-town square stood a small cluster of shops. Away from all the noise and clamour of bartering and hassle we at last found a reason for being here. Like finding an oasis in the desert, we walked into the first shop and drank in the tranquil atmosphere. Our eyes were met by a dazzling array of Turkish "killim" art. All manner of bags, shoes and men's waistcoats were on display. Pat fell in love with a multicoloured shoulder bag. It was beautiful and rich in colour, practical in design, just what she was looking for. The sale was made.

In conversation with a courteous salesman we discovered the bags on sale were made in different areas and mountain regions of Turkey. Each bag or item was an original, not a clone. No two were identical, each was woven with a pattern or symbol that bore a meaning that represented our personal dreams and goals – no two were alike.

In the same way God has created each of us to shine in a way that only we can. Our lives are a song that only we can sing with a purpose and a destiny that is distinct and tailor-made for each one of us.

Everybody is an original. Everybody is important. The secret of our life of grace is to be true and authentic to that person God has made us to be. As my friend Gerald Coates says, "Most people start their lives as originals and end up as copies." God's anointing most surely comes to those who are true to themselves and to their calling.

Whenever you feel that you are just not good enough, grace is the antidote. At some point every one of us feels vulnerable, weak, inadequate, especially musicians I think! Creative people tend to be the most vulnerable because it is their sensitivity which makes them want to create things of beauty, such as music, art, poetry, dance etc. Feelings of low self-esteem can dog us and prevent us from pressing into the very place that God wants us to be in Christ. Inferior feelings, a sense of shame, a sense of failure, are all things that hinder the flow of God's grace in our lives. Again and again the devil will come and try to tell us that we are just not good enough to be doing the things we are doing. "You can't stand up there and lead worship Bilbrough, because of the way you reacted yesterday..." Condemnation will rob us of our identity.

James Dobson, a great thinker and writer, talks in one of his books about the various types of personality that people tend to be attracted by. He says there are "gold coin" type personalities – that is a person who is physically attractive. For a man that might mean someone who is six foot eight, speaks with a deep voice, and is good at all sports, especially rowing! Then there is what Dobson calls "silver coin attractiveness" – that is a person who is intelligent and usually has a gift in a particular area that people want to know about, be it artistic or musical. Naturally speaking, we tend to be overawed by people's giftedness, attracted by their achievement, but this is a worldly way of thinking. Subtly, we allow this kind of thinking to infiltrate the Church and define success based on achievement. Like a Hollywood film set, which can look impressive from the outside but is actually a façade, what we perceive to be successful is in reality a hollow illusion when viewed from up close. God's grace says, "Be who you are" and from that place of rest, achieve what God wants you to achieve.

The value of something is often determined by its perceived worth, and what something is worth will determine what a person is willing to pay for it. The good news for us is that our worth is found in the life that was paid for by Jesus Himself on the cross. Jesus bought us with His own life. Now we can look at God with our heads held high, not because of what we have done, but because of what Jesus has done for us.

We are loved and accepted by God as we are. That doesn't mean there isn't a lot of transformation that still needs to take place in us, but nothing we do can cause God to love us any more than He does already – and nothing we can do can cause Him to love us any less! We will be changed and transformed by Him as we increasingly become aware of His holiness. The more we worship Him in awe and wonder, the more He will be able to change us from one degree of glory to the next.

When God identifies something in us that needs to change, He wants us to take that seriously and respond to Him in obedience. But He doesn't want us to come under condemnation and to struggle and strive. He wants us to respond by saying, "Yes, Lord. I will cooperate with you. I am going to let You work through me and shape me according to Your will." God chose you long before He created the world. He knew you; knew what you would be like; He knew you for who you are. God doesn't just love you in a general "God loves everyone" kind of way, He loves you specifically, knowing all about you. You have nothing to prove to Him today, so open your heart to Him and let the tidal wave of His love wash over you.

Grace and Mercy

Grace and mercy wash over me,
fill my soul with your healing stream.
Here I stand with this prayer within my heart,
take me deeper in the river that flows with
> your love.

Thank you, Thank you,
> Oh what riches are mine in Christ Jesus.
Thank you, Thank you,
> your forgiveness is so undeserved.[2]

[2] *Grace and Mercy*, written by Dave Bilbrough. Copyright 2000, Kingsway/Thank You Music, from the album *Personal Worship*.

How God wants to meet with us

Exodus chapter 25 is a passage that paints a vivid picture of how God wants to meet with His people. He wants us to come to meet Him in His dwelling place by His grace, and for that place to be a place of worship. The first few verses of this chapter mention how God asked the people through Moses to bring a variety of different "offerings" – gifts that would be used in building a tabernacle to house God's presence.

> *"Then the LORD spoke to Moses, saying: 'Speak to the children of Israel, that they bring Me an offering. From everyone who gives it willingly with his heart you shall take My offering. And this is the offering which you shall take from them: gold, silver, and bronze; blue, purple, and scarlet thread, fine linen, and goats' hair; ram skins dyed red, badger skins, and acacia wood; oil for the light, and spices for the anointing oil and for*

the sweet incense; onyx stones, and stones to
be set in the ephod and in the breastplate."

(Exodus 25:1–7 NKJV)

Quite an amazing list! And then God says,

"For I want the people of Israel to make me
a sacred temple where I can live among them.
This home of mine should be a tent pavilion,
a tabernacle. I will give you the drawing of
the construction plan and the details for each
furnishing."

(Exodus 25:8–9 TLB)

God reveals to Moses that He wants to build a
"house" for His presence to reside in and all God's
people are to contribute something towards to
building it. The tabernacle of God's presence is a
foreshadowing, under the Old Covenant, of the
New Covenant "house" of God which is the
"Church" – the body of Christ made up of all
believers. But even more than that, it reveals
Jesus to us in so many ways. We, as the "Church",
are joined to Jesus and "covered" by Him so
that we may freely enter the dwelling place of
God. Covered in Christ we can enter the place
where God's presence rests and be together with

Him, just as the tabernacle of Moses provided an entrance into the very presence of God.

In verse 10 God describes to Moses how the Ark of the Covenant should be fashioned:

> *"And they shall make an ark of acacia wood; two and a half cubits shall be its length, a cubit and a half its width, and a cubit and a half its height. And you shall overlay it with pure gold, inside and out you shall overlay it, and shall make on it a molding of gold all around."*
>
> (Exodus 25:10-11 NKJV)

Acacia wood was very common in those days. It wasn't a particularly special wood, it was a bit like modern-day MDF! It was abundantly available and you could build anything with it. In the Bible it speaks to us of our humanity. It was significant that God specified the use of acacia wood to make the Ark and then instructed them to overlay it with pure gold. Gold speaks of God's divine nature. It is a picture of what God wants to do for each of us – to take the ignoble wood of our humanity and overlay it with His divine gold.

What a picture of God's grace that is for us! The gold that overlaid the wood of the Ark was

pure and very thin – so thin you could actually
see the grain of the wood coming through beneath
it. This is how God wants to grace us – He wants
to allow the grain (our personality) to be seen
through the gold of His divine nature. He doesn't
want to rob us of our individuality and make us
Christian clones!

Verse 12 continues,

> *"You shall cast four rings of gold for it,*
> *and put them in its four corners; two rings*
> *shall be on one side, and two rings on the*
> *other side. And you shall make poles of*
> *acacia wood, and overlay them with gold.*
> *You shall put the poles into the rings on the*
> *sides of the ark, that the ark may be carried*
> *by them."*
>
> (Exodus 25:12–14 NKJV)

The Ark was made to be transportable because it
was meant to be on the move. It was designed for
journeying. It was to be carried around with the
people of God wherever they went so that they
were never without the presence of God. Again,
what an incredible picture for us: we are to
journey through life carrying the very presence
of God with us, covered with His grace.

*"You shall make a mercy seat of pure gold;
two and a half cubits shall be its length and a
cubit and a half its width. And you shall make
two cherubim of gold; of hammered work you
shall make them at the two ends of the mercy
seat. Make one cherub at one end, and the
other cherub at the other end; you shall make
the cherubim at the two ends of it of one piece
with the mercy seat. And the cherubim shall
stretch out their wings above, covering the
mercy seat with their wings, and they shall
face one another; the faces of the cherubim
shall be toward the mercy seat. You shall put
the mercy seat on top of the ark, and in the
ark you shall put the Testimony that I will
give you. And there I will meet with you, and
I will speak with you from above the mercy
seat, from between the two cherubim which
are on the ark of the Testimony, about
everything which I will give you in
commandment to the children of Israel."*

(Exodus 25:17–22 NKJV)

God specified that there should be two angels, one
at either end of the mercy seat that covered the
Ark. If you like they were the grid coordinates for
God's people because God said, "I will meet you

there and speak to you." God wants to meet with you and me at the place of mercy – an incredible picture of the New Covenant. This issue of law and grace is so foundational, so fundamental to our understanding of who God is. It is imperative that we understand His heart towards us. His heart is grace and mercy to us.

The New Testament is full of many things that we need to consider and do as followers of Jesus. Paul's epistles in particular give us much instruction on how to live our lives as believers, but the foundation for all this teaching is the grace and mercy of God. That's why it is so important that we understand who we are in Christ. There are five things that I want to highlight about the Ark that are reflected in our identity in Christ. I hope they will help you to firmly take hold of who you are in Him:

1. We start with the finished work

God designed His tabernacle in a specific order. He began with the Ark which was going to reside in the Holy of Holies. He was designing a glorious temple that He would fill with His presence, but He started at the end. As Christians we are born into the kingdom of God; we are forgiven; we are given a glorious inheritance in Christ. We start at the finish line! We are told to "run the race" but are told we have already run the race in Jesus. We are told to "fight the good fight", but we are told that the battle is already won in Jesus!

God starts His wonderful New Covenant by putting us at our final destination to begin with. Our understanding of worship will be transformed by seeing this. We don't need to struggle and strive in order to enter the Holy of Holies, we need to realise that Jesus has already made that way open to us. All things are attainable through Christ. We start from where we end.

2. The Ark was designed to be on a journey

As we've already noted, the Ark was fitted with special hooks and poles that enabled it to be safely carried from place to place. The poles were designed to keep the Ark stable so that it would not topple over. Have you ever thought to yourself when you look at a married couple, that one person is more stable than their partner? In any marriage you will often find one person who is more emotional and another person who is more constant in their feelings. Have you seen that?

The good news of God's grace is that He is the stable one in the relationship. We may be up or down, sometimes feeling joyful, sometimes feeling unfulfilled; sometimes feeling very positive and sometimes down in the dumps. But God is the One who carries us through. The Ark is a picture of God's stability to us, His constancy. He is not going to topple over on us however much we might waver.

3. The Ark speaks of God's sovereign ability to provide

God told Moses that certain things must be placed inside the Ark and stored there. There were three things that were put inside and each has significance for us.

(i) The two tablets of Moses containing the law
This is a picture of our relationship with Christ. He is the law keeper within our hearts.

(ii) Some manna
Manna was the food that the children of Israel had received from God in the desert, His miraculous provision for them. Manna literally means, "what is it?". God's people were fed by this thing called

"what is it". My life has been a testimony of
God's "what is it". Time and again God has come
and fed me miraculously and I have wondered,
"How did that happen?"

Years ago I belonged to a church that was very
successful and I was given a lot of profile in the
church and was rewarded very well financially.
We used to think that our church was really on
the cutting edge of things, but then over a period
of months, suddenly the whole church dissolved
and broke down. From being in a place where I
was well looked after by the church, suddenly
I was out on my own. I had no financial support
and a wife, one child, and another on the way
to look after. It happened just before Christmas.
I wanted to care for my family whom I loved
dearly, but I had next to nothing. I went to the
local supermarket and could just afford the bare
necessities to get us through the Christmas period.
To make matters worse I spotted another family
from our church there stocking up for Christmas
and resentment rose up in me as I saw what they
were able to afford to buy for themselves. All of
us suffer from this from time to time. I don't know
how it happened, but from that day forward God
began to supply all my needs. The grace of God
kicked in and it was the beginning of many "what

is it?" miraculous provisions. It was the grace of God in action. In His faithfulness, God's grace meets us at our point of need.

(iii) Aaron's rod that had budded

The rod represents God's approval in our lives – in our ministry, our sphere of function, our calling. It is significant to me that those men and women who have really pressed on with God and become pioneers, who have not accepted the status quo around them, have all been people who have known their acceptance and credence comes from God's approval alone. We need to be people who put God's approval first in our lives, far above the approval of others. George Müller, a great man of God, said, "There came a day when I died to the approval of others." God doesn't want us to seek after the approval of others, only to seek after His approval.

4. The Ark of the Covenant testifies to God's unfailing mercy

In the Exodus passage "mercy" is mentioned seven times. Scriptural scholars will tell you that seven is a number of completion. Once you have said something seven times there is nothing more you can say. God's unfailing mercy completes us. It frees us from our struggles and from our guilt, enabling us to lift up our heads high; enabling us to dare to come face to face with God. God's mercy is available to us. May God give us, in our spheres of function, ministries of mercy to others. Even those people who have hurt us, those people who sometimes, even by chance comments, put us down – we need to learn to extend God's mercy to them, to be witnesses of God's unfailing mercy.

▓ 5. The Ark of the Covenant is a witness to unbroken communion with God

God has told us that He wants to meet us at the place of mercy and talk with us. Some versions of the Exodus passage say He wants to "commune" with us. In other words He just wants to be with us and have us with Him in the place of mercy.

The revealed presence of God comes by us simply and adoringly opening up to the God of all grace – a God who loves us unconditionally, freely; a God who wants to put steel in our soul as He tenderises our hearts; a God who has affections towards us that are so much greater than our affections towards Him; a God whom, it says in Scripture, is singing over us with joy

(Zephaniah 3:17). Imagine that! God is singing over us with joy! I wonder what He is singing right now?

"I love you! Open up to my love and forgiveness. Let the sunshine and the warmth of my love come into your heart."

Our Father is a God who sings over us, who sees hope and potential for us; a God who never gives up on us; and as my friend Maurice Smith used to say, a God whose hobby it is to collect failures.

> **"Even though on the outside it often looks like things are falling apart on us, on the inside, where God is making new life, not a day goes by without his unfolding grace."**
> (2 Corinthians 4:16)

He accepts us as we are! He loves us unconditionally! He's ours. The One who puts passion in our soul that sets us free from the inside out; allows us to be unique, to be original, to be everything that He destined us to be. Someone once said that, "the glory of God is man fully alive." Open yourself up to His grace again today. Even though we don't deserve it, even though we fail at times, God still lavishes His grace on us and we are amazed.

> "GOD is sheer mercy and grace;
> not easily angered, he's rich in love."
> (Psalm 103:8)

Grace

It was grace that welcomed me home
I was lost and alone but you threw me a banquet
It was grace that healed all my shame
No words can explain this mercy so free

Grace came down and took all my burdens
Grace came down and lifted me
All my sorrow was turned into dancing
When grace came down and lifted me

Lord your grace comes so undeserved
It just cannot be earned, it's a gift like no other
This grace is mine to receive
As empty and weak I come to You

Grace came down and took all my burdens
Grace came down and lifted me
All my sorrow was turned into dancing
When grace came down and lifted me

I have strayed from your path
I have squandered your truth
I had gone to a land far away[3]

---

[3] *Grace*, written by Dave Bilbrough. Copyright 2005, Dave Bilbrough Songs, from the album *This is My Worship*.

A prayer

"Thank You Lord for Your love and Your
grace. Lord with every fibre of my being I
want to know You, to press on and know You
more and more and to live in the fullness of
Your love and grace. Thank You for smiling
down on me, embracing me, and changing
me by Your grace from the inside out.
Through my life Lord, help me to convey
Your grace to others.

In Jesus' name. Amen."

Dave Bilbrough

This is my worship

New DVD and CD out now!

All new, original songs, filmed as a live concert in an intimate unplugged setting in the historic Spitalfields area of London.

All profits towards developing worship initiatives in parts of the world which cannot afford to host worship events, commonplace in the affluent West.

www.davebilbrough.com

For further information on Dave's ministry, including tour dates and albums visit the Dave Bilbrough website www.davebilbrough.com

Coming soon – Book II: *Worship and Mission* and Book III: *Worship and the Presence of God.*

In addition to regular travelling and touring as a worship leader/speaker in the UK and the US, Dave frequently travels to many of the poorer parts of the world that cannot afford to host worship and training events. His latest album, *This is My Worship* was produced to help raise funds for further initiatives in these regions. If you would like to partner with Dave and Pat in financial or prayerful support of these missions please contact them via email:

strum@davebilbrough.com

or write to them at:

Dave Bilbrough
PO Box 2612
Romford
Essex RM2 5YB

We hope you enjoyed reading this New Wine book.
For details of other New Wine books
and a range of 2,000 titles from other
Word and Spirit publishers visit our website:
www.newwineministries.co.uk

A

light

AMONGST

shadows

DARK IS THE NIGHT: BOOK 1

KELLEY YORK
&
ROWAN ATWOOD

www.kelley-york.com

Edited by Beedoo! Radosevich and Jamie Manning
Cover design by x-potion designs
Interior Design by The Illustrated Author

First Edition June 2018
A LIGHT AMONGST SHADOWS

Kelley York & Rowan Altwood

The hour of departure has arrived and we go our ways; I to die, and you to live.
Which is better? Only God knows.

—Socrates

Father said Whisperwood would be my "home away from home." I rather think it looks like an illustration straight from the cover of a penny dreadful, but I suppose he never insinuated that home away from home would be a *pleasant* one.

The central driveway curves through the grounds to a roundabout just before a wall of hedges the height of two grown men. This is where I exit the carriage, granting myself a moment to look around while the footman fetches my trunk and suitcase. Through the leafy, immaculately trimmed archway of the hedges sits a courtyard, complete with an elegant stone fountain adorned with lions and unicorns reared on two legs, water spilling from their open mouths.

I've grown so accustomed to the intricate buildings of the city that the symmetrical, simple architecture of Whisperwood is both strange and refreshing. Its high stone walls, deep-set, narrow windows, and a grand double-door gives it the look of an old royal countryside estate rather than a school. The pamphlet Mother showed me about Whisperwood said something of its history and the year it was built, but I hadn't paid it the least bit of attention.

A member of staff trots out to greet us, bowing his head politely in my direction before chatting with the footman and preparing to gather my things. I scoop up my suitcase before he has a chance to take it but allow him to hoist the trunk into his arms and carry it off after giving him my name, so he knows to which room it's to be delivered. *Pack lightly*, they'd said in the paperwork mailed with my registration information. How troublesome to have to fit one's belongings into two meagre pieces of luggage.

There were carriages and omnibuses both in front of and behind mine coming up the driveway, and just as many boys disembarking. Other students who have likely arrived in the preceding days are milling about, rushing to see old friends as they unload. I have no one to greet me and, for just a moment, standing in a courtyard of strangers who seem to know one another, I'll admit I'm feeling more than a little isolated.

That will change. I'm an easy-going and friendly enough lad; I know I will find a group to immerse myself in with no trouble and likely little time.

The important thing is that I'm away from home. That's what I repeat to myself to combat the wave of loneliness and nervousness that creeps over me. I'm away from home and I am safe. I will be allowed the opportunity not just to grow back into myself, but perhaps to blossom to an even greater potential. One, perhaps, that will make my family proud of me again.

I linger in the courtyard for the better part of three hours, until my legs have begun to ache, and I've had to give in and steal a seat on the fountain ledge, awaiting instructions as more carriages deliver more students. Finally, just as I've begun to grow more than a little impatient, a voice crows over the top of all the chatter for new students to come inside.

As we're ushered into the foyer of the building by men I presume to be instructors, I find myself crowding shoulder-to-shoulder with mostly boys younger than my seventeen years. First years, I presume. I'm coming in at the beginning of third year, later than most boys would begin at public school. But, surely, I'm not the only one.

Once everyone has been packed inside and the doors closed, an older man with a shock of white, thinning, but neatly combed hair steps to the forefront of the group. Despite his age, he stands tall with his shoulders pushed back and his chin up, surveying the lot of us with a critical eye. If I were to judge based on looks and demeanour alone, I don't think I will much care for this man; he seems the sort to spit in disdain at his own birthday party.

"Hello, gentlemen, and good afternoon. My name is Maxwell King, and I am the headmaster here at Whisperwood."

Ah, yes. Father corresponded with the headmaster through letters prior to choosing this school. No doubt to tell him of my troubles and see if Whisperwood would be an appropriate place for me to go. A place that could *handle* me.

There's a thought that makes me uncomfortable all over again. How much, I wonder, did Father tell him? Would it really have been necessary to divulge my private affairs to as sour a man as this? And, for that matter, I wonder if he's the only one who knows. Are the staff informed why the students are here as a means of knowing how to deal with us?

Nerves promptly begin to gnaw at me. I cannot let it get the best of me, though. I'm over-worrying. Father would not want word of my little mishap getting out any more than necessary for fear of how it might reflect on our family. Certainly, a school such as this would thrive best functioning on the utmost discretion.

The headmaster continues, "Here at Whisperwood, we take young men from all walks of life. Young men who have lost their direction and need assistance finding it again. We offer structure, balance, entertainment, and most importantly—an education that will assist you greatly in life after graduation, especially if your next destination should be university. Our instructors are some of the finest you'll find anywhere."

I want to roll my eyes as far back into my head as possible. Someone ought to tell him that our tuition has already been paid and there's no need to sell us on the school; we've no choice in the matter.

He prattles on. He speaks of the history of the school— built in 1691, largely untouched since then save for some maintenance—and the expectations of the student body. We are to show up to all classes and activities on time and in presentable attire every day. Missed assignments are unacceptable. Our rooms are to be kept tidy, our bedding and laundry delivered to the laundry room twice a week, and the student body alternates weeks for doing said laundry. Mandatory church services every Sunday morning in the assembly hall. A ten o'clock curfew is strictly enforced.

Above all else, Mr. King wishes to instil upon us the blessing of this opportunity we've been given. Hardly a blessing; our parents are paying out of their arses for it. Whisperwood, he says, is our chance for redemption. That statement on its own solidifies my thought that he is a most unpleasant man and I want to do all that I can to steer clear of him.

After his lengthy and self-serving speech has concluded, another neatly dressed gentlemen takes his place and begins barking out orders. "New fourth years, head to the hall down your left and you'll be instructed where to go. Third years, upstairs, to the left. Second years, surnames A through G..."

I begin inching my way through the crowd to venture upstairs, which is significantly less crowded. The bulk of students are, in fact, second and first years who must be split up because there are too many to shuffle into one classroom. The third years like myself, however, are only six in number and we all navigate easily into the room we're directed to.

A classroom in the dipping sunlight is a bit eerie. The windows are open, helping to air out the stuffiness but allowing in the cold along with it, and the sunset outside casts everything in a warm, haunting light. There are enough desks for maybe forty students, give or take. I have a seat at one of them, suitcase beside me, and steal a look at the other third years who appear just as out of place as I do.

The man who steps into our class and shuts the door behind him is tall, middle-aged, bespectacled, and without a hair on his head. He doesn't smile as his eyes rake over the few of us, and then he looks down at a stack of papers in his hand. From the first one, he reads aloud, "Marcus Worthington?"

A boy to my left slowly raises a hand as though he's afraid it's going to be removed from his person. "Present, sir."

The instructor steps forward, without looking at him, and places a piece of paper upon his desk. "James Spencer?"

"Sir." I put my hand up without hesitation, and even offer him a smile when he hands my paper over, although he scarcely glances at me to see it. Glad that the adults here are so sunny in disposition. We're off to a great start.

He proceeds to go down the very short list until each of us has our paper, and I find myself looking at a class schedule. Breakfast at eight, Latin and history before lunch, English and maths after, followed by drill Monday, Wednesday, and Friday. I look around, but the classroom we're currently in doesn't give me a clue as to which lessons are held here.

The instructor stands at the front of the room, before his desk, hands clasped neatly in front of him. "My name is Graham McLachlan. I'm the maths instructor for all third and fourth years, so I'll be seeing a lot of you in the coming weeks. Lateness will not be tolerated. Breakfast is at eight, lunch at noon, dinner at six. From the hours of four to six you are expected to focus solely on your studies, save for days you have drill and sports, in which case, study time starts after that.

"Leisure time begins at seven. Use this time for bathing, socialising, and extracurricular activities. Curfew at ten. No exceptions."

It's a lot of information to take in, however I appreciate the succinct manner in which he relays it. It may not be exciting, but at least it isn't the needless droning of the headmaster and, in that, I find sincerity.

Mr. McLachlan continues, "As third years, your dormitory will be Gawain Hall. Your registration papers ought to have your room numbers. Each hall has two prefects; these are fourth year students who have earned the privilege of residing on the second floor of each dormitory and helping to monitor the goings on. For you, this will be Virgil Appleton and Augustus Smith.

"In addition to your prefects, each building has a staff member located on the fourth floor who serves as your housemaster. This will be Mr. Charles Simmons. He's a recent graduate of Whisperwood and now an apprentice, so he's well-acquainted with how things work here. Any issues with your housemates, you report to your prefects and your prefects report to the housemaster. Any questions?"

A few of us glance at one another, an uncomfortable rustling as some shift in their chairs, but no one speaks up. Mr. McLachlan looks to each of us one at a time, granting us a moment to think of anything to ask. Personally, I can think of none that are serious in nature and it's likely a bit too early in the year to be reprimanded for horsing around. When no hands go up, he gives a curt nod. "In that case, dismissed. I will see you for your first lesson tomorrow."

Upon exiting the school building, I attempt to remind myself again that at least I'm not at home. Certainly, the rules are strict, the atmosphere itself is as cold as the headmaster, and the one teacher I've met comes across as quite humourless, but...

Not home.

Things could be worse.

A fourth year outside directs me to the third years' hall across the grounds. A trampled, gravelled pathway takes me to the large, four-story dormitory. A wooden signpost stands erect in the ground outside, etched with care to read the name *Gawain*. So, this must be the right place.

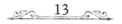

Inside, the architecture is more reminiscent of home. Polished wooden floors, framed paintings done by the student body mounted upon the walls like a gallery, interspersed with sconces, which have already been lit as the sun goes down. An intricate spiral staircase winds up from the ground floor to the first storey, and the steps creak in quiet protest beneath my feet. Boys mingle in the hall and in open-doored rooms, their voices echoing through the old architecture.

My floor is, at least, moderately quiet. A few boys are seated in a large den that appears to serve as a common area, just to the right of the stairs; they're swapping stories of holiday, and not for the first time I feel the niggling concern at the back of my brain that being the new boy here may prove a challenge. There is always the possibility, too, that I'll be stuck with some prick for a roommate, that my teachers will be abhorrent, and that the strict regime I have never been subjected to in my life will wear me down.

But these are not new thoughts. They're thoughts I've entertained the last several weeks since Mother informed me that Whisperwood would be my new home, and I've yet to let it get me down. Whatever I will have to face, I must remember that I've survived worse and come out intact.

Still, I *am* hopeful, yes, that whomever will be sharing my room will be someone I get on with. Oh, I could get on with a rock, if needed, but there's a significant difference between tolerating someone's presence and genuinely *enjoying* their company. Should I be fortunate enough to have the latter, I should be quite pleased.

A friend. That would be nice.

The rooms are each labelled with iron numbers upon the doors. I locate mine down the second hall—room forty-two—and allow myself in.

I'm greeted by the waning sun spilling cider-coloured light through the open window, a bed against either wall, a table and chairs in one corner, a pair of modest-sized wardrobes and a shared chest of drawers and a washing table and mirror. Simple, clean, impossibly draughty.

More important to me in that moment is the boy who rises from his bed. He's already dressed in uniform, sans jacket. A good bit shorter than myself, blonde-haired, blue-eyed, with a sunny smile upon his face that looks to have never shed its baby fat. It's a smile that could do nothing but put a man at ease. If nothing else, it encourages me to don a smile of my own. "Evening. You must be my roommate."

The boy wastes no time in crossing the distance between us and extending a hand. "S'right. Oscar Frances," he says. "You must be James."

"That's what my mum tells me." I grasp the offered hand and give it a firm shake. Oscar, I've already decided, has a good feel to him. That's promising. "A pleasure to meet you."

Oscar draws back, gesturing to the as of yet unoccupied side of the room. "Welcome to Whisperwood. You just come from orientation? Did the headmaster give that god-awful, droning speech about second chances and redemption?"

A chuckle escapes my mouth as I place my suitcase upon the floor at the foot of my bed. Unpacking can wait until staff has brought up my trunk. "I was certainly left with the impression that I ought to check the handbook to see what hours breathing is allowed."

"Between two and four." Oscar grins. As I survey the room, he adds, "Afraid it ain't much, and it's bloody freezing at night, but not so bad once you get used to it."

"You'd think we were sleeping on beds of gold for how that man speaks of this place." I brush a hand over the simplistic iron of the bedframe and then fall face-first onto the mattress. Certainly not the feather bed I was accustomed to at home, but it could be worse. Horse-hair and wool, perhaps, so not altogether horrible.

Oscar has an edge of amusement to his voice. "Trust me, better than what Edlebridge offered. My mum took me there first and we settled on Whisperwood because it was streets above."

"Do you mean this *isn't* a last resort and our only hopes of becoming civilized young men?" I ask, voice muffled into my pillow. No matter how the headmaster tries to sell it, it is, in essence, a place for boys whose families couldn't afford somewhere like Harrow, or boys that somewhere like Harrow wouldn't take.

"They'd like to make us think so. They'd also like to make us think they're stricter than they are." I see Oscar shrug from the corner of my gaze. "Only thing they're big sticklers about is curfew; keep your marks good and don't go wanderin' about after hours, and you'll have a grand time."

I roll onto my back. I don't recall ever having to be ushered to bed before I was good and ready. "They make an awful fuss about curfew. What do they think we'll do, write obscene messages on the chalkboards?"

"This place is full of gentlemen—I use that term loosely, mind— who got themselves in trouble some way or another," Oscar points out. "Stricter they are with us, less opportunities for us to get to doing somethin' we ought to not be doing. Couple of terms ago, some bloke ran off in the middle of the night to meet up with someone from the girl's school down the road. Needless to say, he got expelled and everyone else has suffered with a crackdown on curfew ever since."

"Always one ruining it for the rest of us."

"Always." The other boy graces me with a charming smile. "You as famished as I am? Dinner starts soon."

After a day of travelling on crowded trains and bumpy carriage rides and my nerves only now beginning to settle, I'm honestly not hungry in the slightest. Nor do I fancy staying in this room all by my lonesome. As such, I pick myself up off the bed and smooth a hand down my shirt. "Is the food good, at least?"

"Ain't bad, actually." Oscar leads the way out and back down the hall.

We pass a number of open doors, revealing boys moving in and out as they settle in, reacquainting themselves with their surroundings and each other. It makes me think to ask Oscar, "Have you been here long?"

"Started here at the beginning of second year," he says, lifting a hand in a wave to a pair of boys in the common room who call his name. "What brings you here, anyway?"

Oh, that is a question I expect to be asked plenty in coming weeks and months. *What are you in for?* As though I've been convicted of some grievous crime. (Well...) "My parents thought I needed 'structure,' whatever that means."

"Structure is something unavoidable here."

"What about you?"

A faint frown passes across Oscar's face, though it smooths out quickly enough. "My father was enlisted in the

Army. Serving King and Country and all that. Something went wrong—couldn't tell you what; Mum refused to tell me—but she thought…"

"It was wiser to send her son away?"

He opens the dormitory door, pausing half a second as though considering the best way to answer that. "I was a little difficult to deal with at times, I suppose. She thought she'd be better able to care for my little sister without me in the way. Father's brother does all right for himself and offered to pay the tuition."

That seems unduly harsh. I wonder if there's more to his story than he's telling me or if his mother really is that kind of person. Oscar doesn't strike me as a boy prone to getting into trouble. Then again, we've only just met.

Not going to pry, though. I don't want my personal business dug up, and so I won't needle anyone else for details on theirs, either. "Are most of the occupants here really sent for reform, then?"

"Some, sure. Lads who were too caught up with crime or prostitutes or wouldn't get out of the opium dens. Caught up in scandals, others just…in the way. Got a fair share of boys from illegitimate births, too. Mistresses couldn't keep 'em on their own, father wasn't willing to take 'em in."

"So pay to send them to public school because it appears kinder than simply turning their backs on them."

"About right, yeah."

"Charming." And sad. True, my relationship with my mother and father has been strained as of late, but I have a difficult time imagining either of them turning me away because they did not *want* me. Then again, I've always been a well-behaved boy. Father disliked some of my interests, found a few of my behaviours too foppish for his taste, but I'd never been caught doing anything inappropriate and so I think he still held out hope for me.

I don't know that he still does now.

The sun has about completely set by the time we re-enter the school, whose doors are propped wide open. Even without Oscar there to guide me, all I need do is follow the crowd heading into a set of doors directly across the foyer, between the two staircases that lead to the next floor.

Inside the dining hall, the scent of food washes over me and makes my stomach growl despite my lingering nerves and previous notion that I wasn't hungry. The mahogany tables are draped with cloths, adorned with candelabras spaced between the silver platters of food. I spy ham, rolls with sweet cream butter, vegetables, turkey roasted and dressed, and large bowls of soup. Not as elegant as meals at home, but better than expected. Although I won't be surprised if our everyday spreads are significantly sparser than this, and what we're presented with today is more of a welcome gift. Regardless, it does smell good, and as Oscar and I take up chairs at one of the far end tables near the windows, I think I shall eat after all.

The empty chairs around us fill quickly. Oscar introduces me to the various gentlemen who join us; Preston Alexander, a tall, broad-shouldered, smiling third-year with a handshake like a vice. His roommate, Benjamin Prichard, has some of the loveliest, darkest eyes I've ever seen, and is a quiet and unassuming boy who gives me a polite greeting but seems otherwise content to sit and listen to the conversation with the occasional smile and laugh. A few others fill in the gaps. I'm given their names, where they're from, and at least some information about each of them that I will likely need to be reminded of again later, but I'm largely distracted.

My eyes have traversed the length of our table and come to land on a boy at the very far end of it. Which sounds ridiculous because the table is full of boys, but this one in particular...

There is little about him that would stand out in a crowd, at least from this distance. He's dressed in the same uniform I've seen several of the others wearing, even though it isn't required until the start of classes. His hair—darker than my own—is swept to the side and back, and a few strands threaten to slip down into his face. Perhaps what catches my eye is the way he's sitting, isolated, tucked into his chair as though trying to put distance between himself and everyone around him.

I dig an elbow into Oscar's side to get his attention, gaze unwavering. "Who is that? Why's he by himself?"

Oscar leans forwards to peer around me. "Oh, that's William Esher. He's always off on his own. Not much of a social sort, that one. Bit of a snob." He cuts into his dressing-covered turkey and pops a bite into his mouth even as one of the boys across from us—Edwin Davies, I think his name was—leans over to add, "They say he's here because he murdered his parents."

"Murdered his parents? *Really*." The idea is so preposterous I almost laugh. Seems unnecessary to point out that anyone convicted of murder would be in a jail cell or an asylum, not sent off to public school. Instead, I turn to Oscar. "What makes him a snob?"

He shrugs. "He doesn't talk to anyone if he can help it. Complete prick if you try to strike up a conversation, like he's too good to grace anyone with polite conversation."

"I see."

"Also, heard someone caught him buggerin' about with another student last term, but not sure how true that is."

I arch an eyebrow. "Fancying men is somehow related to being a snob?"

Another shrug as he looks back down to his food. I think he might be avoiding meeting my eyes, but perhaps I'm imagining that. "Just an observation, is all. And a warning. If he gets caught doing anything of that sort, it'll mean a pretty big punishment—if not expulsion—for anyone involved."

Well, yes. Expulsion is honestly the better alternative than being tossed in jail, and I came to Whisperwood aware that my own...interests...were not something to be discussed openly. Still, I keep glancing askance at William Esher as I eat, studying this boy who probably did not murder his parents but maybe did get caught with his hands down someone's trousers. I make a mental note that he is a person I shall most definitely pester later. Even snobs need friends, and I do enjoy a challenge.

2

I'm not a man who has ever really been struck by homesickness. That isn't to say, of course, that I don't miss my family, but I adjust well enough. So long as I have a comfortable bed to retire in at the end of the day, anything else can be dealt with.

The first night at school, however, I don't find sleep easy. Oh, the bed is fine, and even having Oscar asleep in the bed across from me is all right, it's just... I don't know. Some part of me waits for the hour to grow late enough. For the rest of the house to be asleep and for my door to creak open.

I toss and turn. Pull the pillow over my head, toss it to the foot of the bed. Under the covers, over them, on my side, on my stomach. I cannot for the life of me find a position that suits me. Eventually, I end on my back, staring at the ceiling in the dark. Unlike the halls, the dorm rooms are not papered, so I'm simply looking at blank, flat surfaces.

I suppose I'll have to settle for listening to the noises around me, then. The groans of an old building, the soft snoring from my roommate, the creaking of floorboards. All sounds with legitimate explanations behind them, of course, but to entertain myself I create stories about them. Boys sneaking around, teachers trying to catch them.

Then begins the crying.

So soft that at first, I almost miss it as I try to force myself to drift off, but—there it is, someone out in the halls of the dormitory, wailing, long and low, and it could almost come across as the wind shoving through narrow corridors. Hell, I cannot sleep anyway, and now that I can pick out the sound I'm not certain I'll be able to sleep until I know what's causing it. A homesick student? Someone lost?

I fetch my robe, not bothering with a candle because I would sooner not have light to give me away to the prefects or staff while I'm out and about on my first night here. Yet as I step out and ease the door shut behind me, I think that may have been a mistake. With no windows, I'm plunged into near total darkness, and suddenly all the sounds I've been listening to feel a lot more ominous. Shuffling towards where I think the crying is coming from, I swing my gaze from one door to the next. All closed. All silent.

At the end of the corridor, the crying comes to an abrupt stop, and so do I. It ceased so suddenly. No tapering off, just there one second and then silent the next. I allow myself to linger a few moments to see if it picks up again, and when it doesn't, I sigh, turn on my heel, and begin back to my own room.

When my hand comes to rest upon the doorknob, someone steps up behind me. It's subtle. Brief. A hand on my shoulder, the breath of an incoherent whisper against my ear that makes every hair on the back of my neck stand to attention.

I whip around, expecting…something, anything, and finding myself disoriented that the hallway is still pitch black and very empty.

"Hello?" My voice emerges softer than I intended due to my heart having become lodged in my throat. For the life of me, I cannot shake the feeling that I'm being watched. Is this some kind of joke? Someone having a laugh at the new boy? "If you're trying to be funny, you're very dull."

No response. Only the sound of my own breathing and darkness all around and I still have the sense of someone close by, just out of my line of sight, and I can feel the remnants of that breath against my skin. I should go back to bed. Staring at the ceiling is far less foolish than standing in an empty hall waiting for God knows what and—

A loud clang speeds up that decision for me. It comes from somewhere at the end of the hall, followed by the heavy sound of rushing footsteps—right in my direction. My hand twists, the door gives, and I topple backwards into my room and heave the door closed behind me.

From out in the hall—silence.

I've broken out into a cold sweat and I cannot seem to get my breathing to steady. From his bed, my abrupt door-closing has caused Oscar to stir; he pushes himself up onto an elbow to peer groggily and messy-haired in my direction. "Spencer? What's wrong?"

"Nothing," I manage, carefully twisting the deadbolt into place as I straighten up. "Nothing at all. Go back to sleep."

I will not have my new roommate think me utterly insane on my first night here. Especially when I'm still uncertain as to what just happened. No, I much prefer getting back into bed—robe and all—drawing the blankets to my chin and staring at the ceiling for however long it takes me to find sleep.

IF OSCAR RECALLS my racket waking him in the middle of the night, he doesn't say a word about it the next day. Come morning, we're up with the sound of bells from school, shuffling around in an early-morning stupor while we take our turns getting in a proper wash and shave.

I'm accustomed to the servants bringing hot water for such an endeavour, and for someone to be standing by to collect the slop bucket when I'm done, but apparently, we're to make do with a jug of water so cold it's become a bit slushy. I guess delivering hot water to every student *would* be rather difficult, and at least the cold is quick to wake me up. I make sense of my hair, and get into uniform, of which there were a few hanging up in my wardrobe upon arriving. I brought my own underwear, of course, but everything else has been tailored according to the measurements we sent ahead of time and everything appears to fit snugly.

My tired fingers are attempting to make sense of my necktie when I decide to broach the subject. "Did you hear anything odd last night?"

Oscar, hunched over before the mirror with a comb in hand, trying to tame a few bits of hair that refuse to be forced into place, hmms in response. "Don't think so. Why?"

I believe I've tied it all wrong. Damn it. With a frown, I undo it all to start again. This is something I should know how to do in my sleep, but apparently not when I've been without sleep most of the night. "Oh, nothing, just sounded like there was someone out in the halls."

Oscar purses his lips at his reflection. "It's an old building. Makes all kinds of queer noises. Or it could've been the prefects or housemaster taking a stroll to make sure no one was out past curfew. Simmons does so love to catch people nightwandering. He was our prefect last year in Lancelot Hall. Complete prick."

I could tell him that I went into the hall and I know damned well no one was out there. Had I run into our prefect or housemaster, surely, they would have marched right up and slapped me with due punishment. But I was exhausted. First night in a very new place, it's perfectly possible my mind was playing tricks on me and I have no desire to make things awkward between us. "I suppose."

"You'll get used to it," he assures, straightening up and giving himself a last once-over in the mirror. "First month I was here, I didn't sleep more than a few hours a night on account of the noises and it being so bloody cold." He flashes me a smile, opens the door, and beckons me along. Sleeping poorly is not a grand way to start off my first day of classes, so a proper breakfast is most certainly in order.

We tuck in at the same spot we did the night before, surrounded by the same group of gentlemen. Remembering their names is easier this time. Preston Alexander, Benjamin Prichard, Edwin Davies. All pleasant enough in their own right. People who seem to accept me right into the fold.

A glance to one side tells me that William Esher is, yet again, seated on his own at the far end of the table, this time donning a pair of spectacles and with a book in hand as he eats. He's trying to be discreet; I can imagine reading is not permitted while at the breakfast table. At one point, he lifts his head, scanning the room. I think he meets my gaze, if only for a moment, before his eyes dart quickly back to his page.

I really do need to make it a point to talk to him.

During breakfast, and after the headmaster has stood at the front of the room and given his morning announcements and led us in a quick prayer, Oscar, the other boys, and myself compare schedules. Preston and Benjamin share my first lesson, which is Latin. Oscar and I also share a class—maths with Mr. McLachlan.

"He seems intense," I say.

Virgil Appleton, one of the two prefects of my dormitory and who is seated a few chairs down, leans forwards to say, "He is, yes. And strict. But not unfair."

I suppose there's that. Strict can be dealt with, but I have little patience for unfairness. "What about the rest of these?" I pass my schedule down to him and he scans over it.

"Not bad. Mr. Keys is a bit of a brute," he says, referencing my Latin instructor. "Mr. Harrison is dull, but he's also old as dirt and forgets to collect essays half the time." He passes back the paper.

"Mr. Hart's great," Oscar says of my English instructor, taking the paper and placing it back in my hands. "Brilliant, in fact. He teaches second-years, too. I was thrilled to see I had him again this term."

"Good to know." I tuck the schedule back amongst my books on the floor at my feet. With my fourth period with

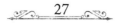

Oscar and the others with some combination of Preston and Benjamin and a few other boys sitting near us, I can take comfort in the fact I won't be stuck all on my own.

Preston and Benjamin accompany me to Latin. My tutor back home was not well-versed in the language, and what I was taught in my younger years has largely abandoned me. When I explain this predicament to Benjamin, he gives me a kind smile and says, "I'm sure Mr. Keys will understand and offer some extra tutoring."

When we arrive at the classroom, I immediately notice another semi-familiar face towards the back of the room. William still has his nose in a book, elbow resting upon his desk, chin in his hand. I think I might sit in the empty desk beside him except Benjamin and Preston take a seat towards the front and it might be rude to abandon them for a stranger when they've been so kind as to try to reassure me I won't be alone here. Instead I take up the desk beside Benjamin, stealing a glance over my left shoulder at William, who certainly doesn't notice me. The way he continues in this manner makes me even more certain that I will very soon be invading his space in order to make myself be noticed.

As Virgil said at breakfast, Mr. Keys is the epitome of a stubborn, traditional old man. Highly religious and highly stuck in his ways. Latin, he says, is a crucial part of any proper man's education. He spends the better part of class passing out our textbooks and lecturing us on this rather than giving any actual lessons, and I find my eyes beginning to glaze over towards the end.

English is a far more enjoyable experience. Benjamin has left for his next lesson and Preston and I sit next to each other. From the moment Mr. Hart rises from his desk to greet the class, I instantly think I'm going to like him.

He's middle-aged, brown hair swept neatly aside and back, and lightly sprinkled with grey at the temples. Even gently lined with age, he has the sort of face I think women would adore. He might be the first instructor I've seen at Whisperwood who knows how to smile, too, and he does so as he speaks fondly to the class.

"While we will be addressing concepts of grammar and spelling, there are a great many things I will be covering over the term," he tells us, all with that gentle smile upon his face. "We shall study some of the classics in both fiction and poetry, and I will very much encourage all of you to do some creative writing of your own."

Oh. Yes. I definitely like this class already. Anything that grants me an excuse to write, especially poetry. For that matter, any class that doesn't involve me simply sitting, listening, and copying down what is written on the board will be better than what Mr. Keys' class is shaping up to be.

During lunch, Preston and I meet back up with Oscar, Benjamin, and a few others as we crowd into the hall to eat. It's only been a few hours, but I'm famished, glad to tuck in and stuff my face so that I'm certain to feel unpleasantly full through my last two classes.

History with Mr. Harrison is nothing of note. He's an elderly gentleman whose hands shake something horrible when he writes upon the blackboard, but he seems knowledgeable of his subject. It beats Latin.

To say that I'm excited for maths is almost laughable, but it pleases me to get to take a seat beside Oscar in the very back row, the two of us exchanging grins. William is in this class, too, I notice. The back row has filled up, so he sits two seats in front of and to the right of me, giving me a grand view of…well, mostly the back of his head, really.

Mr. McLachlan is, indeed, an intense man, but I appreciate that he skims over the typical introductory information the other instructors droned on about and gets right into teaching. He has us scribbling down formulas not even halfway through the lesson, and while I'm struggling to grasp some of the concepts, he slows it down towards the end of class and takes the time to come to each desk, checking over our work and giving patient guidance for those— myself included—who are struggling. Oscar surprises me by grasping the information effortlessly, and I don't notice William requesting help, either.

Overall it's not an overly dreadful class, and though I cannot say it's something I will enjoy, it's not the worst that I've attended. By the time the day rolls to an end, I'm thoroughly worn out. Back home, my days rarely started before eleven and they ended late into the night, whenever I felt compelled to sleep. Having my timeframe for wakefulness yanked forward several hours, on top of piling it full of sitting in place while teachers saw open my head and cram information into my brain, has left me bloody exhausted. At least for tonight, I won't mind the early hour of retiring as much as I thought I would.

After drill class—which, thankfully, consists mostly of being shown the dressing room and being given our uniforms and little actual exercise—we spend a few hours lounging about in front of the fireplace in the common room of Gawain Hall. It grants me a quieter atmosphere of getting to know some of my housemates. Even Virgil joins us for a bit, although he's a very serious sort who doesn't seem prone to joking around, but genuinely seems interested in knowing we've all settled in with no issues, and that we know where to find him if he's needed. He seems a nice enough fellow, but impossible to get a good read on.

I call it a night before curfew draws too near, and Oscar accompanies me. He flops down onto his bed while I wash, change into my nightshirt, and locate a sheet of paper, my pen, and inkwell to take a seat at the table and see if I cannot think of something to put in a letter home.

> *To my dearest parents,*
>
> *I hope this letter reaches you in the best of health. I have arrived at Whisperwood and it is as I think you had hoped it would be. The instructors are strict, the food is decent, and the rooms are quite cold. I've made friends already, but that should come as no surprise as Mother often says I could befriend a rock if I tried...*

I come to a stop there, debating on how best to proceed. Do I ask how Uncle is? Cousins Kitty and Rebecca? Do I ask how the search is going for a new house, and if they have plans to come visit me at school any time during the term? Things with my family were not well when I left. Mother cried as I boarded my carriage to leave, but I received no hugs, no requests to write—although I said I would anyway. These last two months, I have never felt so uncertain as to where I stand with my family. For a boy who has always been on good footing with his parents, it's a jarring feeling.

I slump back in my chair and look to Oscar. He's hunched over on his bed, fumbling with a piece of paper in his hands. After a few moments, his pinching and twisting begins to take the shape of a flower.

"For someone special?"

He lifts his head briefly and a sheepish grin pulls at his mouth. "For my sister, Lily. I've made these for her since she was a baby, and I send them home with my letters."

It makes me smile, too. "How old is she?"

"Ten and two, as of last month," he says, sounding proud of that fact.

"You were on holiday, then, right? Good you were able to be home for such an event."

At that, his smile fades, replaced by a withdrawn look of melancholy. His head bows back over his paper flower. "Ah, no, not exactly. I spent holiday at my uncle's in Lancashire."

I frown. I know I said I wouldn't pry, and yet... "Why is that?"

"Mum was—she said it would be difficult. To have me home." He shrugs, and it's such a small, sad gesture that it truly makes my heart hurt for him.

I place my pen down and cap the inkwell before rising to my feet. "I know we've only just met, Oscar, but I do hope you know if you want to talk about it, I'm here."

The smile he gives me is small but sincere, and he seems unbothered by my overly familiar use of his given name. "I appreciate that, but I'm all right."

"Promise?"

"Promise."

Fair enough. With my letter put on hold until I can figure out just what to say, I crawl into bed and decide to call it an

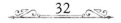

early night. I slept so poorly last night that catching an extra hour or two isn't a bad idea.

Oscar does the same before long, changing into his nightclothes and snuffing out the candles. The room falls into silence, followed soon by the sound of Oscar's open-mouthed breathing.

And, as I begin to doze, the soft sound of someone sobbing in the depths of the dorms.

3

My letter home remains unfinished until the end of my first week, and I don't find the nerve to post it until the following Wednesday when Oscar tells me to stop puttering about and just do it. It's both his encouragement and my growing ease at Whisperwood that emboldens me.

Over the course of my first two weeks, I've carved myself a little niche amongst my new friends that I find comfortable. I'm adjusting to the early hours, the cold water, and busy schedule. Even the late-night sounds have seemed to vanish, or perhaps—as Oscar said I would—I've become accustomed enough to sleep through them.

After fourth period every Monday, Wednesday, and Friday, we attend drill class. Important towards promoting good health, our instructor says, while leading us through an intensive and thoroughly boring round of calisthenics. Only after that are we free to play sports, which is notably more entertaining.

Promoting physical and cognitive wellness may be part of the agenda, however I personally believe it's the staff's way of having us run off some energy given we spend so much time cooped up indoors, listening to our professors drone on about the most uninteresting of subjects.

But as far as sports go, rugby is, admittedly, one of the more entertaining ones. Oscar is in his element here. Short as he might be, he's broad-shouldered and well-toned, and when he ducks low and takes a player by their midsection, they go down fast and with little resistance. Myself included. My back slamming to the muddy ground doesn't feel the most pleasant, but I laugh at the ridiculousness of it all. If Mother were to see me like this, she'd be horrified. Sports, she says, perhaps with the exception of golf, are not gentlemanly endeavours no matter how much wellness they may offer. After an hour of chasing each other around on a muddy, rain-soaked field, the lot of us are equally as rain-soaked and filthy.

Everyone except for William, that is.

Not once in the past two weeks have I seen William participate during sports. He dresses down in grey linens, the same as the rest of us, but throughout drill he remains seated off to the side of the field upon a bench, legs crossed, head down, nose in a book. Preston told me, with a roll of his eyes, that William had a doctor's excuse that got him out of having to do any sort of physical activity, and I'll admit I am curious. He looks healthy enough, at any rate, and I've not noticed anything amiss about him in the classes we share.

Today, as Oscar is knocking me to the ground, somewhere in my peripheral vision I notice William watching us. After picking myself up I steal a glance at Oscar, Benjamin, and the others, who are taking a brief break to catch their breath. While they're doing that, I jog my way across the field to where William is seated.

I don't know why I choose today of all days to approach him. The day I'm wet and sweating and undoubtedly not looking my best, but why not? I've been immensely curious about this boy the others seem to avoid, this soul that is allegedly so unfriendly and who cannot be bothered to participate in sports and speaks so softly only when forced to during classes.

But perhaps it was fate, because as I near, it dawns on me what book he's reading, and I cannot help a smile.

"*Pardon, oh, pardon, that my soul should make, of all that strong divineness which I know,*" I begin, and William stills in the middle of turning the page but doesn't look up. I continue, "*For thine and thee, an image only so, formed of the sand, and fit to shift and break.*"

Did I remember all that correctly? I have a knack for memorizing poetry, but it's been a while since reading *Sonnets from the Portuguese*, so I could be off a bit.

Slowly, William's eyes roll up to watch me. I'm standing in his sunlight, casting a shadow over him, and he simply stares as though expecting me to say something further. This is the first time I have ever seen William up close and, goodness, he does have the most remarkable and intense eyes, doesn't he? "No? Not a good one? All right, how about...

*And wilt thou have me fashion into speech
The love I bear thee, finding words enough,*

And hold the torch out, while the winds are rough,
Between our faces, to cast light on each?—
I drop it at thy feet. I cannot teach
My hand to hold my spirit so far off
From myself—me—that I should bring thee proof
In words, of love hid in me out of reach."

For a long moment, William studies me like a specimen in a jar. Then he drops his gaze and bows his head, and I'm beginning to think he's going to blatantly ignore me.

Just as I'm about to turn away, his quiet voice continues where I left off.

"If thou must love me, let it be for nought
Except for love's sake only."

Truly, I cannot help the way my face lights up. *"Do not say*
"I love her for her smile—her look—her way
Of speaking gently,—for a trick of thought
That falls in well with mine, and certes brought
A sense of pleasant ease on such a day"—
For these things in themselves, Belovèd, may
Be changed, or change for thee,—and love, so wrought,
May be unwrought so."

"Hm." William marks the page he's on with a scrap of paper and closes the book. "Congratulations on your memorisation skills. May I help you with something?"

"Oh, thank you. It comes easily to me, you know. Memorisation. Ask me for basic multiplication and I'm afraid I'm lost, but—well, poetry is a strength. Or a weakness, depending on how you look at it."

William rolls his gaze up to watch me over the top of his glasses. He has remarkably long lashes, I note. High cheekbones begging to be touched and a thin mouth pulled into a tight-lipped line that makes his expression utterly impossible to read. Whatever it was I thought ordinary about him from afar was wrong; up close, William Esher is quite beautiful. "I'll repeat my question: can I help you?"

I take it upon myself to have an uninvited seat beside him, although I do try to maintain a bit of distance to avoid dirtying him with my muddied linens. "I don't know. Do I need help?"

It's a subtle movement, but William seems to shy away from me, an impatient edge to his voice. "What do you want, Spencer?"

Oh! But he knows my name and that's quite nice, isn't it? Granted, we share classes, so perhaps that isn't so surprising. Although I couldn't put a name to every one of my classmates, so there is that. "A pony entirely my own so that I don't have to share with the others," is my sweet and entirely unnecessary reply.

By the twitch of his eyebrows as they draw together, he doesn't appear to enjoy my teasing. "If that will be all, I have reading to do."

This is where manners would dictate I should leave, because this boy clearly doesn't want me here. But when have I ever been known to take a hint? "Which one is your favourite so far?"

William sighs heavily through his nose, pushing his shoulders back. Honestly, I'm surprised when he humours me by meeting my eyes again as he speaks.

"...*How do I love thee? Let me count the ways.*
I love thee to the depth and breadth and height
My soul can reach, when feeling out of sight."

The intensity of his gaze and the melted-butter smoothness of his voice leaves my throat a little dry and my pulse jumping in a pleasant fashion. For someone who projects such a cold front to the world, he's chosen one of Browning's sweetest lines to recite to me, and it makes me wonder if he isn't quite a soft soul beneath all that prickliness. "She has a way with words, doesn't she? A certain sweetness that has so often been lost in all the pretentiousness of many poets these days. She's more focused with the message, less so with trying to prove herself."

He steals a glance down at the cover of the book. "I thought they were translated from other foreign poets?"

"That's what she says, but I don't believe it. Perhaps she merely wanted to maintain some semblance of privacy over her love life. Love sonnets are quite personal, after all."

"Well, regardless of who penned them, they are certainly from the heart," William agrees. "Did you really come over here to bother me about poetry?"

"Was there something else I should bother you about?"

A persistent frown tugs at his face. "I'm not understanding why you approached me at all when I clearly had no wish to be disturbed."

"In that regard, you're a difficult man, William. May I call you William? But you see, I am also a difficult man, and as such I would approach someone who does not wish to be approached. Like attracts like, I suppose, and so here we are. Two difficult people reciting love poetry to one another." A smile pulls at the corners of my mouth at the look of confusion that settles over William's lovely features, and I wonder if he's aware that—or trying to figure out if—I am most certainly flirting with him.

Before he has a chance to respond, Oscar's voice carries across the field. "Spencer! We're waiting on you!"

I lift a hand in their direction but don't break eye contact with William, even as I rise to my feet. "I hope to recite more poetry with you again," I say, flashing him my most charming smile before turning to jog back to where my friends are waiting for me. He says nothing as I go, but any time I glance back, his gaze is still locked onto me.

As I re-join my group, Oscar peers around me in William's direction with an eyebrow cocked. "What was that all about?"

I snag the ball from under his arm, turning and tossing it in Preston's direction; despite being off-guard, he catches it with ease. "Oh, nothing. Just discussing mutual interests."

"William has interests?" Preston muses, spinning the ball lithely in his large hands.

"Of course he does. Do you see him sitting, staring at walls all day? What sort of man doesn't have interests?"

"He's always got his nose in a book."

"There you have it. Reading is one of his interests." I steal a look over my shoulder. William's head is bowed again and that makes me a bit sad. I rather like it when he watches me, and I think I'll make it a point to encourage him to do it much more often.

The next morning at breakfast, during our daily morning prayer, I catch William observing me from a distance. Briefly, of course; he isn't outright staring but he glances up from his clasped hands, locks his eyes with mine for half a second, and averts his gaze when I smile his way.

It's a gesture he repeats in Latin, and again at lunch. It's a curious, calculating sort of look—like he's trying to figure me out. I wonder what there is *to* figure out. I like to think my motives with him were clear: I would like to get to know him better. We might have things in common. I'm very fond of my new friends, but any attempt at speaking of poetry and art and theatre seems to bore them to tears.

Besides, William is terribly lovely to look at. I'd like an excuse to do it more often, up close and personal.

He does it yet again in maths, his eyes raking over me when he enters the room, and his gaze lingers as he takes his seat. But this time, I have Oscar beside me, and he's quick to take notice.

"What was that look Esher just gave you?"

I make a noncommittal noise and shrug it off. Which is fine for the first day, but when it carries into the second and third days of exchanged looks and lingering gazes upon one another, Oscar jabs a finger sharply into my side.

"I'm not imagining things," he whispers. Class hasn't officially started yet, but he keeps his voice down all the same. "He's been eyeing you an awful lot the last couple of days."

I cannot help but smile, pleased. "Maybe he thinks I'm pretty."

Humourless, Oscar frowns. "I warned you about that. Watch yourself around him."

"I think you're worrying too much." I tip my head with a dramatic flutter of lashes. "Besides, you'll always have my heart first."

That coaxes a smile out of him, but there's still worry etched into his features. If he has plans to respond, he hasn't a chance as Mr. McLachlan enters the room and starts right in on his lecture.

A lecture that, twenty minutes in, is interrupted by a gentleman stepping into the room and crooking a finger at our teacher. Mr. McLachlan turns from the chalkboard, looking more than a little miffed at the intrusion. He steps over and bows his head while the man whispers something to him, and the frown upon his face shifts into confusion and then something not unlike concern. He straightens up, eyes roaming the room and landing on me.

No, not me.

"Mr. Frances," he says. "Your presence is requested in the headmaster's office."

Oscar? But why?

I turn my head in his direction. All colour has drained from Oscar's face and his eyes have gone wide. What I do not see, however, is any kind of bewilderment about this summons, and I wonder if he's aware of what he's being called in for.

Slowly, mechanically, Oscar collects his things and slides from his seat. He doesn't make eye contact with anyone, myself included, as he inches down the row and out of the room to follow the man—who I now presume to be an aide to the headmaster. Every set of eyes watches him go, and a protective instinct inside me wants to snap at the lot of them to mind their own bloody business and leave him alone. Oscar's a good lad. As far as I've been privy to, he's not done a thing that warrants getting into trouble.

Mr. McLachlan is uncharacteristically taken aback. He recovers quickly enough, clearing his throat and redirecting the class back on-topic. But my mind is elsewhere, and I'm counting down the minutes until class is dismissed and I can grab my things and hurry out.

I go straight to Gawain Hall but find our room empty. When I meet up with Preston and Benjamin in the common room, they haven't seen hide nor hair of him, either. My concern hits its peak when his chair is empty at dinner. Surely if he'd been called to the headmaster's office, he would have been released by now?

In fact, it isn't until close to curfew—after I've changed for the night and planned on lying down to read—that the door creaks open and Oscar steps inside.

I sit up straight and abandon my book, unable to keep the worry from my voice. "There you are. I was beginning to think you'd been sent home."

To say Oscar looks exhausted is an understatement. He moves slow and stiff, dropping his books to the table and tugging at his neckwear. His hair is dishevelled and like he recently attempted to smooth it back without having a mirror to do so. Yet he smiles at me, just a flicker and then gone. "I'm sorry. Got in a spot of trouble, is all. Everything's well."

I frown at the obvious lie. "What on earth would you be in trouble for? Being too friendly?"

There's shame in his expression as he turns from me to retrieve his nightshirt from his drawer. "Headmaster found out I cheated on one of my exams at the end of last term."

Another blatant lie. I've seen Oscar's work. I've seen him answer questions in class. He's bloody brilliant and puts many of the students to shame. Which likely chafes a fair amount of them, that this low-born, poor boy from London is brighter than them and their rich upbringing.

"You don't need to cheat, Oscar. Why would you do that?"

He heaves a sigh, turning back to me as he begins to undress, although his gaze remains focused elsewhere. "I ain't a good test taker, is all. I freeze up."

Still lying. "Right. So, what was your punishment?"

"Couple of lashes."

Not surprising, and that would explain why he's keeping his back to the door as he removes his coat and shirt and pulls on his nightclothes, and the stiff way in which he moves.

"I'll be watched like a hawk in class and will be reporting to the headmaster's office a few times a week for extra work. Laundry duty every Sunday, too. Any further slip-ups of any kind will result in immediate expulsion."

I want him to turn around so I can survey the damage. Maybe I'm making too much of this, but it feels extremely harsh a punishment for a first offense of cheating. "Ridiculous, but it'll be all right."

Bless him, he does his best to give me a reassuring smile, but it falls a bit flat. "Course." He turns to finish preparing for bed, and he barely utters a good night to me when he crawls beneath the blankets and curls up to sleep before I've even snuffed out the candles.

For a while, I watch him from across the room, that Oscar-shaped lump curled in on himself, and my chest aches. I want to call him out on what I know to be a string of untruths, but what evidence do I have beyond my own gut feeling and what I've gleaned of Oscar's character over the last few weeks? I'm reluctant to brag about the fact that I already know him so well when there's so much about me he doesn't know. People have secrets. Oscar is not exempt from that.

I TRY TO sleep. Really, I do. But it's a night where it's simply not happening for me. Especially after some tossing and turning when I begin to hear the return of noises in the halls.

I've grown capable of pinpointing certain sounds in the dorms. The creaks that are just the wind upsetting old architecture. The sound of Virgil's footsteps—always around eleven-thirty—accompanied by a faint light spilling beneath the doorway from his candle as he does a sweep of the halls. The crying I picked up on the first two nights has been non-existent and I do not hear it now, but instead...

Footsteps.

Not Virgil's. It's too late for that, I see no light beneath the door, and it sounds to me as though whoever the steps belong to are making it a point to be as quiet as possible. It could be, I think, someone sneaking out.

At first, I contemplate ignoring it. Memories of that first night are still fresh enough that my pulse has already begun to quicken at the thought of following that sound, and yet... Ahh, hell. Maybe I'm too nosy for my own good. Maybe it's just something to do since I cannot sleep. Either way, I slide out of bed, fetch my robe, and duck out into the hall. This time, I think to bring a candle with me, willing to sacrifice stealth for a sense of safety to not be bumbling about in the dark.

Unlike my last nightmare adventure, though, I can better determine where the noise is coming from. Down the hall to my left. So that's where I go.

By the time I reach the end, it's come to my attention the door to the common room is ajar. I feel I won't be able to sleep until I see a person's face for myself. Steeling my nerves, I press onward, lingering outside the door only long enough to brace myself before shoving it open.

A figure poking about the bookshelf startles, whirling around with eyes as wide and frightened as those of a cornered animal. With the moonlight pouring in from the windows, I needn't even have my candle to discern William's face in the darkness.

We stare at one another, open-mouthed, and I think his heart must be racing as quickly as mine judging by the look on his face.

"William," I finally manage. "*You're* the thing that goes bump in the night?"

"What? No, I was just..." He slips his hands behind his back, and the movement makes me think that I saw something in his hand that he is now attempting to hide. "I couldn't sleep."

My eyebrows shoot up. "So, you came to fetch a book?"

"I went for a walk," he says, a touch defensively. "What are you doing here?"

I'm feeling a bit rankled from so much secrecy from people tonight. "I was sneaking out to meet my secret lover for a late-night tryst, of course."

He scowls, mouth downturned. Oh, goodness, he's quite precious when he's annoyed. "Well, terribly sorry but I'm the only one here."

"Perhaps that means you're my secret lover," I respond with an amused grin, feeling some of the tension easing from me to know that what I was hearing wasn't something ghostly.

It's difficult to tell in the eerie light, but I think he might be blushing. My teasing seems to have thrown water over the fire of his annoyance, at least. Whatever it is he's holding—a bottle, I think—is tucked carefully into the pocket of his robe as he crosses the room to come to a halt right before me. "Is that right?"

"Maybe." My smile holds as we study each other in the moonlight, which casts the most ethereal shadows upon William's beautiful face and seems to dance in his eyes. I almost wish I were a bolder man that I could push that flirting a step further. "But, in all honesty, and in an offer of peace, I simply heard noises and came to investigate. I do hope you're able to sleep, William. I sometimes have trouble with it in this place, too."

The sudden shift in my tone seems to confuse William as a puzzled frown tugs at his face. "Yes, of course," he mumbles, ducking his head. "This place is full of strange noises to keep one up at night."

"So I've noticed." My gaze drops briefly to that pocket. I'd be lying if I said I wasn't insanely curious just what it is he came here to get, and why it was here, of all places. The bookshelf contains a few knick-knacks, one of which is an ornate trinket box, and I think that may have been what I saw him messing with. The question being, what was in it that he risked being out past curfew to get? *None of my business, that's what,* I remind myself.

"Sweet dreams, William."

I leave him there to retreat to my own room, latching the door behind me. Though as I slip out of my robe, I hear slow, heavy footsteps in the hallway again. They head from right to left, which is the opposite direction William would be going if it were him, and I idly worry that perhaps someone else is wandering around and might catch him before he's had a chance to retreat to his room.

Against my better judgement, I pull open the door and lean out, looking towards where someone ought to be standing and—

Nothing.

The hall is empty, and the steps have stopped. My pulse quickens, and I think that I'm seeing shapes in the darkness that do not exist but chase me back behind the comfort of a closed door and make me jam a chair up beneath the handle all the same. Swiftly, I crawl into bed to sleep, but I'm again left with the unsettling sensation that something is watching.

5

Oscar is slow to get moving in the morning. He's always groggy and not quite his perky self upon first waking, but usually a wash-up does the trick at making him brighten. He scarcely bothers with shaving, and I must catch him to get his necktie on proper before he leaves the room.

At breakfast, I attempt to keep the conversation off whatever it was that happened to him the previous day. Though I do think to say, "I heard someone moving about again last night."

Oscar, not having engaged much in anything the other boys are conversing about, is busy pushing eggs about his plate. "Told you, mate, it was probably just someone out past curfew or something."

Well, last night it certainly was. But then afterwards...
"And yet every time I check, there's no one there."

He sighs. It might be the first time Oscar has ever sounded tired or irritated at me. "Maybe it's one of them ghosts, rattlin' about its chains. Someone ought to tell it to go study."

That certainly catches my interest. "Ghosts?"

He pauses, fork tapping once against the plate. "Nothing. Forget I said it."

"But you did say it. What do you mean?"

"Some people just say stuff. Silly stories."

"Silly stories often start somewhere."

"Sure, with creepy noises in the halls because students are pokin' about when they shouldn't be." He places his cutlery down and leans back in his seat. "Look, there are some tales. Things lads have seen and heard. But I shouldn't have opened my mouth. The staff gets steamin' mad when they hear anyone talking about it."

"What *don't* they get mad about," I mutter.

"Us keeping our heads down and not asking questions," he murmurs, and in that moment, the headmaster—performing his usual post-announcement walkthrough of the hall while we eat—passes behind us and Oscar shrinks in on himself. I think the headmaster makes it a point to look at him as he wanders by.

Prick.

"If there's something going on here," I say, voice low, only after dear old Mr. King is out of earshot, "we've a right to know."

"Nothing for us *to* know, James. They just don't like nonsense stories being spread around."

Oh, he's being difficult this morning. "What if they're not nonsense?"

The look Oscar tosses my way is one of utter exhaustion and it makes me feel all too horrible to needle him further. Ghosts or not, this may be something I need to address on my own.

Oscar takes his leave for his first class a few minutes early. Part of me is immensely interested in heading down the table to chat with William a bit, ask how he's doing as we haven't properly spoken since a few days ago on the field, but... Benjamin and Preston have spent the morning engaged in their usual, easy banter, and something they say snags my attention and swiftly reels me in. Now, before I've had the opportunity to get up and approach William, Preston leans across the table. "Frances seems a bit off today."

"Indeed."

"You're hearing things at night, you were saying?"

I suppose we weren't speaking as softly as I thought, but if he's going to broach the subject, then I'll go with it. "I have. Odd sounds out in the halls at night."

Preston grins. "I suppose if I were a ghost, that's what I would do. Try to give all the lads a fright."

"If you were a ghost," Benjamin interjects mildly, "you'd be the most unbearable one ever heard of. They'd have a priest here immediately to exorcise you."

"First of all, I'd be a basket of fun, thank you very much. Second, that's quite rude; I should not have to do any sort of exercise outside of drill."

"You know perfectly well what I meant."

On any normal day, their banter would be amusing. The pair of them share a close friendship judging by the teasing they dish out at one another. And yet, I've witnessed myself how swiftly Preston comes to his rescue when some of the

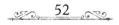

other boys sneer at Benjamin's dark eyes and hair, traits he inherited from his Chinese mother.

Unwilling to allow the two of them to get distracted with their jabs, I say, "The ghosts here don't appear to be much fun at all, though."

Benjamin's raised eyebrow is curious. "No such things actually exist."

"Unless you ask my aunt," Preston adds. "She's a medium. Into all that odd spirit photography and whatnot. Growing up, she always told my sisters and me that the ghosts would come after us if we didn't behave. Even if they did exist, they'd certainly run from this place or risk dying all over again from boredom."

I tilt my head. "Do you think so? I've heard whispers."

"Of course you have," Benjamin says. "We're a school full of young men isolated from the outside world with only work and more work to occupy us. There's bound to be gossip."

Preston nods in agreement. "That's all it is. Someone putting ideas in your head and getting you worked up, Spencer? Don't let them bother you. Some fools around here try their damndest to scare the new boys, but stories are all they are."

Frustration sinks in. I know they don't mean any harm, but even so. "I've heard things, you know. Sounds like there's something moving about in the dorms at night and talking, but any time I go to check, there's nothing there."

Benjamin's tone takes on a gentle, reassuring quality. "Old, unfamiliar buildings make odd noises."

"It wasn't your average creaks and groans."

"It wasn't ghosts, either."

"How do you know that?" I'm no stranger to people brushing off my concerns about much of anything, but I had been hoping for something different this time.

"I just told you, such things don't exist."

"And you've proof?"

"I've a reasonable mind and a grip on my imagination."

"Are you implying—"

"What Benji is *trying* to say," Preston interrupts, attempting to place a lid on this pot before it boils over into something it's not, "is that we've all gone through that in the beginning. New place, bunch of new people, and it's frightening, right? Give it some time. Let yourself adjust. I bet you ten to one, the noises will go away once you grow comfortable here. If not, well, I'll fight the ghosts for you myself."

Despite myself, I chuckle at the mental image. "That would be something to see."

"Why on earth?" Benjamin's mouth curves up. "We don't need anything supernatural to see Preston make a fool of himself."

They laugh it off. I still feel overwhelmingly frustrated, but I bite it back and let the conversation switch gears. I've got nowhere, after all, and I don't feel like I will this morning. Whether my two friends honestly have no idea what's going on or have been fortunate to not encounter anything, I cannot say I know.

IT ISN'T UNTIL lunch arrives that I spot my opportunity to speak with William again. He slips out from the hall early, and I come up with some excuse to do the same, abandoning my meal to do so.

When I emerge outside, the chill bites straight through my wool underclothes, making me shiver. I spot him on the

other side of the courtyard, back to me, perched upon the edge of the large fountain. Although when I descend the steps and begin to circle around, it also comes to my attention that he isn't alone.

Charles Simmons stands before him, hands in his pockets, and although his mouth is moving he's speaking too quietly for me to hear a word of it. I'm not sure what our housemaster wants with William, but the way he's hunched over, almost curled in on himself and away from Charles, looking very much like he simply wants to enjoy his book and be left alone, makes me instantly worry. It isn't the same kind of reluctance he displayed with me the other day. Right now, William looks downright uncomfortable.

I approach without thought, determined to interrupt the situation if it needs to be interrupted. When Charles notices me, he inclines his chin and offers me a vulpine grin. "Afternoon. Spencer, isn't it?"

"Mr. Simmons," I greet him with a pleasant smile in return. He doesn't offer his hand out to me, so I don't offer mine to him. "Terribly sorry to intrude, gentlemen; is this a bad time?"

"Not at all." Charles returns an intense gaze down to William. "Esher and I were just chatting. We've not had much time to do so since the term began."

"Ah, yes. The duties of a housemaster must keep you very busy indeed! Although I'm afraid I'm here to steal dear William away. We've maths work due tomorrow and I had a question about it he offered to help me with, you see. That is, if you still have time, William?"

William's brow furrows. He spares a look up at me and then rises to his feet, and I'm glad he's seeing my offer for help

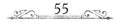

and swiftly taking it. "Yes, of course. Why else was I waiting out here for you in the cold?"

It could very well be my imagination, but Charles' eyes seem to narrow a fraction, though his smile stays in place. "By all means. Good day." To William he adds, "I'll be by some other time to see you," before turning to head off in the direction of the dorms.

The further he goes, the more William's shoulders seem to relax. The urge to touch a comforting hand to his back is strong and I have to fight it back. "Are you all right?"

"I'm fine," he assures, hugging his book to his chest. "Simmons was the prefect for Lancelot House last term when I was a second year. We didn't get on well and he enjoys pestering me."

"Now you're stuck with him for a housemaster. That's a cruel twist of fate."

"Life is full of those." He squints at me, as though he half expects me to have some sort of shifty ulterior motive for assisting him. "Did you really need help with maths?"

"I'm likely beyond help in that subject, I'm afraid." The school bell rings, signalling a ten-minute warning to get to our third lesson. I wonder what class William will be scurrying off to. Regardless, I can at least begin the walk back inside with him. "I do have an assignment for you, though."

"An assignment for me?"

"One of utmost importance. You see, I have a poem memorised, but I cannot for the life of me recall who it's by. Maybe you can help?"

He ducks his head as we ascend the steps, brows knitted together. "Spencer—"

"James."

"—I believe poetry to be a much stronger subject for you than it is for me. I enjoy reading it, but I cannot say I have a single poem memorised nor am I particularly good at remembering who wrote what."

"Fair enough. But it wouldn't be an assignment if it were easy, would it?"

The foyer has flooded with students emerging from the dining hall and scurrying down hallways and upstairs. This is where I'm to head down the left hall, and it looks like William intends to go down the right. He sighs at my persistence, and I decide to take the opportunity to lean in to speak against his ear where he might better hear me.

"*Love is enough: though the World be a-waning,*
And the woods have no voice but the voice of complaining,
Though the sky be too dark for dim eyes to discover
The gold-cups and daisies fair blooming thereunder,
Though the hills be held shadows, and the sea a dark
wonder..."

I pull back to see his gaze lowered and, dare I say, a tinge of rouge to his cheeks that pleases me immensely. "There's more to it, but I'll leave that to you to figure out," I say. And because I need to get to class, and because William is utterly perfect in his shy, flustered state, I'd like to frame this moment and not say another word more that might ruin it.

I NOTICE OSCAR'S discomfort throughout maths. Something that only seems to increase as the time ticks by, but I don't have much of an opportunity to ask him about it. As soon as we're let go for the day, he lingers at his desk even as I'm grabbing my things and eager to get out the door. His hesitance has me pausing.

"What is it?"

He heaves a sigh, sliding slowly from his chair. "Remember how I told you I have to check in with the headmaster for extra work?"

Oh. "Today is one of those days?"

"It is." He sounds so dismal when he says it that it doesn't sit right with me. Sure, it's certainly frustrating, but Oscar acts as though he's being sent to the gallows, and he isn't a man prone to theatrics over things. If anything, he tends to downplay.

"Why don't I go with you?" I offer. The headmaster wouldn't let me into his office with him, no, but—"I could wait for you in the hall."

Oscar's expression softens, and he smiles. "S'all right, but I appreciate the offer. I'll see you at dinner."

We walk together out of class, and I cannot help but let my attention be diverted to William when he slips past us, but only momentarily. I bid Oscar farewell for the time being before heading back to the dorms.

Having the room to myself borders on unsettling. Normally the pair of us sit at the table and do our school work together. Oscar's so bloody brilliant at everything except English, which is perfect because that is the one subject I excel in. Between the two of us, we do well for ourselves. I'll finish what work I can on my own, leaving aside a set of maths problems I've little hope of completing (correctly) on my own, and pull out a fresh sheet of paper to dabble in my poetry for a bit.

It's the first time in some months the words come easily to me. Things at home were so strained, so tense, that I couldn't for the life of me put pen to paper and come up with anything decent. Now, the process still feels disjointed and a little stiff, but the words are coming easier. Perhaps it's because I have something on my mind that does not weigh heavily upon me. For the first time in ages, it feels like, I have something I can think about and it brings a smile to my mouth, a flutter to my chest.

I think of William when I write.

I think of the way his eyes are so beautiful that they should be considered a work of art. The soft curve of his mouth, the way his lips purse together so gently when he is thinking about something. I think of the way his hair will sometimes fall into his face and I am always left with an irresistible urge to lean forwards and brush it back for him.

Stagger me into grace
With such soft eyes
And even softer lips...

I think, most of all, about how at ease I feel with him. For as standoffish as he is, for as odd his tendencies, I feel oddly content simply to have him near. His company feels as natural to me as night and day and I feed off that feeling, that warmth. Ridiculous how I find myself so enamoured, given we've only just met and hardly spoken. But there's something there, a spark, a flicker between us. Shared interests? Shared pain? I cannot say I know.

The time passes swiftly, several pages full of poems— although not all of them any good. I'd expected Oscar to have returned prior to dinner, but since he hasn't, I accompany Benjamin and Preston to the dining hall to meet up with the others. We're all very much aware of the empty seat to my left, and even Virgil and Augustus stop as they pass and give the chair a frown.

"Where's Frances?" Virgil asks.

I'm honestly a little surprised he's unaware of Oscar's situation, but I'm not about to divulge details. "He was summoned to the headmaster's office," is all I say, because any other answer might get him into trouble for missing a meal. Virgil purses his lips and the two exchange a look, but they head to their seats without further inquiry.

Oscar does not show up.

I spot William in his usual seat, and I've tucked one of the poems I wrote into my pocket, having thought that I might slip it to him on my way out, but he exits the hall before I have the chance.

We retire to the common room after we've eaten our fill. Benjamin sits with Preston, patiently going over something they discussed in philosophy that day, and I busy myself watching Edwin battle it out in cards with a few other boys. I sit it out. Boring, I say, because it's not as though betting is permitted, and what's the point of a good game of cards if you get nothing for it?

The hour grows late before Oscar joins us, and it's around that time I've begun to worry a little about his lateness.

Preston looks up from the cards in his hand, which he took up as soon as he and Benjamin had finished their work. "There you are. What took so long? Were you really with the headmaster all this time?"

Oscar sinks down into the armchair beside mine. When he exhales a sigh, he seems to be pushing an exorbitant amount of tension out of his body. "Yeah. Sorry."

I stretch out a leg to nudge one of his feet with my own. "You missed dinner."

"My stomach noticed."

"Are you well?"

"Fine." He flashes me a small smile that is not any more reassuring than it was the last time he spent an evening with that man. Before I can press him on it, he turns his attention to the others. "What are we playing? Deal me in."

Cards, as it turns out, is not as entertaining to watch as it is to play. But I can enjoy the warmth of the fire and the sound of chatter and laughter about the room, which dies down as some people retire for the night when curfew draws near. I could, in fact, almost doze off right there in that armchair, and I'm just about to do so when the sound of footsteps racing down the hall drags me back to my first night here and the unseen presence outside my room and—

When my eyes fly open and I sit up straight, looking to the door, it's William I see stumbling into the room. His sudden appearance draws the attention of all the boys in the den, and the fact that his skin has gone white as a sheet and his eyes are wide as saucers has every onlooker dead silent and still. Immediately concerned, I rise to my feet as he struggles to get words out.

"There was... In the hall, a boy crying and he... It was one of the ghosts. I'm *certain* of it."

The moment the word *ghosts* leaves his lips, most of the boys groan and go back to whatever activity they were previously engaged in. A few others quietly laugh. Edwin sighs with a roll of his eyes. "Looks like someone's a bit overly drugged this evening."

I shoot him a dour glare. "Oh, hush." Regardless of whether anyone cares what he has to say, William is clearly distressed. "Let me walk you back to your room, William. You don't look well." With the utmost gentleness, I take him by the elbow to coax him out the door and away from the snickering from within. Even as we relocate into the hall, William twists towards me, grasping my arms in a tight, trembling grip. "There was a boy—I *swear* it. You believe me, don't you? I promise, I did not imagine it."

"Of course," I croon, putting an arm about his shoulders to lead him down the hall. "Come now, you need some rest."

Together we walk down the corridor, passing by my own door, one of William's hands fisted in the fabric of my coat. He attempts to recount what happened. "I was heading to my room when I heard the crying. I rounded the corner and it was by the stairs. It *grabbed* me, James."

The moment we approach the end of the hall, where it rounds to the right and dead-ends into the stairwell leading to the second floor, William digs in his heels and refuses to budge another inch. He's no longer staring at me, instead he's looking down that direction as though advancing around that corner might mean certain death.

"I believe you," I assure him again in the softest, most soothing voice I know how to use. "I've heard a lot of strange things since arriving here, too. Including the crying."

William drags in a quaking breath. "It was just around there, at the base of the stairs."

I think back to the first night. The breath against my skin, the impossible to ignore sensation of someone standing behind me. Those horrible rushing footsteps that sent me scurrying into my room like a frightened child. It could all be nothing. It could be something. Either way, I steel my nerves and untangle myself from William to slowly walk the rest of the way to the end of the hall. Despite his fear, William dogs my heels, hands wrung together, watching me intently as I lean forwards and look around the corner.

Just a dark, empty stretch of hall and an even darker stairwell. Why aren't any of the candles lit? "There's nothing there now."

William doesn't relax, but he does crane his neck to peer around me to confirm what I've said. He uncurls his hands, rubbing at his left arm, and then he undoes his cuff and pushes up his sleeve with a wince, and we both look on in mixed horror and shock. There, upon otherwise unblemished skin, is a set of dark purple bruises in the shape of fingerprints.

My heart struggles to climb its way up into my throat and I have to force it down, attempting to remain calm and comforting for William's sake. "Let's get back to your room."

For the remainder of our trip upstairs, William is silent. I've not had cause to go up to the second floor yet, but it's a great deal quieter than any of the others. Both prefects reside here, along with the pricier single rooms for students. None of the second-floor boys need to share with a roommate, meaning William's family paid a hefty sum for him to have his own space.

Still visibly shaken, the moment we step inside he releases his hold on me and hurries to his dresser, rummaging in the top drawer and retrieving a bottle. I recognize it as, possibly, the same bottle I saw him sneaking into his pocket that night from the bookshelf. Now in proper lighting, I can sort of make out the label that reads *laudanum* across the front. Edwin's earlier comment makes a bit more sense now, and while opium use is hardly uncommon, I think the faculty might have something to say about a student smuggling it in and taking it without a doctor's permission.

I close the door and lean back against it. "Are you going to be all right?"

"Just fine." He uncorks the bottle and makes quick, practised work of putting several drops into his mouth. I get the impression this is not something he'd do in front of someone in any other situation.

That done, he closes the bottle, takes a deep breath, and turns back to me. Some of the colour is returning to his face. "You've heard the sounds before, too? Really?"

"A few times. At first, I thought it was a homesick student."

William looks away. Now that he's begun to calm down, he seems embarrassed. I wonder if he's second-guessing himself and what he saw. He tucks the laudanum back into the drawer and re-examines the bruises upon his arm. Those alone prove *something* strange happened. "I've heard that sound—the crying—many times since coming here," he softly admits. "From the very first night."

"But not just crying, right? Whispers, scratching, footsteps?"

He hugs himself. "Yes. Like nails clawing at the walls. My doorknob rattles at times, like someone is trying to get in. Ever since, I've kept a chair jammed up beneath the door knob while I sleep."

My head drops back against the door as my gaze rolls to the ceiling. "It's so strange no one wants to discuss it. I would think they'd use it to make this place seem more interesting."

The look William shoots me at my attempt to lighten the mood is an unimpressed one. "I could do without spirits causing my heart to stop, thank you very much."

"Better than dying of boredom... no? Just me?" I smile. "Do you think you'll be able to get some sleep?"

William opens his mouth as though to say something, catches whatever it is and shoves it back, biting his lower lip. He ducks his head into a nod. "Yes. Thank you, James."

I wish he'd ask me to stay longer; I would gladly oblige. Should I offer? Would it be too forward? "Happy to help," is all I say, tipping my head to him before letting myself back out of the room. William steps into the hall after me and watches me go, as though wanting to ensure I get down the steps without incident. As I descend the stairs, I hear his door quietly close, and I'd be lying if I say I don't walk a bit more briskly than is necessary to my own room.

Oscar is hunched over on his bed, reading by candlelight, and his head snaps up with a worried pull to his features when I enter. "Everything all right?"

He likely won't want to discuss it, will he? But I've made it a point to be as honest with him as I'm able, so— "I really think he saw something."

His mouth turns down and he slowly closes his book, running a hand over the cover that reads *A History of Pendennis*, by W. M. Thackeray. "And if he did, what're we supposed to do about it?"

A good question, and not one I really know the answer to. "I suppose...we try to figure out if anyone else has had similar experiences and have been too frightened to talk about it."

A tilt of Oscar's head shows his dubiousness. "Then what? Staff still won't want to hear it."

Sighing, I begin to strip out of my clothes to dress for bed. "And then we get the ghosts to *make* the staff hear it, Oscar, I don't know. But something has to happen. Poor William has *bruises*."

That gets his attention, eyebrows darting up. "Bruises?"

"Yes, where the ghost grabbed him."

Oscar sinks back against his pillow, bed frame giving a poignant creak. He appears to be mulling this information over. Truthfully, I half expect him to drop the subject and simply go to sleep, so he surprises me when he says, "All right. I don't know that there's ghosts runnin' about, but I trust your judgement, so if there's somethin' I can do..."

I pull my nightshirt over my head and swivel around to face him, unsure what's made him finally agreeable on the subject. A pleased smile splits across my face. "You're the best mate in all the world, do you know?"

He responds with a quiet laugh. "Not so sure about that. I know I've been a beast to deal with lately. Suppose we get some shut-eye for the time being, though? Maybe you can get some more information out of your darling Esher tomorrow."

6

The next morning, I have every intention of catching William at breakfast to talk to him, but his seat is noticeably vacant. The headmaster's announcements include a stern reminder about curfew, and I'm concerned it's William he's referring to until he turns a sharp look towards a group of first years. He also reminds us—not for the first time in the last few weeks—about the end of term. Exams, the importance of studying and, of course, the Christmas party.

Every teacher has brought it up at some point recently. Each year at the end of first term, just in time for Christmas, Whisperwood hosts a ball and invites a nearby girls' school. Mr. Hart said it's a means of rewarding us for a semester well spent, and a learning experience for those of us who have little practise in engaging in social events. I cannot say I'm looking forward to it.

I don't see William until Latin, where he arrives with only seconds to spare. He hurries in with his cheeks flushed red and his hair mussed, as though he ran to get here on time, and I smile to myself.

After class, there's not enough time to corner him if we both want to get to our next lesson, and at meals there are simply too many people around to have a discreet conversation. Lunch, then, after we've eaten. William tends to slip out early and sit near the fountain to read. At least, that's the plan until Oscar blindsides me with the fact he'll be reporting to the headmaster's office again after maths.

I twist in my seat to turn my full attention to him. He's scarcely touched his food, and he spoke the words so softly that I gather they were intended only for me.

"It's nearly the end of the bloody semester. How long does he intend to keep this up?"

"I don't know." He furrows his brow down at his plate as though it's caused him some distress.

I've done my best not to pry, but this situation cannot be ignored forever. "Oscar, what's going on? What is he *doing?*"

"I told you; I have to—"

"You've told me a string of lies," I interject, feeling only mildly bad that I'm accusing him of such things. "Something isn't right, and I want to be able to help, but I cannot if you won't even admit what's going on."

Oscar sets his fork down, stealing a glance at the others around us who are, thankfully, engaged in their own conversations and have not taken notice of ours. He draws in a slow breath, leaning in towards me to speak with his voice low. "Look, it's...complicated. The headmaster thinks that I did something I didn't do, and he's intent on pressing me until I admit to it. Which I bloody well won't because I've done nothin' wrong."

That makes a little more sense than the idea that Oscar would ever do something like cheat on an exam, but it's still difficult to grasp. "So, you're—what, being interrogated into confessing to a crime you didn't commit?"

"Something like that," he admits quietly.

Out of reflex and an urge to comfort, I reach to put a hand upon his back and note the way he immediately flinches, pained, from my touch. Any and all good humour I began my day with quickly vanishes. "Oscar..."

"I've got it handled, mate." He collects himself and grasps my shoulder as he offers me a smile. "All I can ask for right now is for you to be you. Make me laugh when I come home at the end of the day, maybe save me some dinner now and again if you think you can get away with it."

I swallow hard, studying his face. There are shadows beneath his eyes, a bit more definition in his cheekbones than I remember there being the day we met. I don't like that. And I don't like that he feels he cannot confide in me when I so desperately want to help. I cannot force Oscar to talk to me, so if all I can do is what he asks, then I'll give him a smile of my own. "I'll see what I can do."

WHEN I FINALLY do get the opportunity to seek out William, it's after maths when Oscar slips away to endure

another round of—I guess—interrogation by the headmaster. I saw William steal out of the classroom, though he met my gaze briefly before doing so, and I'm quick to follow after saying my goodbyes to Oscar.

Outside, it smells thickly of rain. This time when I spot William at the fountain, there is no Charles looming over him, and he appears to be waiting specifically for me because he meets my gaze as I approach and, oh, God, he *smiles*.

It's a small smile. Not grand in the great history of smiles, but it's far more than he's ever granted me before and I have to bite back the urge to return it with a dopey smile of my own.

What's more, he gestures to the spot at his side, a silent invitation for me to join him rather than the usual uncertain, sullen stares I've grown used to. I take the offered seat without a second thought. "Lovely day out, isn't it?"

"It looks like rain."

"I like rain."

"Mm." He folds his hands atop his lap. "I have something for you."

Oh, dear William is *full* of surprises today. "Is it a hug? I do like hugs."

With a roll of his eyes, he reaches to the other side of himself and retrieves a book, which he then offers out to me with a downcast expression I can only describe as shy. Upon the worn cover is the title *Stories that Might be True, and Other Poems* by Dora Greenwell. I desperately want to take his face in my hands and tell him what a perfect creature he is, and it's only with great constraint on my part that I refrain. I can think of no other way to split my heart open and show him what such a gift means to me, especially coming from someone so reserved as him. I settle for taking one of his hands in my own, sliding my thumb across his knuckles and savouring the way that William doesn't instantly pull back from me.

He bows his head with a blush, but his voice is crystal clear when he speaks.

"... *When closer ties have failed us,—meeting here,*
Both born in Yorkshire, we are friends at once,
Old friends as we had known each other all our lives;
And if you still will talk to me like one,
I will put off my journey to-morrow,
Just for the sake of hearing you."

"And you told me you weren't any good at memorisation," I tease, still positively beaming as I release his hand. "Thank you, William. Such a sweet and thoughtful gesture, and it means the world to me."

"It's only a book," William says, but the way he keeps his head down and fusses absently with his tie while his mouth twitches up at the corners suggests he's quietly pleased. "I had worried you might run low on poetry to recite to me. Fresh material."

I stick out my tongue at him and clutch the book to my chest, over my heart. "Me, run out of love poetry? Perish the thought."

"Do you make it a point to recite love poetry to all of your friends?"

"Only you."

He lifts his eyes to meet mine, and not for the first time I am struck by the clear blue of them, how they always convey so much even when the rest of his face remains so well-guarded. "Why is that?"

"Because you like it. And because I want to make you truly smile; it would be quite lovely to see, I think." And—yes, there it is again. A brief uptick of the corners of his mouth.

"If you want to make me smile, you could accompany me to the Christmas party tomorrow."

"I'm looking forward to that about as much as I'm looking forward to exams."

"That's too bad." William absently circles his thumb across one of his cufflinks. "I've found myself thinking more than once that I'm disappointed I won't be able to ask you for a dance."

I study him with the utmost curiosity. Where has this sudden boldness come from? I wonder if it has something to do with me escorting him to his room last night, if that encounter knocked down some unseen wall between us. "Not the *actual* dance, no. That may be a call for expulsion. Quite a shame, that."

"A shame indeed. I enjoy dancing, and I think I would especially enjoy doing dancing with you." The look he gives me is nothing short of inviting and—dare I say—flirtatious. At least, as flirtatious as I believe William is capable of being. Those eyes of his could reduce any man to a puddle.

"Ask nicely and perhaps you'll get a dance in private."

"I'll hold you to that." He shifts his position to uncross his legs and cross them again the other way. In the process of inching closer, his hand brushes mine, and I wonder if it was intentional. "I've been meaning to ask you, by the way. What brought you to Whisperwood?"

The smile I offer this time is cheeky. "Certainly not for murdering my family."

That gives him pause, and then he sighs. "Ah. Is that the story you've heard?"

"I daresay that makes you quite legendary, being here for such outlandish reasons."

"Not a doubt in your mind that it isn't true?"

I chuckle without meaning to. "I've never even entertained the idea. I imagine the truth to be far less exciting."

William's mouth twitches. "If you wish to know, my parents disagreed with some of my…hobbies. They sent me here with hopes it would encourage my interests to stray elsewhere."

Really, I didn't need him to say that aloud for me to assume as much. "Hobbies like dancing with boys and reading poetry?"

He glances at me, thoughtful. "Amongst other things. You've heard the rumours; not all of them are untrue."

I've now born witness to his laudanum use, yes, and although I've not overheard anyone speaking of it, Edwin's single comment last night was enough to tell me that others are, apparently, aware of it. "Vague and intriguing, as usual."

"More information than you've given me," he says with a tilt of his head.

More information than I intend on giving him any time soon, too. "Misbehaviour is why I'm here, dear William. Quite boring."

"Vague and intriguing," he mirrors my words, but doesn't look particularly bothered about my lack of clarity. For that, I'm grateful. He rises to his feet, fingertips touching briefly to my knee as he goes. "Now if you'll excuse me, I have some studying to get to."

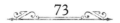

Without thinking, I catch hold of that hand, unwilling to relinquish his attention just yet. "Allow me to walk you back. We're going in the same direction, after all."

His gaze flicks down to my fingers wrapped about his. He slides smoothly from my grasp but permits me to begin walking back with him to Gawain Hall. Truthfully, I would love nothing more than to keep the conversation on good things, but I did seek him out to inquire about the spirits. When I do, William seems almost disappointed I brought it up.

"I'm afraid I've told you all I know," he says, casting a look skyward as the first few raindrops begin to fall. "I've heard noises since I started here at the beginning of second year. I initially attempted to speak with some of the other students and one of my prefects about it, but it didn't go well."

"They didn't believe you?"

"The other boys laughed me off. Our prefect at the time, he…" He purses his lips, and I wonder if he's ever had to discuss this subject with anyone before. "…He said my medication was clearly causing me to hallucinate."

I cannot say I know enough about laudanum to know if that's possible. Mother keeps a small vial of it for her terrible headaches, but she takes it sparingly. I'm getting the impression William's use is more frequent than that. "That prefect—you mean Simmons, don't you?"

"That would be him."

"I see."

"At any rate, it's been worse this term, in this hall." He rolls his thin shoulders back into a shrug. "It makes going out at night all the more terrifying."

He's proven it doesn't stop him; he goes out to fetch his medication, which says something about how desperate he is

for it. "Yet so many people either aren't hearing anything or won't speak up about it. You don't find that peculiar?"

"Of course I do. I presumed some were not as susceptible to otherworldly influences. Perhaps they don't see what I see."

That would be an explanation for it, but I'm not entirely convinced. Then again, beyond ghost stories in books, what experience do I have with this sort of thing? I wish Preston had been more open to discussing it, given he has a relation with a background in the supernatural.

My silence must bother William, because when we reach the dormitory entrance, he stops me and places a hand to my chest. I swear I can feel the warmth of it even through my clothing.

"Everything's going to be all right," he assures.

I want to believe him, but something nags incessantly at the back of my mind. Never the less, I smile reassuringly. "Of course."

"I should be getting to my studying."

"Naturally." Before he can withdraw that hand, I cover it with my own, holding it to me. "We must do this more often, though. Tell me you'll have breakfast with me."

A slight pink tinge rises to his cheeks and his gaze lowers. "With you and your friends, you mean."

"Well, yes. You'd be welcome with us, William."

He pulls back, and I reluctantly let him go. "We'll see," is what he answers, but the way he smiles as he ducks inside leaves me with hope.

7

I put serious contemplation into dragging Oscar up to William's room in the morning, intending to walk with the two of them to breakfast. In the end, I chicken out of doing so, although I do find myself dressing quickly and standing outside his door, crouching down to slip one of my folded poems beneath it. If that doesn't solidify my invitation to him or make my intentions clear, I don't know what will.

Oscar has waited for me, and he says nothing, although he raises an eyebrow because he likely knows where I've been. I only offer him a sheepish smile before falling into step beside him as we walk to breakfast.

I'm famished enough that I load up my plate a good deal more than is proper, not wanting to risk the buttered bread being eaten up before I've had my fill. Oscar seems tired, but isn't in a bad temper, and I enjoy the sound of his conversation with Preston as the two of them discuss the Christmas party.

I notice Edwin frowning deeply in my direction, but then realise—he isn't looking at *me*, but past me. I twist around to see William standing just a few paces away, looking extremely uncomfortable and as though he wants to turn tail and run. He glances at the seats around me and I realise he wants to sit with us.

With *me*.

My heart must grow three sizes at this ridiculously darling man tackling his awkwardness on behalf of my invitation.

"Do you have a problem, Esher?" Edwin inquires.

I greet him with a bright smile. "Yes, do you have a problem, dear William? Standing there like that and not taking a seat." To the boy sitting next to me I say, "Budge over one, would you?" so that he shifts into the empty seat to his right.

Edwin startles. "Seriously? You're asking a—"

He cuts off with a yelp, and I think Oscar has kicked him beneath the table to demand his silence.

"If you have a problem, there are plenty of free seats elsewhere," I say without taking my eyes off William. He takes up the newly vacated seat, and I desperately wish I could reach out to touch his nervous-looking face. "I'm glad you decided to join us."

He settles in his chair, hands in his lap and lashes lowered almost shyly. "It seemed rude to ignore such a gracious invitation."

I laugh, discreetly brushing my fingertips against his knee beneath the table where no one can see. He even attempts to

give me a small smile in response. I turn my attention back to my food and address the group as a whole. "Is anyone prepared for the upcoming maths exam? I don't think I'll ever be."

"That's because Mr. McLachlan is a slave-driver," Oscar says absently, pushing his food around on his plate. He's hardly touched it, which is worrisome.

William has served himself a plate of eggs, bread, and gravy, and he eats while being the epitome of manners. He pauses between bites, dabbing at his mouth with a napkin before speaking. "He's not so bad."

"Are you good at maths, William?" Benjamin asks, and I'm grateful he isn't giving William the same distasteful scowls some of the others are. "I find it such a disagreeable subject."

William looks alarmed that anyone other than me has addressed him. "I don't find it enjoyable, but I can navigate it well enough. If someone needed some extra help..."

"Frances helps us out when we're struggling," Edwin says, not unkindly but the undertone is there of what he means. *We don't need your help.* I want to throw him into a lake. If he makes William regret coming here even for a moment...

"I could always use the extra assistance," I'm quick to say. A cover-up that William seems to recognize for what it is, but his expression remains soft at the edges, so I think he's all right.

William eats his breakfast, silent except when I ask him a direct question. Yet I don't take his quietness as a bad thing. He lacks the pinched, anxious look to the corners of his eyes and the tense pull of his lips I've grown accustomed to seeing. On the contrary, he seems at ease despite the negative energy from those who don't want him here. I do my best to include him without swivelling the spotlight onto him directly.

He excuses himself before the rest of us, though he does so with a polite nod of his head and a promise that he'll see me in Latin. As soon as he's out of earshot, Edwin leans forward to speak. "Fair word of warning, mate; you might want to keep that one at arm's length or you'll be waking up with him crawling into your bed and a hand under your nightclothes."

I pin him with an intense, unamused stare. "Are you jealous that it wouldn't be your bed?"

Disgust visibly settles across his face. "What? No—only trying to look out for you. The headmaster is not kind about buggery in this school."

I smile although it's forced. "The headmaster is not kind about much but thank you for your concern."

Next to me, Oscar shifts uncomfortably and puts his fork down, and it sounds oddly loud even in the busy hum of the dining hall. He pushes his chair back. "I'm gonna get to class, too," he says. I follow him with a worried gaze, but don't give chase.

"Is it just me," Preston says, "or has he been acting odd as of late?"

My chest tangles itself into knots. "It's not just you."

I WAIT UNTIL we've retired to our room that evening before trying to pin Oscar down about his behaviour. He wanted me to be myself, to leave it to him to handle whatever it is he's going through. His slow decline has me thinking I need to try, yet again, to step in. "Are you all right?"

Oscar deposits his school books upon the table. "Why wouldn't I be?"

"Oh, where to start. Your moodiness, your lack of appetite? You look like hell, too, by the way."

Oscar pauses and drags in a deep breath, pushing a hand back through his hair. "I appreciate all the concern, but maybe you ought to focus on keeping yourself out of trouble right now."

I frown. "What? I'm not doing anything."

"Yeah, James, you are." He turns to me, a scowl overtaking his entire face. "Runnin' around with your talk of ghosts, not being the least bit careful if anyone else hears you. Being all good company with Esher when you've been warned about the type of person he is. All it takes is him to slip up once, to get caught screwing around with some other bloke, and you'll have earned yourself a reputation for being the same as him."

He breaks my heart. This isn't the Oscar I know, who is always so kind and cautious about what he says. "You disappoint me, Oscar. If any of you took thirty seconds to actually get to know William instead of relying on rumours and nonsense, then you'd know he's a very lovely person."

Oscar's brows twitch together, mouth pulling up into something furious. "And if *you'd* take thirty seconds to notice the way he's been undressing you with his eyes in the middle of class, you'd realise that everyone around the both of you can see it, too. Including and especially the staff."

For half a second, I almost—*almost*—wonder if what he's displaying is jealousy, but that isn't the impression I'm getting. No, he sounds worried, afraid, and I feel like there's a reason behind it that I cannot pinpoint.

"William would do nothing without my permission. Upon which, it would be my choice and my responsibility." I rise from my bed to step over to him. He doesn't flinch away when I put a hand upon his shoulder, but he looks as though he might want to. "I'm your friend, Oscar, and you matter a great deal to me. I haven't a clue what you're going through right now—by your hand, might I add, because God knows I've tried to find out—but I'm doing my best to be here for you. All I ask is that you please stop taking your frustrations out on me and treating me like some ignorant child."

Oscar opens his mouth to respond, but I can see the anger seep right out of him. An immediate look of pain and fear overtakes him. He runs a hand over his face and turns away, slipping from beneath my grasp. "...I'm sorry."

Of course he is. Yet still, he's offering me nothing to go on, and I'm feeling a bit exhausted with it all. "Mm. I think I'll get some sleep."

"James," he sighs, sinking to the edge of his bed with his head in his hands. "What I'm going through right now, I cannot... You're the type that wants to fix things, and this isn't something you or anyone *can* fix. You're right. I've been taking it out on you because I don't want to see you slip into the same pit I've fallen into. I'm scared for you."

That's enough to give me pause and turn back to him, and it nibbles its way through my own irritation. What in the world has the headmaster accused him of? How does it relate to anything I'm going through? Is it possible that Oscar himself is inclined towards men, and I had absolutely no idea? I'd feel quite foolish if that were the case; we could have confided in one another. It would be good for us both, I should think. "I have no fear of what anyone in this place would do to me, Oscar. Nothing you nor anyone else says will change that. No matter what I do, no matter where I go, life finds a way to punish me, so at least this time, let it be for something that I want."

Oscar lifts his head. His eyes look glassy. Just a bit. I think he wants to ask me what that means, which is perhaps why I say it, so that he can begin to grasp how heart-breaking it is to want to know your friends and help them and being held at arm's length. Perhaps some small part of me is hoping he'll then tell me what I want to know.

"I've got your back," he says quietly. "No matter what."

"And I've got yours," I say without hesitation. "Now, get some sleep. You look like you could use it."

8

Oscar wakes the next day and, by some miracle, is almost back to his usual, cheerful self. Which is an act, I'm sure, but he's making an effort.

To make things even better, William joins us again at breakfast, a fact that has me grinning from ear to ear. Even when Oscar has to part from me to go to class and I head to Latin alongside Preston and Benjamin, William falls into step beside us. There's little that feels quite so lovely as him at my side, his quiet presence something calming.

He joins us again at lunch and dinner, and although he still doesn't speak much, the others seem to be growing accustomed to his unobtrusive presence. Even Edwin has stopped glaring at him and instead has settled on ignoring his existence.

When William excuses himself from dinner, he sneaks a folded sheet of paper into my lap. I make a point of tucking it into one of my books beneath my chair for later reading. I catch Oscar watching me with a raised eyebrow; it's difficult to get anything by him when he's sitting directly beside me, it seems.

I should wait until I get back to my room to read it, but my curiosity gets the best of me. As Oscar and I head back to Gawain, I give in to the temptation and pull the note from my book to open it. William has such elegant, flowing writing, every word a piece of art.

And this day draw a veil over all deeds pass'd over,
Yet their hands shall not tremble, their feet shall not falter;
The void shall not weary, the fear shall not alter
These lips and these eyes of the loved and the lover.
—William Morris.

The other half of the "assignment" I gave him. I hadn't actually expected him to figure it out. The fact that he did, that he went through the effort to do so, has my heart feeling full to bursting.

"What in the world is that look for?" Oscar asks.

"What look?" I reread the note.

"*That* look. You have the most ridiculous smile on your face." He cranes his head, trying to take a peek. "Is that from Esher? I thought I saw him slip you something."

I'm quick to draw the paper to my chest, sticking my tongue out at him. "Perhaps, but it's for my eyes only."

He rolls his eyes. "The two of you could not be any more obvious."

"Perhaps you're jealous that I have an admirer and you don't."

"Who says that I don't?"

My eyebrows lift. "Oh?"

Oscar pockets his hands, flashes me a cheeky grin, and shrugs. Curious. Though with that silly smile upon his mouth, he could very well be taunting me.

Later that evening, after Oscar has fallen asleep and I've tossed and turned myself into exhaustion, I think I hear the crying again. Soft, far away, but it makes my pulse race and my stomach twist.

I pull on my robe and slip out into the hall, not with any intention of searching out the source of that noise, exactly, but to sneak my way upstairs instead. Coming up here is frightening all on its own, because it requires me to sneak past Virgil's room to reach William's door. For that matter, I have to knock very quietly, desperately hoping that he answers quickly because I have that sneaking feeling of being watched again. After a moment of no answer, I knock again and lean in close. "Dear William, please let me in before the ghosts eat me?"

Not a second later, I hear the sound of something scraping against the floor, and the door opens. I'm greeted by William's startled and lovely face. He grabs the front of my robe and drags me into the room. "What are you *doing?* Are you mad?"

Fear aside, I have to stifle a laugh. "Not at all. I couldn't sleep and it was cold."

"I thought you were…" He trails off, making swift work of closing the door and using one bare foot to shove a blanket up against the bottom of it, which I realise he does to prevent candlelight from seeping underneath it and getting him into trouble for the lights not being out past curfew. Sneaky. He also shoves a chair up and under the door knob with the practised ease of someone who does it often. "So you decided to see if my room was warmer, did you?"

"It would appear that way." I wink and head right over to his bed, not bothering to ask permission before I crawl beneath the blankets.

The blush that floods William's face is worth the anxiety of sneaking up here. "What are you doing?"

"I told you, it's cold." I smile sweetly. "Oh, you do have nicer blankets up here."

William stares at me like I've lost my mind, tempting fate like this. I suppose I might be giving him the slightly wrong impression; I'm not here to try to get my hands beneath his clothes—though God knows I've thought about it. Especially when he's standing there in nothing but his nightshirt, bared collar bones looking delicious enough to kiss amongst the dipping shirt collar. "Mother insisted I have a single room because she thought it better than me sharing with another boy."

I chuckle. "People are rather ridiculous, aren't they?"

He rubs at one of his arms before shuffling over to the bed and, after a moment's hesitation, he slips beneath the blankets beside me. Although his mattress is made of the same materials as mine, his is significantly larger and fits two more than comfortably. "I suppose it's a fair enough concern. According to the rumours, I have trouble keeping my hands to myself."

"I have been warned on occasion about your sinful nature," I purr, and it makes William's eyes drop to my mouth and bite gently at his own lower lip.

"It's true that I do have a bit of a weakness for a pretty face."

"Is that why you spend so much time alone? Because you just cannot resist yourself?"

William blinks, retrains his eyes upon mine, and snorts. "More like I cannot tolerate most of the people here."

"Does that mean you can tolerate me?"

"As I said…" He slowly brings a hand to brush a stray strand of hair from my forehead. "I have a weakness for a pretty face."

I have half a mind to kiss him. "I'll have to remember that."

William draws his hand back and I'm already aching for its nearness. "Hm. Why couldn't you sleep?"

"I suppose I've just had a lot on my mind lately."

"Care to talk about it?"

"Ghosts. You. Well done figuring out that author, by the way."

"Thank you."

"Quite. Also, Oscar has been acting very strange lately."

He props himself up on his elbow, cheek against his palm. "Strange how?"

Oh, where do I start? "Withdrawn, moody. He said he would help me investigate the spirits, but he gets uncomfortable anytime I try to discuss it."

William hmms. "Frances has been here a few years. It's possible he's simply seen one too many boys punished for 'spreading rumours.' There was one boy who wrote home to his parents that the head cook was serving us rat and got into trouble. The staff views it as students trying to undermine the credibility of the school. Or perhaps something more is going on. Wasn't he summoned to the headmaster's office a few weeks ago?"

It's Oscar's personal business and I've not even shared information with our mutual friends. But this is William, and who in the world would he tell? If there's anyone besides Oscar that I trust, it's him. "He said it was because he got caught cheating on an exam last term."

"I wasn't aware Frances had any issues with his marks."

"He doesn't. Later he admitted that was a lie. Something about the headmaster accusing him of doing something he didn't do. Whatever it is, King has been making his life miserable. He's been caned or whipped or something more than once."

"Any thoughts as to the truth?"

A frown tugs at my face. "He's been quite adamant about me being careful around you. About me being caught with another boy."

"You're thinking perhaps he was caught engaging in something salacious, is that it? Though why they would not automatically expel him for it is beyond me."

"I don't know," I admit with a sigh. "He won't tell me anything. I've been fraught with worry."

William touches me again, this time his fingertips stroking down my cheek in an impossibly soft gesture that makes my entire body thrum pleasantly. "You are a wonderful friend, James. The best Frances could ask for. If he isn't willing to talk, then all you can do is support him if and when he needs you."

My eyes drift shut. "It doesn't mean I won't worry."

"That's part of what makes you a good friend," he says softly. "Perhaps he thinks if he denies and ignores whatever it is that's happened, he can make it go away. Not an uncommon defence, I should think."

Oh, I understand that all too well, don't I? Though I won't say as much. Instead I yawn, drawing the blankets up and over my head. "Why is your bed so much warmer than mine?"

"Because I've been lying in it awhile," is William's all-too-practical response. "Why don't you get some sleep, if you plan on staying?"

I shouldn't. The risk of getting caught is ever-present, yet the mere idea of sleeping here alongside William is far too tempting to pass up. "I cannot answer that if I'm already asleep."

I hear him make a sound not unlike a laugh as he pulls the blankets away from my head. He leans in, lips brushing my forehead as he murmurs, "Good night, James," before rolling onto his back and closing his eyes.

As I lay there in an unfamiliar room with someone mere centimetres from me, it occurs to me the level of trust I'm placing in William to share a bed with him. I watch him in the dark long after he's fallen asleep. The delicate line of his mouth, lips slightly parted, long lashes resting against the tops of his cheeks and his normally immaculate hair all in his face. At some point, when I shift, he stirs, and his hand finds mine, weaving our fingers together.

It's embarrassingly easy to fall asleep this way.

Even as I move about during the night and eventually sprawl out across him, shoving my face into his hair and breathing in deep, dear William doesn't budge at all. I wonder idly if it's the laudanum that does that, or if he naturally sleeps like the dead.

I would gladly waste the day away, just like this. When was the last time I rested so well or comfortably, and without a single nightmare? But come early morning, I begin to stir because the back of my mind is reminding me that I cannot be found here. In fact, I slept far later than I meant to.

With a displeased sigh, I begin to untangle myself from William to get up. He doesn't budge, at least not until I rise from the bed and then he makes a soft sound and reaches blindly for me in the newly vacated spot beside him. There's something so sweet and innocent about that gesture that makes me smile. I smooth a hand over his hair before sliding the rest of the way out of bed. "I'll see you at breakfast, yes?"

William only sighs plaintively, curling in on himself to go back to sleep. I bite my lip to keep from chuckling at him.

I take great care in sneaking back downstairs. The halls are significantly less intimidating in the early morning, and noticeably quieter, save for the stirring of some boys behind closed doors. I make it back to my own room without incident.

However, the moment I slip inside, Oscar is up off his bed with his eyes wide and fraught with worry.

"Christ almighty, where have you been?!"

I startle, though really, I should have expected as much. Poor lad, waking up and finding himself alone. I really ought to have warned him and I hadn't been thinking beyond wanting to see William. Though it's still early and I'm feeling half-asleep, so coming up with a good excuse isn't happening. "Um... With your mum?"

Oscar frowns deeply. "I don't care if you want to sneak out at night, but at least let me know so I can make sure I've got a cover story for you, yeah?"

My smile is a sheepish one. "Apologies. It wasn't planned. I couldn't sleep."

His shoulders relax a little, some of the concern ebbing out of his face. "So, what, you went for a stroll?"

Lying might be a wiser option; it's not like I'm not good at it. But, well, if Oscar put his mind to it, he'll know damned well where I've been. "I went to bother William."

Oscar blinks, taking a seat back upon his bed. His hair is quite a mess although he looks as though he's already washed up and gotten mostly dressed for the day. I feel a little bad, wondering how long he's been up fretting over me.

I'm also expecting a lecture. Bracing for it, even. But perhaps our previous tense conversations did some good, because Oscar just smiles a little instead. "You really do fancy him, don't you?"

From the main building, the bell begins to ring. I suppose that's my own cue to begin washing up. "Maybe," I admit, shrugging out of my robe. "He really is quite nice to look at." Which is glossing over all the other things about William I find quite nice. Like the sound of his voice, the feel of his hands, how utterly brilliant he is about most every subject and the way he likes poetry.

"He's all right, I suppose." Oscar begins to run his hands through his hair to try to make some sense of it. It's such an off-handed comment, really; it could mean nothing, but it feels like it means something, and I think that something is Oscar's way of telling me it's okay to discuss this with him, that he isn't judging.

I really do wish hugging were a more acceptable form of affection here, because I would very much like to gather him up and squeeze him tight. "Not as pretty as you, though."

Oscar smirks. "Well, of course not. Look at this face. Plus, my sense of humour is better."

I strip out of my nightshirt with a laugh. "Now, that's just not fair. William doesn't have much of a sense of humour to compare." Which isn't entirely fair either, I suppose; I should think that he does, it's simply a very dry sort of humour.

"I'll make sure to tell him you said that. You ready for the dance tonight?"

The water jug delivered to our rooms each morning is, as always, utterly freezing. I fill the basin and set to scrubbing myself clean. These last many weeks, if nothing else, have certainly acclimated me to the cold. "As ready as one ever is for something they have no interest in."

Oscar steps up behind me with a brush in hand, trying to steal a sliver of the mirror to see what he's doing as he works on his hair. "I hear it's an excuse for good food. King goes all-out, likely to make us look better in front of the girls' school."

I glance at his reflection. "Are you looking forward to it?"

"Hm. I don't know. Food, pretty girls to dance with, no school work…"

I'm in need of a shave, I note, but I'll save it for tonight. I'm too tired to care, and it isn't enough to warrant being lectured by the staff. I think. "I'm certain all of the ladies in attendance will flock to you." Which isn't me being patronizing, either. Oscar is a good-looking lad.

"Why wouldn't they?" he muses, although the prospect doesn't sound as though it overly excites him. He sits long enough to pull on his shoes. "If nothing else, it's the last day of the term. That's something to celebrate."

True enough, I think, as I finish with my washing and fetch a uniform to dress. "Did your mother ever end up writing? Will you be returning home for holiday?"

Although I'm not looking at him, I can hear the good humour fading from his voice. "Ah, no. Not home, but I'll be going to my uncle's. I leave first thing in the morning."

Something to do with his poor relationship with his mother, I'd wager, which is unfortunate. I see him writing home to his sister quite often, always tucking those paper lilies into the envelopes. I've never seen him receive a letter back. "It will be quite lonely without you."

"What about you? Going home?"

I direct a sunny smile at him. "I'd rather throw myself from the roof."

"None of that." He gives me a pointed look. "The others always leave, but it might please you to know that I think Esher usually stays around during holidays."

By the sound of it, a fair number of boys do. When they're unwanted boys whose parents have discarded them here, their families have little interest in seeing them. It's the same reason why few relatives come to visit. "I'm glad I'll have someone to pester." Two weeks of time to myself? In a largely empty school? Much of the staff leaves, too, with only a skeleton crew to manage meals, clean, and watch over the students who remain behind. Which means largely unsupervised time with William. That sounds quite nice.

I finish dressing, still fussing with my neckwear as we exit the room. It's there Oscar nearly runs into—literally—William standing in the hall, and the pair of them startle and

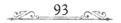

blink widely at each other before William's attention turns to me. "Ah, good morning, James, Frances. I thought I would walk with you to breakfast, if…that's all right."

My mouth spreads into a wide grin. Every time I grow accustomed to the nearness and attention William offers me, he closes the gap a little further and it never ceases to please me. "Only if you give me your leftovers."

"You'll get fat," William says dryly. "You already eat Frances."

"Is that a problem?"

"If you're fat and cannot fit into your desk, you'll fail all your classes. It would be a shame for you to lose your figure."

"Admiring my figure, are you?"

"You need to have something going for you."

"Ooh, that wounds."

"If you two are done flirting," Oscar says patiently, "we're gonna be late, and then the headmaster will be sending us all home for Christmas in pieces."

I laugh and fall into step between them, thinking I could live happily if every morning began this way, between my two favourite people in a place far from home.

Final exams are headache-inducing, but I believe, thanks to Oscar's tutoring, I manage to pass each of them. I look forward to sending word home of my good marks. During maths, after our test, Mr. McLachlan lectures on the etiquette and manners expected of us at the Christmas party. The proper way to approach the ladies, the manner in which we are to dress, the polite forms of conversation and what topics are appropriate versus what we should avoid. These are all things I already know; I've been attending such events since I was a child. I imagine for some—like Oscar—this is a very new thing indeed, and I see him leaned forward in his chair, listening intently.

Oscar needn't run off to the headmaster's after we're released, and he seems to be in a jovial mood as we sit down for dinner, which is held directly after classes today. This will be our last meal together like this for a few weeks. I sit amongst my friends and enjoy their faces, the sound of their voices, the warmth of William at my side, even if he says little.

Dinner is a brief affair, however; we're ushered out, so the staff can begin clearing the room to decorate for the party. And, of course, to grant the students time to ready themselves. Which is what Oscar and I are planning to do as he, William, and I head back to Gawain. William retires to his own room to change, and I cannot help but wonder what he'll look like done up like a proper gentleman. This is the one night where we're granted permission to dress in our finest rather than the school uniform.

I have my outfit laid out upon my bed, and I make it a point to get Oscar's out of his wardrobe for him, as well. Upon closer inspection, I observe his second-hand waistcoat is frayed and not of the best quality, and I can see where his shirt has been poorly repaired at the seams—not something anyone would notice beneath his coat, but even so. It's a reminder that Oscar is only here because his tuition is being covered by a gracious uncle, and not because his parents are well-off. He's had a rough time of it, I think, even though he'd never say as much. After he's washed and begun to dress, I debate with myself. I have a spare waistcoat that is much nicer than his, but I'm unsure if offering it to him would come across as patronizing. I lay it beside his clothes, just in case, as a silent invitation.

I strip down to my undergarments and wash up for the second time today. Not because I really need it, but just because

I did a rather lazy job of it this morning when half asleep, and tonight is a special occasion. Not to mention, I skimped on shaving, so that's a must. From the corner of my gaze, I see Oscar examine the extra waistcoat, glance my way, and admire the embroidery upon it before hesitantly slipping it on.

I still have shaving soap upon my face when someone raps at the door minutes later. Oscar—fully dressed and finishing with his hair—exchanges a look with me with a frown. He answers it, blocking my view of whoever is on the other side. The smooth voice that reaches my ears is familiar enough.

"Evening, Mr. Frances. The headmaster has summoned you."

Scowling, I swipe the remaining bits of soap from my face and step around the open door, tall enough to look over the top of Oscar at Charles and his smarmy smile. "What on earth for? The term is over."

Charles' gaze slides slowly over to me, as though he finds it annoying to have to address me at all. "Be that as it may, his presence is required."

God, he has a face only appropriate for punching. "Give me a moment and I'll go with you, Oscar."

"No," he says quickly, smoothing his hair back one last time. "It's all right. Finish getting ready and I'll meet you there, yeah? I'm sure it won't take long." He smiles, and were it not for the fact that he looks far more confident and certain of himself than he has in days past, I might argue with him. But it doesn't mean I have to like it.

"I'll see you there?" I ask, noting the uncertainty in my voice.

Oscar steps out into the hall, adjusting his necktie and flashing me a wink. "'Course. Save me a dance."

A laugh bubbles from my throat. "I'll save you all the dances, mate."

I watch as they disappear down the hall together, trying to stamp down the discomfort edging its way into my chest. Slipping back inside, I run a hand across my jaw to ensure I didn't miss any spots and then set to refilling the water basin to wash up and dress myself.

My own outfit consists of all black, with a striped red-and-black silk waistcoat, matching cravat, and shoes shined to perfection. It's been so long since I've worn such an ensemble that it feels odd at first. Where my finer suits are made of higher quality cotton and silk, the uniforms are mediocre wool designed solely to protect from the elements. Useful and practical and easy to make in large numbers to cover all the student body, and certainly cheaper, but hardly the peak of fashion.

With my hair parted and swept to the side, cologne placed sparingly behind each ear, I peer at my own reflection and think that I make a decent enough picture. I look more like the me who grew up in the busy city, who attended all the big parties alongside my parents. The me who had a promising future, once upon a time.

Now, I haven't a clue what will be in store for me after graduating. Will Father be willing to shell out the funds for me to attend university? Will I be expected to join the Army? I have the fortune of being his only child, and the only male amongst any children even in the extended family. Should he want to pass on his estate and business to someone with his name, I'm his only hope of doing so.

But given recent events, maybe I've tipped the scales too far out of my favour.

I'm stunned by how abruptly that hits me. That I haven't a clue what I'll do after leaving Whisperwood, and that everything I've built in the short time I've been here—the friendships, the relationship I've forged with William—will come to an end.

The future is uncertain, and that bothers me. Immensely.

I turn away from the mirror, drawing in a deep breath. Tonight, I refuse to dwell on such dismal things that are out of my control. Even if I don't care to humour a bunch of girls looking to flutter their lashes at me all night, I do think I will enjoy myself by spending the evening with my friends. I will admire William and the food and being in a social setting that I am familiar with, and it will be good.

Given the hour, I have a little bit of time to kill. Which I will do by taking a seat at the table, bowed over a few sheets of paper, a pen, and an inkwell. The words flow easily. Even if not everything is usable later, the fact that I have my muse back is a beautiful thing. I wonder if William received the poem I slipped under his door, and what he thought of it.

Eventually, the bell chimes six o'clock. Thirty minutes until the party begins, which means it's due time for me to give myself one last look in the mirror before heading upstairs to see how William is getting along.

He answers the door and I give myself a moment to simply appreciate the sight of him. William always looks so elegant and put together, but this takes it a great step beyond the norm.

His hair is parted and combed back, bandoline ensuring that not a single strand is out of place. Beneath his jacket is a gorgeous silk waistcoat in cobalt blue, adorned with silver embroidery of the highest quality and intricate detail, and a similar, silvery silk cravat. There is something to be said for how a man looks in a finely tailored pair of trousers and coat, and William's has definitely been fitted well.

He bears the scent of orange blossoms, though not so much to be overpowering. Just enough that it makes me want to duck my head and bury my face against the crook of his neck to breathe him in. I desperately want to run my hands through that hair and pop every button on his clothing to get at him. Such a beautiful piece of art begs to be properly ravished.

I settle for smiling instead. "Good evening, dear William. Are you ready to accompany me to the dance?"

It occurs to me that while I was admiring him, William seems to have been admiring me, as well, as he lifts his gaze back up to my face. "You say that as though I'm to be your suitor for the night."

"Isn't that what you wanted?"

His mouth twitches into a brief smile. "Where is your shadow?"

I shrug helplessly in response to that. "Meeting us there, it seems." The headmaster has to make an appearance at the dance, doesn't he? So, Oscar won't possibly be kept all night.

William lowers his lashes. He extends a hand, palm against my chest, smoothing over one of the lapels of my coat and making my heart skip a beat. "I'll enjoy having you to myself for just a bit, then."

"We can cut out early, if alone time is what you're after."

William sidles closer, the hand upon my chest sliding its way north until his palm is cupped to my cheek, and it sends every inch of my body alight in both nervousness and delight. It's been a long time since I've wanted someone to touch me.

"Planning to steal me away from the ball, are you?" he hums.

I cannot help but tilt my head into that touch. "That was my intention, yes."

His lower lip tucks itself between his teeth briefly, and I have half a mind to kiss him senseless. I think that I just might, or that he might kiss me first before I've had the chance.

Except the door to our right swings open and Virgil steps out just as we're swiftly putting distance between us to avoid looking as though we were mere seconds away from engaging in anything improper. He looks quite sharp in his outfit and with his hair slicked back, and he gives us a most intense stare before nodding once in greeting and heading for the stairs.

Alone again, but even so that rather interrupted the mood, didn't it? "Let's go before we're lectured on punctuality."

As we head downstairs, we're greeted with the bustle of others also venturing out. How strange to be amongst my peers and see them wearing such finery in contrast to their uniforms. It's a reminder that we all existed outside of Whisperwood before, and that we will all exist outside of it again someday. Some of us undoubtedly better than others.

Outside the building, many of the boys linger, craning their necks to peer down the long driveway and keeping an eye out for the arrival of our guests from the girls' school. They're all ushered inside in short order by staff. I spot a few of my teachers, Mr. McLachlan and Mr. Hart among them, and it's even stranger to see them dressed so finely than it is to see my peers.

The dining hall has been luxuriously transformed. An impressive fir tree towers in one corner, adorned with paper chains, candles, and handmade ornaments. One quarter of the room has been arranged with tables and playing cards, encouraging those who don't wish to dance to still sit and socialise. What other few tables remain are pushed close to the walls, draped with cloths of a vibrant red and lined in garland befitting the upcoming holiday. The windows are trimmed with more garland and tinsel and ornaments, and the musicians have set up at the head of the room; even the grand piano from the foyer has been relocated in here for their use.

On silver platters and trays is a spread of food ranging from cakes and pastries and sweets to sandwiches, eggnog, fruits and more I cannot immediately make out. I would have preferred a proper sit-down Christmas feast, but it *does* look delicious.

Given that I'm not returning home for the holidays, a Christmas dinner isn't in the cards this year. I'll admit, it's a holiday I'm going to miss spending with my family. Watching my mother and cousins create their own Christmas crackers out of patterned paper and stuffed with treats, while the smell of cooking turkey and pigeon and potatoes filled the entirety of the house.

I steal a glance at William, who is observing the room at my side, and wonder if I shouldn't do something special to ensure the holiday isn't utterly dismal for the both of us. Without our family Christmas traditions, we ought to create some of our own.

What I don't see, as I look around, is Oscar. Or the headmaster, for that matter. My stomach twists into an uncomfortable knot.

"This is silly," I mumble under my breath. "This entire event reeks of wanting to show off."

"Is that not why most anyone throws lavish parties?" he responds, leaning in so I can hear him over the sound of other conversations. "My mother has a tendency towards grand galas, too. Always ridiculously expensive and for no reason other than to appeal to her peers."

"Some people throw parties just to have fun, don't they?"

"I hardly see what's fun about them. Except the dancing, I suppose."

At long last, the doors open back up and the headmistress from the girls' school steps into the room, followed by her stream of third and fourth-year girls, every one of them in the most beautiful dresses. Their cinched waists, discreetly painted faces, and complicated hairstyles must have taken hours. I feel the utmost sympathy and am grateful corsets on men faded from popularity when I was still a child. The girls move so stiffly, without the practised elegance of older women who are well accustomed to moving in constricting clothing and wide-backed skirts.

I notice William watching them with a mild spark of interest in his eyes. The already anxious feeling in my chest takes an abrupt, jealous turn. "Will you ask the girls to dance, then?"

He tilts his head. "It would look rather silly if I danced by myself, wouldn't it? I'm certain there are some lovely dancing partners in there."

"I think it would be fun to watch you dance by yourself."

"It would be ridiculous, I assure you. What about you?"

"Better to dance than stand around bored, I suppose."

When William looks to me and smiles faintly and allows his fingers to brush the back of my hand, it quells some of the building bitterness at the idea of some girl he's only just met having his undivided attention. It's not a pleasure I'm able to indulge in, as much as I would love to dance with him in front of every person in the room.

I notice, then, as the girls' headmistress moves to the front of the room, that she's accompanied by our own headmaster. My friends have found me amongst the crowd, Benjamin and Preston flanking my left while Edwin lingers just behind. Mr. King speaks in his strong, commanding voice that brings everyone's conversations to a halt and their attention to him. But as he announces and introduces himself and then headmistress Vivienne, I'm busy scanning the room for any sign of Oscar. If the headmaster is here, then he should be, too, right?

After the introductions, King gives us leave to enjoy our evening. Boys all around me fidget and linger, awkward with the situation they've been thrown into, but several break from the herd and gladly cross the room to begin their night of socialising, eager to have their first pick of dance partners. Among them are most of my companions; I spot Benjamin trotting through the crowd, shyly approaching a young woman and greeting her with a sweet smile that I think any girl would find irresistible. Preston comes up behind me, clapping a hand on my shoulder before advancing through the throng of people.

William, however much he said about wanting to dance, lingers. "Would you like to enjoy a snack before we get to putting our names on dance cards?"

That sounds like a glorious idea, although Edwin behind me has to interject his unwanted opinion by muttering, "Keeping an eye out for the manliest-looking one, William?"

I shoot him a venomous stare. "A shame you don't fall into that category, hm?"

Edwin takes note of the lack of humour in my voice. For the things he sometimes spews from his obnoxious mouth, he's not a confrontational person, and my sharp retort is enough to make him lower his eyes swiftly. But William's expression becomes pinched, mouth pulling into a thin line. He levels an unimpressed look Edwin's way and turns on his heel. I watch as he navigates the room, approaches a lovely girl in a dress of maroons and silvers—her outfit compliments his nicely—and I see the soft smile he offers her, the elegant bow of his body, and when he extends a hand, she gladly places hers in his.

I want to laugh at the sullen scowl that crosses Edwin's face.

"I'm afraid with a face like yours and a face like dear William's, he will come out ahead every time."

I leave him there with every intention of throwing myself into the fray and finding some enjoyment in it. And because I want to enjoy myself, and I want whomever I associate with to enjoy themselves, I seek out a girl on the outskirts of the room. She keeps fussing with the ringlets of hair framing her face, and up close her dress appears a little worn. Passed down, perhaps. Her face is nicely powdered, but it's obvious she's painted her cheeks, something likely looked down upon by the other girls who strive to look as natural as possible despite that they use the exact same products and simply have more skill at using them subtly. When I approach, she scarcely looks up. I will say, the natural red of her hair may make others turn up their noses, but I find it quite lovely.

"Good evening," I greet, wearing a smile I know from experience women find charming. Her eyes dart up, nervously, and then glance from side to side. When she realises I am indeed addressing her, she straightens her spine and forces herself to lift her head.

"Oh. Yes. Um, good evening."

"It appears to me you don't wish to be here. A sentiment I can sympathize with, by the way." I place one foot forward and bow my head, extending a hand in her direction. "That being said, would you grant me the honour of a dance?"

Her green eyes widen a fraction and she looks to take my hand, pausing just shy of it. "You flatter me, but I feel I should warn you that I'm quite an atrocious dancer."

I remain poised, hand outstretched. "Then I shall be an atrocious dancer with you."

The upturn of her lips and the hopeful glint in her eyes makes me smile, and she places her hand in mine.

As it turns out, my companion—Juniper, her name is—is not all that horrible a dancer, she's simply unconfident and spends too much time trying to look at her feet out of fear of stepping on mine. I manage to coax her into trusting me to lead her appropriately, and she fares much better after that. By the time we've shared two dances, I manage to catch Benjamin's eyes from nearby and he steps in to ask for the next one.

I take a dance with another girl who I think has not been asked, followed by another and another. I pause briefly to fetch myself a drink, and converse with a group of women and fourth years for a while before returning to dancing. Every now and again, I spot William and our eyes meet, smiles are exchanged, and that envious feeling of wanting to be the one dancing with him returns to gnaw at my insides.

The hour grows late. I steal one more dance with Juniper, and afterwards grant myself a brief reprieve by the refreshments table. It's close to the musicians and the noise is a bit deafening, but it means no one tries to bother me while I scan the room. First, I search for Oscar, who is still noticeably absent, and then for William, whom I spot standing amongst a group of four women, engaged in conversation.

It's fascinating to watch. Dear William, always so quiet and the bearer of dark expressions, has the ghost of a smile upon his face and whatever he's saying has his audience entirely enrapt. They giggle and hide smiles behind their hands, demure as can be. It would appear he has quite a knack with the fairer sex. Perhaps he's simply eager to prove Edwin wrong.

A hand comes to rest on my shoulder, and I realise I've been staring after William most intently and didn't notice anyone coming up on my right. I turn, expecting...well, any array of people. Oscar, Preston, Edwin, Benjamin. Instead, I find myself eye to eye with my English teacher, who looks a few years younger in his simple but expensive suit.

"Mr. Hart," I say, trying to mask my surprise that he's approached me in the midst of all this when all the other staff seem to be keeping to the side lines and merely observing.

"Mr. Spencer." He offers me the quietest of smiles, and I could swear there's a bit of worry present in his eyes as he wrings his hands together. "I apologize for interrupting your evening, but I couldn't help but notice the absence of Mr. Frances. Since the two of you room together, I thought you might have seen him?"

An odd question, to be certain; then again, attendance to the party was mandatory. "He was summoned to the headmaster's office hours ago. I thought I would meet up with him here, but he has yet to make an appearance. I'm beginning to worry he was banned from attending."

A concerned frown swiftly chases the smile from Mr. Hart's face. It's a brief look, that worry and alarm, but I take notice of it before he tries to smile again. "Is that so? In that case, I shall inquire with the headmaster. Thank you."

"Enjoy your evening, sir," I say, even as he disappears into the crowd. Rather than seek out the headmaster, however, he heads for the doors and I don a frown of my own. What's more, it isn't long after that I see William heading for those doors, as well. He touches a hand to his forehead and the reasoning for his departure becomes clear: his medicine has undoubtedly worn off after the last few hours. He's told me that large groups are too much for him without it.

Without thought, I abandon my glass and skirt the perimeter of the room to head outside.

It's pitch dark out, save for the gas lamps lining the pathway out to the road. Out towards the dormitories, though, is little more than ghostly shapes beneath the moonlight. I don't spot Mr. Hart, nor William.

"James."

The voice comes from my right, and I turn just in time to see William disappear around the corner of the building. I follow, concerned and curious, having to squeeze into the three-foot gap between the building and the hedges that line it to where William awaits me. He leans into the wall, head bowed, and eyes rolled up to watch me. A come-hither expression like that is enough to make my stomach do pleasant little somersaults but doesn't abate my worry.

"Are you well?"

"Just needed a brief reprieve," he assures. "Although now that you're here, I find no reason to hurry back inside."

"You seemed to be enjoying yourself." I shift closer to him, very aware of the privacy we have here despite being outside. We're out of sight of anyone exiting the building, and should anyone venture too close to our location, we would hear them as they cross the dewy grass.

"I was enjoying seeing your friend's sullen face as I danced with every lovely girl who wouldn't even give him a second glance." A cheeky little smile plays across his mouth and I cannot help but laugh. At least until he says, "And watching you watching me. I enjoyed that, as well."

Not surprising that he noticed, and not something that bothers me. "Perfectly justifiable for me to be a bit jealous, isn't it? All the women fawning all over you, having your undivided attention…"

"Not a one of them had my undivided attention, James. Not when I always kept half of it on you."

I draw in a slow breath as William presses his palm to my chest, fingers splayed out against the fabric. "Really. No interest in any of them, then?" The jealousy is showing, I know it, and I cannot quite bite it back. Or maybe I just want to hear him say it. *You're the one I'm interested in, James.*

William sighs, sliding the lapel of my coat between his thumb and forefinger. "Oh, darling, I like women just fine. It just so happens I like you far more."

As he speaks, as he leans closer, I only have a second to process what's about to happen. He grasps my lapels in both hands and drags me in until his mouth crushes against mine. A surprised gasp escapes my throat, but this is hardly a surprise I can complain about. I've been waiting for this exact moment, and I waste no time in slipping my arms around William and tipping my head, slanting our mouths together as he flattens his back against the wall and holds me against him.

Everything about him tastes and feels as heavenly as I could have imagined. My head is positively swimming. I'm hyper-aware of everything about William's body; the press of his torso against mine, the low, delicious moan that escapes his throat when I catch his lower lip briefly between my teeth, and the desperation in which he clutches at me for dear life. He kisses me until we're breathless and flushed and I can feel my heartbeat in my ears. Everything is fine, perfect.

Until I feel his hands wander down, hiking up my coat, and his fingers against the fastens of my trousers.

Somewhere in the recesses of my mind, a door opens in the dead of night. Footsteps enter my room, and the smell of alcohol and cigars flood my senses...

My mind blanks. Not in a pleasant way.

I've grabbed his wrists before I've even realised it, a firm and resounding "No," upon my lips.

Just like that, we both go impossibly still save for our ragged breathing. William shrinks away from me then, although he hasn't really anywhere to go, and I realise the grip I have on him is painfully tight. He draws back sharply once I've released him, his eyes impossibly wide in confusion, and I contemplate the merits of slamming my own face into the wall in a mixture of embarrassment and irritation at myself.

"I'm sorry," he says softly. "I didn't..."

I force the monstrous anxiety deep down into the pits of my soul, because I cannot stand to see William look at me that way, nor do I want to have to explain to him what just happened. The smile I offer suggests I'm not bothered in the least. "You'll have to forgive me, dear William. I'm a bit of a romantic and this isn't quite the setting I'd envisioned for us." Because I *have* envisioned it. More times than I would like to admit.

William doesn't look convinced, still appearing chastened. "My apologies. I was overly forward."

I tuck my fingers beneath his chin to coax him into looking at me again. "I'm not searching for an apology. I promise, it's all right."

He drags in a slow breath. "But kissing is permissible?"

My mouth curves into a smile. "I'm not sure. Kiss me again so we can find out."

After a look of uncertainty has passed across his face while he nurses his wounded confidence, William brings his hands to my face, cupping it ever so gently between his palms, before leaning up to kiss me again. He's far softer this time, and it isn't any better or worse than before, just…different. Warm and affectionate and it sends a shiver straight down my spine. Kissing William, I decide, is my new favourite thing in the world. I could stay where we are all night.

Were it not for the sound of something on the other side of the hedges causing us both to freeze. Have we gotten so distracted with each other that we didn't hear someone approach?

"What was that?" I whisper.

William licks his lips, breathless and beautiful even as he's straightening up and attempting to orient himself. "Footsteps?"

We fall silent, listening. There's definitely someone out there. Not back around the front of the building where I would have expected anyone to be, but behind us, on the other side of the hedges, where there is nothing but grass stretching out across the grounds towards Gawain and Lancelot Hall.

It could be any number of things. Another boy sneaking about while most of the staff are distracted with the party, for instance. I twist away from William, inching down a ways until I get to a spot where I can part the dense branches between the juncture of two hedges and try to get a glimpse.

"James," William hisses, keeping at my heels and catching hold of my arm.

Through the shrubbery, I have a view of the dewy fields between here and the dorms. In that field, is a boy. Even beneath the moonlight, it's difficult to determine age, but he's wearing a uniform—although something about it does not look quite like our own. Most peculiar, though, is the slow, sluggish way in which he walks, and the hunch of his shoulders.

Something is amiss. My heart has begun to race again, this time out of discomfort rather than the excitement of kissing William. I swallow past a dry throat, take a breath, and push my way between the hedges to advance out onto the grass. Of course William follows suit, never relinquishing his fierce hold on my arm.

Maybe we should have kept hidden. Maybe this is a terrible idea. The closer I walk towards the shambling figure, the quicker my pulse races and the tighter my chest becomes. I stop with plenty of distance between us, observing a moment longer before cautiously calling out, "You there! All right?"

The boy ambles to a stop. Slowly, he turns to face us. The second we get a good look at him, every ounce of blood drains from my face.

Whatever it is we're looking at has not been alive for a very, very long time.

His skin pulled taut across his bones, ashy grey in colour, and his stringy hair clings to it. Never will I wipe the image of those milky, sunken eyes from my mind. The voice that comes out of his cracked lips and blackened mouth is hoarse and quiet.

"If I'm late to class, he'll punish me."

I cannot move. I cannot speak. I'm sorry I said anything at all. William trembles beside me. I cannot move an inch myself to do anything about it.

But the boy has no lingering interest in us. After he speaks, he turns again and resumes shuffling away. The darkness swallows him up and before long, I can no longer see him at all.

I remain silent for a long moment, trying to figure out what has just happened or what we should do about it, and the only thing I can think to say in my nervousness, "Do you think he didn't turn his maths homework in on time?"

William's gaze slowly turns to me. He hits my arm.

"What! Mr. McLachlan is quite strict about those deadlines!"

"We've just seen a corpse walking across our school grounds and your response is to make jokes?!" His voice cracks at the end, fractured by panic.

I frown, rubbing at my arm. "I'm terribly sorry, William; I forgot to consult the etiquette book on spirit sightings."

"Well, maybe you should have," he snaps, despite that such a statement really makes no sense. "What are we supposed to— what if it comes back? It saw us and what if it—"

"What if it wants to be friends? Maybe we can help it with its maths work."

"Oh, Christ's sake..." William turns away and doubles over, hands upon his knees. I'm reminded of the night he came bursting into the common room and cannot help but feel a little niggling sense of guilt for prodding at him when he's obviously far more frightened than I am.

"Let's get you back to your room," I say gently, touching a hand to his back. "I think you need your medicine."

William doesn't reply with anything but a nod. He's shaky as he straightens up, and I wish I could risk holding onto his hand as we begin the trek across the grounds towards the dorms.

With all the third-years at the ball, Gawain is deathly silent. The sconces are still lit, so it isn't too unnerving heading up to the second floor to get William to his room. Inside, he promptly begins to yank at his cravat and the buttons of his coat. As he does so, I spot the bottle of laudanum atop his dresser and fetch it for him, taking a second to look it over.

One DRAM, Tincture of Opium. Soothes all ailments. Dose: Adults, 1 teaspoonful.

The label is adorned with a small red poppy flower next to the brand name. He turns to me as I offer it out to him and he wastes no time in uncorking the bottle and sipping straight from it. It isn't much, truly, but it is without a doubt more than one teaspoon. I start to reach for it with a frown. "Easy."

William only waves me off, disregarding my concern. I try to remind myself that he has far more knowledge about his dosages than I do. He sits on the edge of his bed while I remove my shoes, jacket, and waistcoat, and say, "Let's lie down for a bit, darling." Just long enough for his medicine to kick in, I think. Enough for him to calm down.

William has not moved to get undressed further, so I go to him and coax him into standing so that I can help him along with it. Even given the situation, there's an intense intimacy in helping another man undress. William fusses with the buttons of his waistcoat while I slide the cravat from his neck, and he drops his arms to the sides when we get to his shirt and I begin the process of unbuttoning it for him. I'm distinctly aware of his eyes focused on my face.

"Has it hit already?" I ask, curious, when I've taken notice that he's stopped trembling and a quiet, glazed look has passed over his tired face.

"Starting to," he murmurs.

We get him down to his undergarments and William seems to decide that's good enough. He falls into bed and I join him in short order. As I lay on my back, William tucks himself against my side, head upon my shoulder, and I put my arms around him protectively.

It's hard to ignore how it feels, having him pressed against me. Even through my own shirt and his undershirt, the warmth of him sinks into me. He rests a hand upon my chest, fingers splayed out as he draws in a deep breath. "So, what do we do now?"

I frown at the ceiling. "I'm not sure. It isn't as though anyone else has shown any level of willingness in speaking about any of this. Don't ghosts usually have a reason for lingering?"

"I've heard that, I think."

"Certainly cannot be because they loved this place so much that they cannot pass on."

"James."

"Right, right. Perhaps we should start by doing some research on the school."

William has closed his eyes, his breathing beginning to even out. "The library," he murmurs, voice slurring the slightest bit as the laudanum has begun to fully take hold. "Perhaps some of the old student books…"

I feel my expression softening as I look over at him as best I can from this angle. Rather than try to continue the conversation, I allow William to fall asleep, stroking my fingers back through his hair. For the next hour, I lie there with him, just listening. Convincing myself, I think, that he's all right, and savouring the comfort of him being near.

But I need to get back to my room. With Oscar not having shown up to the party, I want to see if he's there and make sure he's all right.

When I get to the room, however, it's empty and silent. I frown to myself, wondering if maybe he was set on chores of some sort for the evening. But after so many hours, that would seem like a bit much. Maybe he's at the dance now and I simply missed him. I'll get some rest, and surely, he'll be here when I wake in the morning.

Where else could he be?

10

Since arriving at school, not once have I ever woken up to an empty room. Oscar has always been there, usually still fast asleep. His bed is vacant, and nothing appears to have been touched. I wash and dress. The rest of the dorm is abuzz with noise and movement as students bustle about, eager to leave for break. By tonight, I expect most of the school to be empty.

I stop by the room that Preston and Benjamin share, and find them readily packing their things. Benjamin greets me with a smile and a good morning.

"Getting out on good behaviour?" I say.

"Glad to see home for a few weeks," Preston agrees, turning to flash me a grin. I haven't expressly told any of them

I won't be going home myself. I'm fine keeping it that way for now. No sense in getting into it.

I lean against the door frame. "I don't suppose either of you ran into Oscar last night?"

The pair of them exchange looks, then turn frowns in my direction. Benjamin says, "We didn't. I meant to find you and ask where he'd gone off to, but you were noticeably absent."

"I cut out early," I say dismissively. "He got called to the headmaster's office yesterday and said he'd meet me at the party, then never showed up."

"That's worrisome." Benjamin closes and latches his trunk. "Have you asked the headmaster?"

"Would *you* ask the headmaster?" Preston muses.

"Fair enough." He tips his head. "I'm sure he's fine, James. Maybe he was sent home early."

Without any of his things? With no warning? Ridiculous. But the two of them have even less of an idea of what Oscar's been going through in recent weeks than I do, and I suppose I don't want them to spend their holiday concerned over something they cannot help. Which is why I smile reassuringly. "You're probably right. The two of you have a safe trip home and I'll see you in a few weeks."

Entering the nearly empty dining hall—which has been put back into its pre-party layout—is a little surreal. Most of the students won't bother to eat this morning, too busy getting ready to leave. When Oscar fails to show up for breakfast, my worry kicks in full-force. True, he was due to leave school for his uncle's today, but he would not have left his things behind.

William joins me after a while, slightly dishevelled with shadows beneath his bright blue eyes. It seems like he might not have slept off the full effects of his medicine, and he shows little interest in his breakfast. Yet, he's still focused enough to observe, "You look troubled."

"My shadow is still missing." I frown down at my own food, which isn't looking the least bit appetizing. "I'm worried. I've not seen hide nor hair of him since before the party."

"You don't think he went home early?"

"Not with all his things left behind."

"Ah. I'll help you look. He's got to be around somewhere."

I jab my spoon into the bowl of porridge, stomach turning anxiously. "I hope so. I told you he's been acting so strange lately. What if something's happened?"

William touches a gentle hand to my leg beneath the table, and neither of us end up taking more than a few bites of our food. When we depart, the courtyard is full of boys with their belongings, being shuffled onto carriages and omnibuses to take them to the train station. We bypass the lot of them to return to the dorm while I'm trying to determine how we even begin searching for someone in this school. Perhaps starting with our room is our best bet. When we step inside, I'm struck with the fact that someone has been in here.

All of Oscar's things are gone.

It's the books I notice first, and the trunk at the foot of his bed. My chest cinches tight. I march over to the dresser, yanking open drawers—all empty—and to the wardrobe— also empty.

"What in the hell..." I turn to William, trying not to let panic overtake me. "All of his things are gone."

"Everything? Is anything at all left?" William frowns, stepping further into the room and shutting the door. He moves to the dresser to go through the drawers while I begin searching around his bed. The row of books that used to sit beside it, his inkwell, his papers, shoes, clothes. I almost give up, until I think to look beneath Oscar's mattress. There, a book is tucked safely, and my heart sinks. *The History of Pendennis.*

"This is his," I whisper when William steps up beside me. I pick it up, turning it over in my hands.

"Could he have forgotten it?"

"Absolutely not. He wouldn't have. It was one of his favourites; he said it was a gift from someone special."

William touches my shoulder as I continue staring at the cover. "Let's ask around. Maybe one of the teachers knows something."

Don't panic. I swallow hard, drawing the book to my chest and trying to breathe around the thought that something is *very* wrong. "Right. Let's ask Mr. McLachlan." I don't know why he's the first that comes to mind. Maybe because I spotted him this morning, so I know he's still on school grounds.

I realise I haven't moved yet, still inwardly battling with my nervousness. William takes my face in his hands, drawing my attention to him. "Deep breaths, darling," he murmurs. "We'll figure this out."

It's such a simple thing, but I feel like I can breathe again. I grant myself a few moments to lean down, resting my forehead against William's, soaking up the comfort his presence provides. When I feel as though I can focus again, I pull away, place Oscar's book beneath my own mattress, and lead William back out of the dorm and to the school.

I don't know if Mr. McLachlan is one of the teachers who leaves for break, honestly. But he was here earlier. By some grace of God, we find him in his classroom, seated at his desk and bent over a stack of papers as he grades the remainder of final exams. He doesn't notice our presence until I speak. "Sir, are you busy?"

He lifts his head, peering at me over the tops of his spectacles. "How may I help you, Mr. Spencer?"

I move into the room. "We were just wondering if you've seen Oscar, by chance? The last time I spoke to him was yesterday before the party. He wasn't in bed this morning and now all of his things are gone. I'm concerned."

Mr. McLachlan's expression doesn't change, exactly, but there's a brief, subtle way in which his pen stops against the paper. His voice is quiet. "My apologies, but I don't believe I'm allowed to divulge personal information regarding students to other students."

Then he *does* know something. "I'm not asking for personal information, sir; I'm just trying to find out why my best friend is suddenly missing and if he's well."

He sighs a heavy, tired sigh, and leans back in his chair. He slides off his glasses and runs his hands over his face. "I've been informed that Mr. Frances is no longer a student at Whisperwood."

That does not do a damned thing to quell my worry. "What is that supposed to mean?"

"It means exactly as it sounds." The look he gives me is sincere in its regret. "I'm sorry, but that really is all I've been told."

I want to ask him to tell me more. That surely there's *something* else, that he knows why and how and when. But I don't get the impression he's lying to me, and if he honestly doesn't know, then pestering him is pointless. I lower my gaze, feeling sick to my stomach. "Thank you, sir."

He watches us as we turn to leave. Before we can get out the door, he sighs again. "James. Do you have any reason to think that something is off about Mr. Frances' departure?"

Of course something is off. Isn't that the whole reason I'm here? But the way he words it, the hesitation in his voice, I get the impression he's trying to ask—in the subtlest manner possible—if something about his absence is suspicious.

I turn back to him. "I *know* there is, sir."

His mouth presses thin. "What makes you say that?"

William and I exchange looks, uncertain just how much I ought to say. "A number of reasons. His mum didn't like him being around; she never liked him coming home for holidays, so he was going to his uncle's for holiday. But that means she wouldn't have been the one to pull him out of school. He also left something precious behind in our room. And..."

"And?"

"He's my best mate," I say, quietly. "He wouldn't have left without telling me goodbye. Even just a note..."

Mr. McLachlan breathes in deep through his nose. "Thank you for the information. I assure you, this will be a matter I look into."

"I hope that you do. Thank you, sir." I bow my head before turning to leave again.

Outside of the class, I step to the railing overlooking the foyer below, bracing against it with a heavy sigh. William leans his hip into the railing, arms folded. "I'm sorry. I had hoped that would be more productive."

"There has to be someone other than the headmaster who knows what happened," I say. "We just have to figure out who." Asking headmaster King directly? Horrible idea. Given what he's been putting Oscar through, I have no doubt he would take our asking as insubordination and dole out punishment.

"Any of his other teachers? Friends?"

"Benjamin and Preston hadn't seen him. And—" My spine straightens. How could I have forgotten? I turn to William. "Didn't you and Oscar have English together with Mr. Hart?"

He blinks, mulling that over. "We did, yes. He seemed rather fond of Frances, now that I think about it."

"He asked me about Oscar last night at the party. He seemed a little concerned and when I said Oscar hadn't shown up, he left."

"I've not seen him today. If he isn't in his classroom, we might find him in the teachers' dorms."

A search of Mr. Hart's class and the dining hall yields no sign of him, so to the teachers' dorms we go. Although the staff quarters are not expressly out of bounds for students, it's highly frowned upon for us to be traipsing about here without permission. Desperate times, desperate measures, right?

It's been threatening snow for weeks, and the sky has finally let loose. William keeps close to my side as we cross the grounds, our heads bowed. Most of the teachers who live in the dorms are either at the main building or have gone home for holiday, so I'm hoping we'll not have any issues getting in and locating Mr. Hart's rooms.

Inside, while the layout of the building is reminiscent of our dorms, the similarities end there. The wallpaper is different. Newer, I think. It feels more like one large house than the student dorms do, complete with a large parlour and sitting room and a full kitchen, all of which we pass as we look around. Much to my relief, each set of rooms appears to have a placard upon the door with a name engraved. We locate Mr. Hart's on the ground floor at the far end of the hall, and glance at one another uncertainly before I lift a hand to knock.

It's silent for so long that I begin to give up hope of getting a response. Maybe he's out. Maybe we missed him, and he did leave the grounds. Then the door opens and my first thought upon seeing Mr. Hart is that he looks like he hasn't slept in weeks. The dark circles beneath his eyes, the unkempt manner of his hair catches me off-guard.

Almost as off-guard as Mr. Hart looks to see two students standing at his door. He sticks his head out into the hall, glancing both directions as though he expects someone else to be with us. "Can I help you boys?"

"We need to discuss something important with you, Mr. Hart," William says. "May we have a moment of your time?"

For a moment, he looks as though he might just close the door on us without commentary, but then he sighs, steps back, and beckons us in.

Some part of me is hoping we'll find Oscar here. Seated at the table, stuffing his face or something. We'll find this is all one big misunderstanding and my worry has been for nothing. But Mr. Hart appears to be alone.

He gestures to his sitting room, an elegantly decorated space with a collection of fine, red plush chairs and a sofa in front of a burning fireplace. Hanging from every wall are paintings and framed, glass cases of insects. Butterflies, mostly.

"Please," he says, "make yourselves comfortable. I was just about to pour myself some tea."

William and I share another look before taking a seat upon the sofa, hip to hip. His gaze wanders, surveying the room, while I keep mine locked onto Mr. Hart as he steps out of the room into the adjacent kitchen. When he returns a moment later, it's with a tray and tea set, which he carefully places upon a table. "So, how may I help you gentlemen?"

No point in mincing words; might as well get straight to it. "Do you know what's happened to Oscar Frances?"

I could swear that Mr. Hart flinches. "What have you heard?"

"Only that Oscar is no longer a student here."

His mouth pulls taut. His attention swivels to the tea, to filling each cup. "That is all there is to it."

Irritation tugs at my features. "It seems peculiar a student would leave so abruptly, sir. Especially without prior knowledge of the staff. Considering you asked me just last night if I'd seen him, that leads me to think there is more to his departure."

Deep breath. He straightens up, offering out a cup to both William and myself, which we take out of habit. "The staff is not always privy to matters that are ultimately up to the headmaster."

"You seem bothered, though," William presses. "Mr. McLachlan did, too, when we spoke to him."

"It's unfortunate when a well-liked student leaves without warning," Mr. Hart responds. "It's not the first time it has happened, and I doubt it will be the last. He's likely at home with his family, preparing to enjoy Christmas with them."

I curl my fingers around the tea cup and look away, frustrated that we're running in circles with no answers. Mr. Hart *knows* something, I know that he does. William meets his gaze, unflinching. "You knew Frances well enough to know that he really did not have a home to go to."

As my gaze is diverted, something catches my attention upon the fireplace mantel.

A paper lily.

Mr. Hart opens his mouth to reply to William and I set the cup of tea aside, completely untouched, cutting him off. "Thank you for your help, Mr. Hart, but we should be going."

William, just about to take a sip from his own tea, frowns. "We should?"

Mr. Hart, too, studies me in confusion as I pluck the cup from William's hands, set it back upon the table, and coax him to his feet. "Yes. We've bothered Mr. Hart long enough, I think."

William looks like he wants to object, but he exhales heavily. "Thank you for your time, sir. Enjoy holiday."

Mr. Hart sees us to the door where he gently says, "Please try not to worry about this too much, boys. I'm certain Mr. Frances is all right."

I don't bother trying to smile. I'm going to crawl out of my own skin if I don't get away from him immediately.

It isn't until we've retreated outside that William asks, "What was that about?"

I continue briskly through the cold evening air towards the dorms. "He had a paper flower on his mantel."

"A paper flower?"

"His sister's name is Lily; he'd make them for her when he wrote home. That man definitely knows more than he's saying, but I don't think we'll get him to admit it."

"Then, what, you think Oscar and Mr. Hart were...?"

"I don't know what I think," is my honest answer. "Except that I'm certain he was somehow involved in Oscar's disappearance."

It is, truthfully, difficult to think. Mr. Hart has always seemed to be such a gentle and sweet man, but what do I *really* know about him? What would any student really know about a teacher?

I'm beginning to feel more and more like I don't know much about anything.

COME THE NEXT morning, it's blissful to get to skip out on our usual Sunday morning services, seeing as the chaplain has departed while school is out. It leaves us free to eat breakfast and head straight to the library, which we've decided is our best bet to finding any information.

The selection is not the best I've ever seen, but it's far from the worst. We're only here for one thing anyway, and that is the student yearbooks. We find them on a shelf in a far back, dark, and ignored corner of the library.

"What are we looking for?" William asks.

"Dirt." Even as I realise it's likely a useless endeavour and I don't know what, precisely, I'm wanting or how we should go about it. But I must start somewhere. "Something, anything."

William swipes a finger along the dusty shelf. "Plenty of dirt to be had," he says dryly, before we begin plucking the booklets from the shelf.

They're thin books, thirty, forty pages at most—less for the oldest volumes. Each one is hand-bound and carefully penned. These books are not distributed to every student, but are kept as a means of records, really. Each volume lists every student in attendance that year, along with class and staff photographs. Although photos, of course, are a more recent development. The earliest volumes consist of drawings and writing only. Seated at the nearest table, we begin the arduous process of thumbing through each one.

How long we sit there, poring over them, I lose track. Neat the handwriting may be, but after staring at it for the better part of two hours, my eyes have started to blur, and all the photos begin to look the same. Eventually, William slides one of the books over to me. "Look; the year Mr. Hart began teaching here."

I take the offered book, peering down at the staff photo upon the page, and the names written beneath it. "Huh. Mr. McLachlan used to have hair."

William blinks and leans over to look. "Oh, I'd not even recognized him. Do you think the stress of the job caused him to lose it?"

That gets a chuckle out of me. "I can see him up late, grading papers, just ripping out his hair by the handful. *Why don't these children understand such simple concepts!*"

"Look, then you aren't the first student to drive him utterly mad," he teases, turning his attention back to his book.

"I hope I'm the best at it, though." I skim over the short few paragraphs about the 'new teacher,' Mr. Hart. "Christ, this man is boring."

"Apparently Oscar found something about him interesting," William murmurs as his eyes travel over a page. He pauses then, frowning. Before I can ask him what it is he's found, he holds the book up towards me. "James..."

The faint trembling in his tone catches my full attention. At first, I haven't a clue what it is I'm supposed to be looking at. The photo is worn with age and I scan over the numerous faces, trying to determine what William wants me to see.

Towards the bottom, I see him.

"Is that our friend who failed maths?"

"It is him, isn't it? This volume is dated eleven years ago."

I take the book so I can study it closer. The name beneath it reads *Timothy Chambers*. I'd be hard-pressed to have forgotten that face. The boy in the photograph is most definitely the boy we saw the other night, out on the field, and my insides begin doing somersaults out of nervousness and excitement. Obviously, this person existed, which means we did not, in fact, lose our minds and imagine things. "I would think most of the current staff was around back then."

William flips back several pages to the staff photos. "Asking any of them might be a poor move on our part, don't you think?"

I sniff a little. "Let's hear your better idea, then."

His lashes lower and he returns his attention to the book. "That photo tells us he lived. Perhaps we need some real confirmation that he died. The cemetery?"

"A cemetery? What kind of school has a bloody *cemetery?*"

"Schools that are home to people many parents don't want, I suppose." William shrugs. "I've only been once; I've heard it was largely for boys who died from illness and whose parents couldn't afford—or simply didn't want to pay for—a burial elsewhere."

"What's to say he's even buried there?"

"I don't know, but it's something to try. If we're seeing him on school grounds, then logic says it's possible his body is somewhere near here, too."

A fair enough conclusion to come to. I grin as though he's just suggested a picnic. "This should be fun."

"You are entirely too cheerful about this."

"Much better than dwelling on the unsolved disappearance of my best mate, isn't it?"

"Fair enough."

We push our chairs back and return the books to the shelf.

Snow fell lightly all through the night and has continued into the morning. We both were smart enough to put on our warmest wool jackets; I even abandoned my uniform in favour of a linen tunic not unlike the ones they have us wear for drill. "It's always so cold here. Do you think that's what's got the ghosts all worked up?"

William shudders from the chill. "Somehow I doubt that."

"You're no fun."

"I'm allowing myself to be dragged to a graveyard not forty-eight hours after we encountered a dead student not far from here. I should say I'm loads of fun."

"Would you feel better if I carried you instead of dragged?"

"My legs *are* tired," he laments, not without a small smile despite his displeased tone.

"Maybe if you exercised more, you wouldn't tire so easily."

William snorts. "I've never been a physical sort of person." We've passed the dorms, venturing into a section of the school I've only ever seen from afar. The looming iron gates surrounding the small cemetery are in view, inky black where they jut up from the snow.

I laugh, although my gaze remains fixed on the gates in the distance. "Should we have you run laps 'round the graveyard? I bet we'd find what we're looking for faster that way."

"You will never see me running unless my life depends on it."

I'll keep that in mind.

Silence falls over us as we near our destination. It's a small, isolated stretch of land, though it's clearly been tended to over the years and is not overgrown. The fence stretches a good half a foot over my head, the gates a bit more. When William opens them, they give with a strained creak that chases a shiver down my spine. I cram my hands into the pockets of my coat.

"If I die while attending this school, don't let them bury me here. Throw me out into the forest or something less depressing."

He shoots me an anxious glance while slipping inside. "Don't say things like that."

The snowfall has been just barely persistent enough that there's already a blanket of it coating not only the ground, but the gravestones, as well. There is little remarkable about this place. Even the stones are small and unimpressive, the kind of stones one would see in the overcrowded city cemeteries of London. Depressing indeed.

We linger there a moment, surveying the area. William fidgets, and I watch as he slides his laudanum from his coat pocket, uncorks it, and deposits a few drops upon his tongue. I don't think I've seen him cart it around with him before; perhaps it being holiday has something to do with it. Or maybe it's the ghosts exacerbating his anxieties.

"Why are you so nervous, dear William?"

His brows furrow as he moves to the nearest headstone and bends forwards to read the faded, chiselled lettering. "Should I not be nervous where restless spirits are involved?"

"For what it's worth, I don't think we'll encounter any here. We've never seen one during the day, right?"

He doesn't look convinced, and I see him absently rubbing at his arm where, weeks ago, the ghost in the hallway grabbed him. "Small blessings, I suppose."

I place a hand briefly against his back. "Shall we split up?"

"Go on, then."

After offering a reassuring smile, I head to the opposite side of the cemetery. Still close enough we can see one another, can converse if we raise our voices. I begin the process of moving methodically throughout the rows of graves, brushing snow off some of the headstones and taking note of names and dates engraved upon them.

What was it like for some of these students, I wonder? Certainly, illness and accidents happen at school, but for them to have been abandoned here by their families... What did they do to deserve such a thing? If I were to suffer such a fate here, would my family, too, decide it was easier to leave me here? Would I be yet another poorly marked grave to be forgotten about?

I almost pass the headstone by, having to stop and backtrack a few paces to have a second glance. *Timothy Chambers*. The date of death listed matches up to his years of attendance, too.

"William!"

He crunches through the snow and frosted grass to my side, a little winded as he does so.

"Do you think we should try a séance?" I whisper.

"Don't you dare." He crouches, running his fingers over the etching. "No cause of death listed."

"There has to be a record somewhere, don't you think?"

"Well, yes." His head tips back to look up at me. "There's the records room. I believe the headmaster is legally required to keep a file on every student, although I wouldn't know how far back those date."

Ah. Joy. "How likely do you think it is he'd let us in?"

"Maybe if we asked *very* nicely..." He rolls his eyes and rises to his feet, hugging himself tightly. "However, if it is a key we need, I can handle that."

"How in the world are you going to get a key?"

He squares his shoulders, looking moderately pleased with himself. "I know where the maids keep their master set. If I were to *borrow* them and return them by morning, no one would ever know."

That sounds significantly more dangerous than a séance, honestly. "And if you get caught?"

"I won't. One of the girls, May, has been procuring my laudanum since I started here, and I pay her handsomely for it. I'll ask her for the keys. If she wishes to continue being paid, she won't speak a word of it."

"That doesn't sound the least bit shady and concerning."

William's smile is impossibly soft. "I find it endearing when you worry about me."

I sniff a little at that. "Who said I was worried about you?"

"Oh, weren't you?" He draws his hand back. "I suppose I won't give you a kiss to calm you, then."

Try as I might, I cannot help the upward curve of my mouth. "Don't blackmail me for your kisses."

"My kisses do not come easily," he says, indignant. "Do you think me some kind of harlot?"

"My harlot," I hum in response.

William curls his fingers into the front of my jacket, murmuring, "You're quite rude," before he leans in to brush a kiss against my lips that leaves me warm all over.

"And you are quite a harlot," I respond, grabbing him up in my arms to drag him back for a proper kiss that makes William's breath hitch and his arms instantly go around me. For a few moments, anyway, I am content to let the rest of the world fall away around us, savouring the warmth and softness of his mouth.

The only thing that drags us apart is a cold flurry of snow that rushes past us. Even then, William's eyes linger on my lips as he licks his own. "We should get back."

"We should," I agree, despite wanting to remain where I am and continue kissing him for another hour or ten. "Lead the way, harlot."

He gives my chest a playful shove before drawing back. "If I'm a harlot, I'm severely undercharging you."

I follow him with a grin. "And here I am, taking full advantage of that."

"Not full advantage yet," he points out, pushing the gates open while casting a suggestive look in my direction that makes my insides flip-flop and an exorbitant amount of blood rush south.

"Would full advantage mean coercing you into having a séance in the middle of the night here?"

His expression turns sullen. "Not what I had in mind, no."

"During the witching hour? On All Hallows' Eve?"

"I'll break your legs and leave you here in the snow, James Spencer."

I laugh, swinging an arm about his shoulders and drawing him to my side as we walk away. "Why are you so mean to me?" He scoffs at that, but I sense him shrinking in on himself a little and so I ask, "Did I say something wrong?"

"I've been told I'm an unkind person before," he says, looking away. "Am I truly? Am I unkind to you?"

"So awfully unkind," I tease, but the wounded look that crosses his face tells me this is obviously a Serious Conversation.

"Were you to honestly feel that way, James—"

"Stop being so serious," I chide, gently pinching his side. "You are not an unkind man, William. Standoffish, unapproachable, perhaps…"

He relaxes a little, leaning into me. "Now who's being cruel?"

From the school, the lunch bell begins to toll. Food sounds good right about now. "Oh, yes. I'm a regular beast."

"Funny, then, that you should kiss like such a gentleman."

As we pass the dorms, I remove my arm from around his shoulders. "I am but a wolf in sheep's clothing."

"What does that make me? A sheep?"

I flash him a mischievous smile. "Depends on whether or not I can manage to eat you up."

William deadpans and tries to swat at me, and I dance out of his reach with a laugh.

THE REMAINDER OF our day is spent lying low, save for a few probing questions of the staff to ensure that the headmaster has, in fact, taken leave of school grounds. One less thing to worry about. But we haven't a clue how long he'll stay gone and sneaking about in the main building at night seems a terrible idea while he's around. It's for that reason we decide that the breaking and entering of the records room needs to happen tonight.

For a few hours, then, we mull over a plan. Then William drags me into his bed, pressing soft kisses along my face and neck while I hum poetry against his ear. Impressively, his hands remain above my waist at all times. I suppose my rebuke the other night stuck with him.

When the hour grows late, I return to my own room in time for curfew and wait. I'm to leave just shy of midnight and meet William at the records office after he's retrieved a key. He refused my insistent offer to go with him, claiming if he were to get caught, it would be easier if he were alone. I've a million questions and concerns about this plan, but he hasn't given me much choice.

Sneaking to and from William's room in the middle of the night is one thing. Sneaking out of the dorm altogether, crossing the grounds, and slipping into the main building? Entirely different. My heart is in my throat and it's painfully cold outside and my eyes are trying to take everything in at once, wondering if I'll encounter something in the halls or the fields. I arrive at the building with no problem, and the doors are unlocked, likely because servants have to come and go late at night and early in the morning.

The records room is located in the far back of the building, down a series of dark, unsettling, windowless hallways. I've never had reason to be here, but I follow William's directions and find it without difficulty. The minutes tick by on my pocket watch, and I grow increasingly anxious up until I hear quiet footsteps in the darkness and, a moment later, William comes into view, candle in hand to light the way. He smiles briefly, lifting a hand from which dangles a set of keys.

The door opens without a sound, immediately subjecting us to the musty, damp scent of a room that's been locked up far too long. William lets out a noise somewhere between a cough and a sneeze. With no windows to let in moonlight, the candle does little to illuminate more than a few feet around us.

The room is lined with rows of cabinets, each marked with the school year, of which the most recent appears to be closest to us. William lingers near one of the cabinets, and I catch his hand and wrap my fingers around it.

"Nothing those old bastards could say about us would be any good," I say, suspecting he might be wondering what our own files contain. "Let's find what we're looking for and get out before we're caught."

William drags in a deep breath and nods, heading further into the room, scanning labels until we come across the one that reads 1860-1865. "This ought to be it."

He places the candle atop the cabinet while I open the first drawer and begin to rummage through. Thankfully, whoever is charged with organization has done a bang-up job, because Timothy Chambers' file is right where it should be alphabetically. I pull it out with care, propping it atop the drawer and opening it. "This is him, right?"

He leans in as we begin going through the papers together. Registration, class schedules, grades—which aren't flawless but are far from horrible. Through most of Timothy's record, there is nothing of interest. He seems to have been a normal boy.

"Must not have been stressed over maths class after all," I murmur. "His grades look fine."

William abandons my side, and a glance tells me he's wandering a few cabinets down to look around. I flip through a few more pages. "Seems our boy was a thief, though. And an attempted runaway."

William halts in front of a bookshelf at the end of the row, touching the spines and running his fingers along them as though searching for something in particular. "Goodness, I cannot imagine why anyone would want to run away from this place."

"Too bad he didn't make it out. '*Punishments administered as documented in the black book.*' And his death is the last thing in here. Unknown illness."

"I've got it right here." William plucks one of the books from the shelf and opens it up.

"What's in the black books, exactly? Isn't that where they keep track of who gets into trouble?" I slip Timothy's file back in its place.

"Every housemaster has one," William says, head bowed as he flips through the pages. "Any time a student is caught breaking a rule, the prefects are to dole out the appropriate punishment and record it in the black book. I imagine this would include anything the headmaster does, too."

That snags my attention. I fetch the candle and head over to his side. "Would Oscar's be here?"

William shakes his head, offering out the book to me. "For this year? No. Simmons would still have it for our house."

I begin to flip through the book while William removes another from the shelf; it appears to be last year's. It takes me a few minutes to find what I'm looking for, but when I do, I pause, disturbed.

"What is it?" he asks.

I turn the book to show him, not knowing how to put it into words. In neat writing down the pages—and there are two or three of them—are a list of punishments Timothy underwent over the course of the school year. Canings, lashings, waterboarding—something they surely would not get away with these days. William frowns deeply. He places his finger on the last entry. "This here... Isn't the date of this last punishment the date he died?"

"It is." I lift my head to look around the room, feeling a sense of unease, as though we aren't alone.

"So, they were beating him while he was ill? That reeks of something suspicious." He looks up at me, brows furrowed. "Do you remember any of the other names we saw at the cemetery? I want to cross-reference."

"If I didn't have a bad feeling about all of this before, I certainly do now," I mutter.

William scours the black books until he locates another familiar name, tapping the page. "1854, Jonathan Harrison."

I head to the corresponding cabinet and locate Jonathan's file, flipping to the back. "Cause of death listed as suicide. December fifteenth. Another supposed thief."

The way William frowns suggests the dates correspond again. "All right. 1843, Mitchell O'Connors."

It takes me a few minutes to locate it, but—"Caught out past curfew two days prior to his death. Listed as suicide. Second of April."

The standard punishment for nightwandering isn't so bad. A student might be made to stand out in the hall for the remainder of the night, depriving him of sleep. The housemaster or a prefect would make note of his name, and so long as it did not happen again, not the end of the world, right? At worst, a handful of lashes.

"Suicide seems a bit extreme a reaction to getting caught out at night," William says.

"This also says his body was found in the tunnels." I look at him. "What tunnels?"

He blinks. "There aren't any tunnels that I know of."

"According to this, there are. *The deceased was located by head gardeners in the access tunnels beneath the school.*" I'm trying to think if anyone has ever mentioned them, even in passing. "Perhaps they aren't in use anymore?"

"Because a student killed himself down there?" William places the black books back upon the shelf.

"I doubt it's anything that simple." I slip the file into its place, turning to William as he comes up to my side. The firelight makes the shadows across his face look more pronounced, increasing the expression of worry he bears. "You aren't going to like my next suggestion."

He drags in a deep breath. "I imagine that I'm not, no."

"I think we should try to find these tunnels."

William's face blanches. "Pardon?"

"Where else might we find any answers? Should we ask the teachers? Staff?"

William opens his mouth with a protest upon his lips, and I fully expect him to say no, that it's a stupid idea and we're delving too much into something we cannot begin to grasp. "I suppose you'll be doing this with or without my help."

As much as I don't want to do this alone... "I have to. It might help me figure out what happened to Oscar."

I wouldn't blame William for saying that I'm on my own. The ghosts have him spooked, and he's already done so much.

He sighs, taking hold of one of my hands, and there is little hesitation in the way he says, "Then I suppose we have some exploring to do."

I grasp his hand tightly, unable to work past the lump in my throat at how grateful I am for that. "Thank you."

It's growing late, and I don't want to keep us out longer than necessary. I take up the candle and, hand in hand, we head for the exit. William stops me at the most recent cabinet, however, and despite my questioning look, he begins rifling through the current students. At first, I assume he must be looking for our own records, but I realise he's thumbing through the last names beginning with F. I crowd in alongside him, and it only takes us a few moments before realization dawns and I'm fighting back the urge to be sick.

Oscar's file is missing.

11

For the next week and a half, we set about exploring every inch of the school that we can. My suspicions are proven in that finding the tunnels is not a simple task, and we have no one we can really ask. William contemplates needling his contact amongst the maids, or even pestering some of the gardeners, but I tell him to hold off for now. The moment staff gets involved in this will be the moment they shut us down and we find ourselves in the headmaster's office answering for our nosiness.

The number of hours we spend wandering the grounds, the hours in the library trying to piece together information that just isn't there... We've come up on a week of searching and are no closer than when we started. All I have are dismal gut feelings, and those gut feelings are pointing me in the direction that something dark has been happening at this school, and that Oscar was somehow dragged into it.

But, oh, I am infinitely grateful for William's presence. I know he doesn't want to do it, and the idea of what we might encounter should we manage to find the tunnels terrifies him—hell, it's frightening for me, too—and yet he never hesitates. Although he complains now and again, he always does so while at my side, willing to go wherever I wish or do whatever I think needs to be done to get us a little closer. He is steadfast in his loyalty.

It's why I decide a day off is in order. We can hardly spend our Christmas day surrounded by books and theories we've no proof of, after all, and I owe William a thank you. We both slept right through breakfast this morning, likely due to having stayed up late the previous night. I arrive at William's door around lunch time with a basket in hand, a blanket slung across my bent arm. The snow has let up; it will be cold and wet and slushy, but I think I know of a place to take him where it won't matter so much.

William answers the door adorably ruffled and sleepy-eyed despite the late hour. He's never quite at the top of his game when he first wakes, still sluggish with the effects of his medicine. "You're here early."

"It's nearly noon." I spread my arms wide, showing off that I am both bundled up and have the picnic basket and blanket in hand. "I thought we'd earned a day off and could start by enjoying a quiet lunch together."

He blinks, rubbing at his face as his gaze drops to the basket. "You're taking me on a Christmas picnic?"

"If you'd be so kind as to join me, yes."

A small smile pulls at his mouth as he takes a step back, so that I'll step inside to follow him.

"Will there be kissing involved on this outing?"

I ease the door shut behind me. "I've no mistletoe, but if all goes according to my evil plan."

"Your evil plans are quite enticing."

"And thus you fall right into my trap."

I wait patiently as William resumes getting ready. I caught him in the middle of washing, and I admit, I am unabashedly studying him as he hunches over his washbowl, scrubbing himself down, envious of the droplets of water that slide down the lean lines of his body. I have half a mind to slip up behind him and suck some of the moisture from that beautiful neck of his, but I'm afraid it might put us in a position I know I cannot deal with just yet. It's tempting all the same.

He votes against wearing his uniform today, which is the first time I've seen him in anything quite so casual. But he dons his heaviest coat, buttoned up high, and scarcely bothers with his hair beyond giving it a quick brush back. Rumpled William is quite possibly my new favourite thing.

The extra layers of clothing are welcome as we head into the woods. I've taken this walk a few times before, and the path is worn and leads the way. The cold aside, it's a lovely morning. William falls into step beside me, our strides matched. "What brought this idea on, anyway?"

"You've been so kind, I thought I should return the favour."

He chuckles. "'Kind' is not a word I think I've heard used about me...ever."

"That's because no one else knows you very well," I say, and he smiles at that response.

Just a quarter mile into the woods is a pond, largely frozen over, and a patch of frosty grass that has been modestly protected from the snow by the overhead canopy of trees. I hand the basket to William so that I may spread the blanket out. The wool ought to prevent the snow from soaking through, at least for a while. Once I've taken a seat, I turn to flash William a grin. "Come over here," I say, and when he joins me, I lean into him, shoulder to shoulder. "What should we do today, do you think?"

William closes his eyes for a moment, tipping his head to ghost his lips against my cheek. "I can think of a number of things."

The feel of his breath against my ear makes me shiver. "Like...swimming?"

"We'd freeze to death attempting it," he muses, pressing a soft kiss against my skin.

I breathe in slowly. "Then we'd be the ghosts, I suppose."

He nips at my jaw for that remark. "Not funny."

It evokes a laugh from me, and I sling an arm around William to draw him to me. "I'd haunt you every day of the week, darling."

"I would much prefer you to be alive and pestering me in this world rather than the next."

"You're no fun." I turn my head just enough to kiss him properly. Even when I draw back, William has a slightly dazed, warm look upon his face. His entire body has seemed to melt against me.

"I am plenty of fun, I'll have you know."

"Are you?" We're so close that every word I speak has our lips brushing together. "I'm not certain."

"I am," he insists, cupping his palms to my face as he shifts closer. He catches my bottom lip briefly between his teeth, and it sends a jolt down my spine.

"How do you figure that...?"

"Who else would follow you out into the cold just for the chance to kiss you?" One of his hands has dropped from my face and come to rest upon my waist. "I would say that's fun."

"Almost as fun as the way you squeal like a child and cling to me when you're frightened."

"I do not squeal like a child," William says in the most indignant-sounding voice imaginable. His annoyance is overshadowed by the fact that he's slipping into my lap, an action that catches me off-guard, but not in an unpleasant way. Having him atop me like that, straddling me, thighs against my sides, it makes me think all sorts of inappropriate things I should not be thinking.

I swallow hard. "Yes, you do."

He sniffs, expression close to a pout. "I do not. And if you wish to continue being kissed, you'll not be cruel."

I pinch lightly at his side. "I'm not being cruel. I'm teasing. I do so enjoy you flustered and indignant."

"Cruel," he mumbles, covering my mouth with his before I can taunt him further.

His fingers are in my hair, and the subtle movements of him in my lap are enough to make my mind blank. William is impossibly warm and comfortable in every imaginable way and, oh, Lord, I would very much enjoy getting to continue this. To slide my hands up beneath the layers of clothing to touch him, to see just what he looks like to have my mouth all over him.

But it's ruined by that dull, rising sense of anxiety in the pit of my stomach, fuelled by bad memories nipping at my heels and making it difficult to concentrate. I know fully well what I want and how I want it and who I want it with, but maybe…maybe it isn't time yet.

Breaking away from kissing him is the most difficult thing I've had to do in a while. He was being so good, even, not allowing his hands to wander, and I feel guilty for the chastised and worried look that immediately crosses his face when I say, "Let's eat, hm?"

A lovely flush has risen to his face, and that coupled with the way he licks his lips and his breathing is coming just a little quick, not unlike my own, makes me desperately want to just…continue kissing him. I'm almost waiting for him to be angry with me. Instead he says, very softly, "All right," and slides out of my lap to sit beside me once more.

The last thing I want is for William to think this is about him. I catch his chin in my fingers and draw his face closer so that I can kiss his forehead. "I promise, you've done nothing wrong. Trust me?"

He breathes in deep and lowers his lashes. Admittedly, that's a rather cruel thing to ask him because of course he won't say no. He nods once and swiftly embraces a change of topic.

"What did you bring us to eat?"

"All of the goodies I could steal from the kitchen." Although the cooks were more than willing to give me some of the treats they had available, being that it's Christmas and all.

William smiles a little. "Sneaky of you, darling."

Opening the basket, I begin removing the various things I procured to spread them out on the blanket with care. Some sandwiches, sweets, pastries. "I'm a very sneaky individual."

William goes straight for one of the pastries, a flaky, glazed sweet with some sort of filling in the middle. I know from meal times spent together that he has a bit of a sweet tooth, especially for baked goods. "You know, I've been meaning to discuss something with you."

I snag one of the sandwiches for myself and lay back on the blanket as I take a bite. "Hm?"

He looks down at me only briefly. "What do you plan to do after leaving Whisperwood?"

There's a loaded question. One I've thought about plenty but have yet to come up with an answer for. "Why do you ask?"

He tears off a piece of his pastry and tucks it into his mouth. "It was just a question."

"I haven't a clue, if I'm honest."

"You don't like to discuss your family," he points out. "It dawns on me that I don't even know if you are an only child. If you have a business or an estate to inherit. If your parents expect you to enlist or continue on to university..."

Dear William knows how to weigh an atmosphere down, doesn't he? I cannot entirely blame him. He's hinted at wanting to know more about me more than once, and I've been less than forthcoming with information. "I don't know that I'll have anything to inherit, William," is my honest answer. I've not received a single letter from my parents, despite that I've forced myself to pen several to them. I haven't the foggiest idea what awaits me even during the summer holiday, let alone when I graduate from here altogether. "I don't know where I stand with my family, and so I don't know what I'll do when I leave here."

William has turned to watch me as I speak, so enrapt in what I'm saying and eager for any shred of information I'm willing to offer. He opens his mouth and I think he might beg me for more, ask me to clarify things that I'm not sure I can yet, but he hesitates. "You could come with me, you know."

I have another bite of sandwich in my mouth and nearly choke on it in my attempt to say, "Pardon?"

"I don't pretend to know what my family has in store for me after this. My elder brother will inherit the estate and the family business, my sister will be married. But knowing my parents, I'll likely be given a stipend and sent off, so long as I'm out of their way." His gaze drops to the pastry in his hands. "So, if you wanted to join me, wherever I go, it would please me to have you along."

It's a ridiculous thought, when it comes down to it. I would be abandoning my own family to...what, to go live with another man and hide our relationship forever? On the off chance either of us can find the means of which to make a decent living?

Yet, the offer has my mouth splitting into a wide grin and I'm immediately overcome with excitement, and perhaps that says something. Because the truth of the matter is that I have no interest in returning home after this is over. Because if *that man* is there, I don't believe I could convince myself to do it, anyway.

And because I could envision myself with William, the two of us living quite happily, no matter how much of a secret we must make of our relationship.

Without thinking, I sit up and drag him to me, leaning in so that I can rain kisses across his startled but hopeful face. "Nothing would make me happier, you ridiculous man."

He leans into the affection gladly. "Really?"

"Really." I duck my head to kiss him solidly on the mouth, a gesture which makes him whimper softly.

"I cannot promise how well it will go. I just know that I want to wake up beside you every morning. Whatever I must do to make that happen."

When thinking back to the first time we spoke, how guarded he was, how cautiously he'd studied me, how he'd recoiled anytime I drew too near... This is incredible. I find myself very fortunate that William has chosen *me*, of all people, to show his true self to. "How very romantic of you."

"I am quite romantic, even if I don't have the flair for poetry that you do."

I want to crawl all over him and smother him in kisses. "That can be forgiven in lieu of your other romantic qualities, I think."

"In a rather unromantic fashion, I would like to point out you made me drop my food." He gives a forlorn look at the pastry, which has indeed landed on the blanket, glazed side down, and the pout upon his face makes me laugh without meaning to. I can definitely see myself spending an exorbitant amount of my life with this man.

For several hours, we lounge there by the water, talking about nothing of consequence—school, places we'd like to travel or live, books, theatre, art... I lie down with my head in William's lap and he strokes my face, combs his fingers through my hair—he has the loveliest hands—while I recite him poetry and let him guess the author. He only gets about half of them right, but to be fair, I slip a few of my own poems in there and don't disclose to him that fact. We eat when we get hungry, and despite the cold, we're content to linger there as long as we can, which is well past lunch and into the afternoon. It's begun to grow overcast and makes it feel later than it is.

As loath as I am to hear it, William eventually suggests, "We should get back, so we aren't out past dark."

I heave a heavy sigh. "So we aren't encountering ghosts, you mean."

"That was the idea, yes." He's lying beside me on the blanket, tucked close to my side, head upon my shoulder. His head tilts so that he can smile at me. "I would hope to keep our wonderful day wonderful rather than have it ruined by unhappy spirits."

I push myself up onto an elbow and lean over to kiss him briefly. "Well, if you're going to be difficult, then let's get going."

Together we pack up what remains of our food and the blanket and begin the trek back to the school. It's a bit like leaving one world to step into another. Being able to be together and enjoy peace and quiet without interruption is lovely, and not something we shall ever get at school.

But it could, I think, be something we could have after Whisperwood. After we've made our escape. In some little home in the countryside, perhaps. We shall have to conjure up some story about why we're living together. Business partners? Siblings? No, that latter would be too easy to disprove.

It doesn't matter yet; we'll figure it out.

By the time we've reached the dorms, the sun is just about set, and the look of relief on William's face is noticeable. Even I find myself relaxing a bit.

I walk William to his room. On most past occasions, I would often stick around for a while. We would lie on his bed together or I would stay with him until he's medicated himself and fallen asleep before returning to my own room. Today, however, something nags at me that we've tempted fate enough together, so I give him a smile instead. "Good night, dear William. Thank you for a lovely Christmas. We're back to fun and games tomorrow."

I wonder if he's disappointed that I'm not staying; it's difficult to tell, although he does look briefly perplexed if nothing else. His expression is soft, and although he doesn't risk leaning in to kiss me, he does ghost the backs of his fingers against my cheek.

"Good night, James. Sweet dreams."

12

The library has been scoured from top to bottom, and neither William nor myself find a single mention of the tunnels. Or the school grounds in general, for that matter.

We've searched the school itself, too. But the building is vast, and with school back in full swing, we're reduced to having to watch every movement out of fear that we'll be caught poking around somewhere we aren't allowed. My frustration level is through the roof. Even if we found nothing about the ghosts, I had hoped to learn more about Oscar and his whereabouts.

Nothing. There's absolutely fucking nothing.

I lay awake most nights, listening to the quiet sounds of scratching, shuffling, crying in the distance. They've become so mundane they no longer frighten me.

I've begun asking other students questions. I know I must be careful about it, not able to simply jump out and demand to know if they've seen ghosts or heard anything about student mortality rates. That would get me in trouble quickly, I think.

Instead, I try to make it seem more like I'm interested in the school experience. Casual, easy. *What has been the best thing that has happened at school while you've attended? What's been the saddest? What's the strangest thing you've ever heard? The scariest?* That, I find, makes it easier for some of the boys to open up a little. Not that anyone gives me too much information, and almost every single ghostly encounter I hear about is framed as a ridiculous story that someone told them and of course absolutely did not happen to them. I manage to get a few cases of confirmation. Mostly sounds in the hallways, voices when they were otherwise alone...

There are a few, though, who turn their face away as they speak, refusing to look at me. They hesitate, swiftly excusing away their experiences, and it's their demeanour as they recount those experiences that tells me more than anything else.

After days of asking around, and knowing we've run out of places on the grounds to look, the next step of action is—discreetly—questioning the staff. The teachers might not be the best idea just yet, but the maids, the cooks, the slop men, the gardeners... Surely some of them have been here for some time. The chaplain might have been my first choice, but he began here only last term, a replacement for the previous one who passed of old age.

However, I know for a fact that our resident physician, Doctor Mitchell, was here even before Mr. Hart and Mr. McLachlan. I've only met him once, sent for treatment after getting a hefty cut down my shin during a rugby match earlier in the year, and I found him to be a feeble, scatter-brained old man who likely should have retired a decade ago.

He is, however, completely unassuming and unthreatening. When I enter the infirmary where he sits behind a desk and scribbles away on charts, he doesn't even notice me until I clear my throat. "Doctor?"

He lifts his head, the spectacles on his face so thick they make his eyes look big as an owl's, and the smile he bears is wide and void of a few teeth. "Ah, good afternoon. Feeling under the weather?"

"Not exactly." I glance about, making note that the few beds here are empty, and we seem to be alone. "But you can help me. I wondered if you remember a boy from many years ago. Timothy Chambers?"

He adjusts his glasses and leans back in his chair. "Timothy Chambers. The name sounds familiar, now that you mention it."

I take a seat in the chair across from him, wanting to come across as pleasant and as approachable as possible. Not prodding, not prying, right? Just a curious student and nothing more. "He died here about eleven years ago. He's buried in the school cemetery, actually."

Doctor Mitchell squints, then his eyes go wide, and he nods fervently. "Yes, yes. I remember Mr. Chambers now. Very sad to have lost such a bright young man."

Such a statement sounds insincere, especially since—
"Bright young man, was he? I heard quite the opposite. That he was a thief and a runaway."

His smile turns sympathetic. "Many boys who come to Whisperwood have problems to deal with, lad. That doesn't mean they aren't intelligent and talented."

A fair enough assessment, and it brings a number of my friends to mind, all from various backgrounds—not all of them something to be proud of—but each of them quite sharp in their own ways. "Then, if you recall him, do you also recall the manner in which he died?"

He strokes a hand over his snow-white beard. "Mr. Chambers had, I believe, an illness, if memory serves. What has you so interested in this particular boy?"

I expected that question and had time to think of a suitable answer, a pleasant and easy smile upon my mouth. "I'm merely interested in the history of the school. The headmaster was so inspiring in his orientation speech, I've been looking into the numerous success stories the school has created. In the process, I came across his name."

He nods slowly. "Yes, Whisperwood has many stories that please the soul, but unfortunately, even we are not immune to the odd tragedy now and again."

I dare to venture a little further. "Does illness take students often here?"

"Not terribly." He looks proud of that. "Every now and again the cold months will hit us harder than usual, and we had an outbreak of cholera once or twice, but for the most part, I'm quite pleased to say that I have been able to keep my files of deaths at the school—student or teacher—to a minimum."

"We are lucky to have you, then." I tilt my head as I watch him, trying to gauge where I stand and where I should be careful. "While I have you here and we're on the subject, though, would you mind terribly if I asked you a couple more questions?"

"Of course not."

"You're so kind. Have there been any accidents during your tenure here? I know the building is very well maintained and secure, and the staff works tirelessly to ensure our safety, but has any boy managed to get himself into trouble?"

The doctor leans back in his seat as he considers it. "We had a drowning, once. And many years ago, decades, now that I think of it, we also had a student who decided it would be amusing to him to climb the bell tower. Poor lad made it to the top and lost his footing. Nasty accident. Terribly unfortunate, too; he was quite charming."

I'm not certain if he honestly thinks so highly of the students or if he wants me to think that he does. I also feel sceptical about whether this unnamed boy fell by accident or not, and though I desperately want to ask him to expand on that, I don't feel it would be smart to overplay my hand. The last thing I need is for him to be suspicious of me.

"That's horrible," I agree instead, seeing the opening and taking it. "I suppose that would explain why the tower is off limits now. Is it the same for the tunnels beneath the school?"

Doctor Mitchell's smile fades this time, and my heart about stops in my chest in fear that I've stepped a little too far.

"The tunnels," he repeats, folding his hands in his lap. "Well, those were sealed off long ago. Where did you hear talk of them?"

They *do* exist. I knew it. "Oh, some of the student yearbooks in the library. I was surprised. I'd never heard mention of them from anyone, and it seemed a strange thing to exist below a school."

"There's a great many things strange about this school. None of us can pretend to know what the original architect had in mind when he built it."

By the way he's studying me, I think I ought to reel it back in, and I do so with a smile and a swift redirection of topic. "I see. But, tell me, what about success stories? Any boys stick out that you thought weren't going to make it, but did?"

His eyes brighten, and I believe I've succeeded. "A student joined us just a few years ago and injured himself after falling from a horse. I worked on that boy for days; we weren't certain he'd make it."

"But you didn't give up on him."

"I didn't give up on him." His smile here is warm and, I think, sincere. Not that I know how his sincerity works, the depth of it, or its intentions. "The headmaster took a particular shine to him, as well. Saw fit to give him plenty of guidance. Despite his unfortunate background, he's now serving as an apprentice here. Perhaps he'll become a teacher one day."

Simmons. He's talking about Charles Simmons. I smile, fighting back the urge to make a disgusted face. "Well, Doctor, we are definitely lucky to have you and headmaster King both. I'm afraid I've wasted enough of your time already. I should probably be going."

He gives me an absent nod. "Of course. If I can be of any further assistance, please feel free to let me know."

"Thank you, sir."

Not that I think he'll be of any further use to me. He seems too tied to decorum, the school's reputation, and his own handiness.

It hasn't been an entirely useless endeavour, though. I did get confirmation that a student lived and died within these walls, and that he wasn't the only one. I'm also more certain now that I am going to have to be crafty in coming up with answers because it's apparent none of the staff will be of any real help to me. More importantly, he admitted to the existence of the tunnels.

It's a reassurance that William and I are not simply letting our imaginations run wild on us.

LATER, I RECOUNT the conversation to William, who responds by looking up from his schoolwork with a patient gaze and a frustratingly logical point of view: "So you've confirmed what we already knew. Now what?"

Now what, indeed. We know others have seen the ghosts, even if they won't discuss it openly, but we don't know the truth behind their deaths. We know the tunnels exist, but still not where to find them.

And still, I remind myself, no new information on Oscar.

"Now," I begin, brow furrowing. "Now...I think I'd like some dinner. Cannot possibly think on an empty stomach."

He chuckles and returns his focus to his paper. "Go on, then."

"Not coming?"

"Not tonight; I haven't much of an appetite."

It won't be the first meal William has skipped, and I've lectured him on it endlessly to no avail. The laudanum bottle beside his inkwell on the table has my mouth pulling taut. "That medicine of yours seems to do that, I've noticed."

The pen in his hand comes to an abrupt halt. It isn't like me to comment on his drug usage, and I'm uncertain if I ought to feel guilty for it or not. I worry for him endlessly, and yet I don't want to be like his family or even the other students, looking down on him.

With a sigh, I step forward and bow down to rest a kiss upon his head, a hand upon his shoulder, which I feel instantly relaxes at the display of affection. He touches his fingers to mine.

"I'll eat twice as much at breakfast tomorrow, if you insist."

No, he won't, although I imagine he would try. "I'll see you in a bit," I murmur, giving his shoulder a squeeze before I depart.

I make quick work of eating, much to Preston and Benjamin's dismay when they realise I'm taking my leave quite swiftly. I have schoolwork of my own to tend to, and I never enjoy leaving William on his own for long.

"Spencer," a voice calls when I step into the foyer. I turn to see Virgil trailing after me, and I don't like the worried pull to his brows. "The headmaster is asking for you."

I go still, a wave of anxiety-induced nausea sweeping over me. "Did he say what he wanted?"

Virgil shakes his head. "No, sorry. Just that he wanted to speak with you."

"Wonderful." I flash a smile that is all teeth and no real humour, because there is no way this meeting is going to be anything good. "I'll head there promptly."

Virgil always looks terribly sombre, but even more so as he claps me on the shoulder and says, "Good luck."

The headmaster's office is on the second floor of the main building. I've never had cause to be in there before now, and I'm surprised by the sheer number of books lining the walls, and the scent of a fire crackling in the hearth is comforting only for half a second before my brain recalls just where I am.

Headmaster King is standing behind his desk when I enter, gazing out the large windows over the grounds. I refuse to show my nervousness. "You wanted to see me, sir?"

King turns with a pleasant smile and his hands clasped behind his back. "Ah, Mr. Spencer. Come in and have a seat. I hope the new term has been treating you well."

Did Oscar have meetings that started this way? Completely unassuming and normal, wondering what he did to get called here in the first place?

Let's face it: I know why I'm here. It could be any number of offenses, from my nightwandering to getting involved with another boy to prodding around the school to see what secrets about Oscar or ghosts shake loose. I take a seat as directed. "Quite well, thank you."

"Excellent." He studies me thoughtfully, and I wonder if it's on purpose that he doesn't sit despite that it would be politer for him to do so. "It's been brought to my attention that you've been inquiring about some things with students and members of the faculty. Things regarding your previous roommate's whereabouts?"

A lump begins to form in my throat, but I meet his gaze unflinchingly. "Yes, sir."

He nods once, and his eyebrows lift. "Doctor Mitchell says you had a lot of questions pertaining to past students who met untimely ends, as well, although I'm not certain how the two are connected."

"I'm not entirely certain myself, sir."

King turns to fully face me, though his smile has mostly faded. "I feel I don't need to explain to you that this is concerning, Mr. Spencer. First and foremost, the spreading of lies and stories is unacceptable."

"Are inquiries and stories the same thing?" I tilt my head. "Perhaps you should have a conversation with Mr. Hart, if so, because he must be teaching us incorrectly."

The downturn of his mouth is subtle. I'm treading dangerously here, I know, and this not a situation in which my flippant attitude is going to win me any points. "There is not a staff member or student in this school who has any information as to Mr. Frances' departure save for myself. What became of him is not for public consumption, and you do him a great disservice by trying to pry into his personal affairs."

I should watch my mouth. I should bite my tongue and agree and say all the pretty things the headmaster wishes me to say. But he's just told me that he knows what's become of Oscar, and I'm so desperate to know I want to fling myself across the desk and shake the information out of him. "I daresay I do a greater disservice to my friend by not trying to ensure his well-being."

We are at a stalemate, staring at one another with an intensity that makes me sick to my stomach and overcome with anger all at once. I think he might dismiss me, or punish me, or—hell, maybe this is grounds for expulsion, I don't know.

Finally, he says, "I had reason to believe Mr. Frances was engaging in inappropriate behaviour with a member of the staff, although he would not admit to it. He was due to be expelled and disappeared before we had the chance."

He may as well have thrown a bucket of cold water on me.

I cannot fathom this. Oscar and a member of staff. Worded like that, the headmaster could mean anyone. A maid, a cook, or...a teacher? A man old enough to be his father? Because only one person comes to mind: Mr. Hart. The flower upon his mantel. The disparaging look upon his face to even speak of Oscar...

For as incredulous as the idea is, it would also explain so much. The reluctance to speak to me about it. The extra work he put into the assignments for Mr. Hart's class. The reason Mr. Hart asked about him the night of the party, too.

"Not something you knew about, I presume?" he inquires with a cold edge to his voice. "Surely if you had, it was something you would have brought to my attention."

My mouth draws into a thin line. "As per instructions, I would never spread stories and lies, sir."

King purses his lips and nods. His hands unfold, placed upon his desk as he leans forwards slowly. "Given what I know from your mother and father, James, I am very aware that you are on thin ice back home, and that this school may be your only chance at redemption in their eyes. As such, I strongly advise you to watch your tongue."

I'm going to crawl out of my skin. I don't give two shits about who this man is or what power he feels he possesses; I will not be so easily cowed. "Of course, headmaster. I will file your advice under things to ignore."

He lets out a long, low sigh from his nose and straightens up. I hadn't noticed the birch rod resting against the edge of his desk until he reaches for it. "The punishment for such blatant disrespect is twenty strikes, Mr. Spencer."

My eyes do not waver from his face, even as my heartbeat is deafening in my ears. "Should I stand, or do you prefer your boys bent over?"

Mr. King doesn't balk at that, but his voice does come out significantly darker. "When I'm through with you, you will have difficulty standing. Jacket and shirt off, hands on the desk."

"Promises, sir," I respond, a bitter little smile gracing my lips.

It's a response that may or may not add to the intensity of lashes, but I am beyond caring and, at the end of the day, there is nothing this man can do to me. He can lecture, he can threaten, he can beat me bloody. I will not give up on finding out what happened to my friend, or any of the other boys lost at Whisperwood.

I shove back my chair and rise to my feet, slipping out of my coat and shirt, and bracing my hands against the edge of the desk. I do not break eye contact with the headmaster until he's out of sight behind me.

This is not the first time in my life I've been on the receiving end of a birch, days long past as a child getting whippings on the backs of my legs and bottom, and to be struck on the back and against bare flesh is a new level of cruelty. It's been long enough since the last time that the intensity of it catches me off-guard. The first strike comes down across my back with such force that my eyes snap shut, my head ducks, and it takes considerable effort not to cry out.

"Count," the headmaster says.

I swallow hard, sucking in a deep breath. "...One."

Again. The crack of the birch against my skin making my eyes blur.

"Two..."

Again.

And again.

Eight, nine, ten.

"Twenty."

By the time the headmaster is through with me, every nerve in my body is alight with pain. Standing up straight is indeed difficult, and it's with trembling hands that I gingerly slip my shirt back on.

Headmaster King watches me with the most displaced, cold, calculating stare imaginable. "I pray this serves as a good lesson for you, James."

"Of course. I do hope we can do this again." I curse how my voice comes out hoarser than I want it to. "Have a wonderful evening."

I leave with my head held high, desperate to get back to the dorm. To William. I want to see his face, to curl up beside him, listen to the sound of his heartbeat and feel his hands in my hair until the pain begins to fade.

I don't knock because William will have been waiting for me. What I don't expect upon opening his door is to see him pressed against his dresser, shoulders hunched, looking very much like a cornered animal, while Charles Simmons looms over him with a smirk on his face.

I haven't a clue why he's here, but I don't care. Mouthing off to our housemaster is likely to set me up for another beating, and I cannot care about that, either. "Get lost, you parasite," I snarl, thinking if he doesn't put some distance between himself and William, I'm going to throw him out the bloody window.

Charles turns to flash a toothy smile as he straightens up. "Evening, Spencer. I was just delivering a message from the headmaster."

The sound of those words makes my body stiffen, which in turn makes the welts and bruising across my back throb. "Lovely. Message has been delivered, I presume, so if you'll excuse us…"

"Of course. Nice talk, Esher." Charles winks at him, and as he passes me by to leave the room, he makes it a deliberate point to clap a hand on my back. The jostling makes pain shoot into every inch of my body. I jerk forwards a little, teeth gritted to refrain from whirling around and slamming a fist straight into his face.

The door closes with a resounding click behind him, and I take a deep breath. "Are you all right?"

William slowly pushes away from the dresser, rubbing at one of his arms. He looks rattled. Not in the usual, annoyed way he does when Charles has been bothering him, but something more that I cannot quite place.

"Yes." He shakes his head, hesitating, and I know the next words that come out of his mouth are not going to be ones I want to hear. "James, why did your parents send you to Whisperwood?"

My jaw clenches. "Misbehaviour, dear William. As I've said before. Do you think we could lie down? I've had a long evening."

The slightly glazed look in his eyes as he stares at me, like he doesn't quite understand, makes me inwardly sigh. His medicine is in full effect, I see. While he does move to turn down the blankets for me, he also quietly says, "That's not what I was told."

He gestures to the bed, but I don't move just yet, my gaze still locked upon him. I cannot recall the last time I've felt this tired. "Tell me, William, what did reliable old Simmons tell you?"

Silence falls over the room. I can see his inner debate as clear as day; the way his gaze flicks to the floor, to the bed, down at his hands. The slight, uncertain hunch of his shoulders. I'm praying he'll drop the subject, that we can just curl up in bed together and that will be it.

William clasps his hands loosely before him and doesn't look up at me. "He said that you set fire to your family's home with your parents, uncle, and cousins inside."

There it is.

Something Charles should not have known, and yet he did, because the headmaster undoubtedly informed him. The beating was only a formality; this, here, was the real punishment.

A defensive urge to snap at William rears its ugly head, and I fight it back. "Do you believe him?"

Hesitantly, he lifts his eyes to my face, a little bit of hopefulness creeping into his features. "I would believe you over him any day. You know that. So, it isn't true?"

I drag in a deep breath that makes me hurt all over. "Why does it matter why I'm here?"

"Maybe it doesn't, but your evasiveness is troubling. I'm only asking for your honesty."

"And my honest answer is that it honestly does not matter. We have other things to worry about right now."

The stillness that befalls him, the slight widening of his eyes, makes my stomach coil up into a tight little ball. He's waiting for me to say *no, it's not true*, and I know damned well he'd believe me in an instant. It would be so easy to lie and brush this aside.

But the truth would come out eventually.

"I guess that answers my question."

God, I should have just gone to my own room. "Do you truly think I'd hurt anyone?"

He steps towards me and his voice is gentle despite the confusion and concern writ across his face. "No. I don't. But you aren't giving me much to go off of right now."

The softness of him makes my chest ache. "And how would you feel if such a thing were true?"

Directly before me, he comes to a stop, and gives that a long moment of thought. "I...I think I would be disappointed that I don't know you as well as I had thought, and that you didn't trust me enough to tell me the truth."

I don't flinch away from our eye contact. I knew, of course, this conversation had to eventually happen if he and I were to be anything to one another. But I had wanted it to be under different circumstances—*my* circumstances—and those circumstances did not include me being so exhausted and in pain. I wanted time to figure out how to put into words things I cannot even bring myself to think about most of the time, but...

Here we are, and the anxiety washes over me in waves unlike anything I've seen since before I came to Whisperwood. I am trapped, cornered into this conversation, and like a cornered animal, I am an utter beast ready to lash out.

Which has me leaning in closer to William, our faces a mere few inches apart, and the voice that comes out of my lips sounds too detached and cold to be my own.

"Since you are so insistent, then yes, actually. I was sent here because I set fire to my family's home while everyone slept inside, and my only regret is that the lot of them managed to escape, because I wish to God they had died in there."

By some miracle, William does not recoil from me, but the look of horror and confusion that floods his features only infuriates me further. "*Why?*"

Why? Every moment that led up to that decision is racing through my mind like a nightmare finally broke free and I will not—absolutely *will not*—expose myself in such a way. Not here, not now, perhaps not ever, and fuck William for putting me in this position, and fuck Charles Simmons for opening his mouth, and fuck everything. "I don't know, William; perhaps for the same reason you cannot get through a day without drugging yourself into a useless stupor. Perhaps our families didn't love us enough."

That does it. William flinches away, a hand to his chest as though I've physically stricken him and that was both my goal and the complete opposite of what I wanted.

Never did I want to be a source of pain for him. Ever. And yet here we are.

I don't wait for him to respond. If I don't leave now, I'm going to be sick and perhaps I will say more cruel things I never wanted to say.

William does not try to follow me as I flee.

13

YOU'RE *SUCH A GOOD CHILD, JAMES.*

When I first tried to present the truth to my parents, it was that statement that gave me the courage. It was a refrain I'd heard my entire life. From them, from everyone.

And I was, wasn't I? A good child. I did my best. Certainly, I had my flaws, but in the grand scheme of things I did well enough in my studies, I helped around the house, assisted my father in the dealings of the family business. I wasn't prone to misbehaviours nor was I involved in anything scandalous beyond things of normal boys my age. If they had any complaints about me, it was simply my extreme fondness for the theatre and the arts. Father seemed to be wilfully oblivious to my blatant disinterest in women, and mother—I think she just turned a blind eye to it and hoped for the best.

When I told my parents what happened to me, when they refused to even consider that I was telling the truth, it struck me that being the Good Child mattered for nothing. Being good all my life hadn't saved me, and it hadn't lent any credence when it came to my parents saving me, and now...

Lying in my bed with the blanket pulled up and over my head, I don't think I'm a good child at all.

How could I be after what just happened? I'd deflected and lied for so long to someone who absolutely deserved to know the truth, and what did I do when inevitably confronted with it? Instead of apologizing and explaining myself, I've allowed William to think my issues were somehow his fault.

I don't begin to know how I could have been so cruel to him. To the man who cared for me, who has been at my side, who has meant so much to me. *You're such a good child, James.* I hear Mother's voice in my head, but it's William's face that I see. Horrified and wounded and making my chest ache.

There's a distinct part of me that wants to go back to his room. I want to throw myself at his feet and beg his forgiveness, to tell him how frightened I was to have him know such a dark part of me and see the most shameful aspects of who I am. I cannot bear the thought he would think less of me.

I cannot go to him. And I don't. Not that night, and not in the days to follow. My shame and fear are both too great, and any time I so much as think of approaching, my lungs constrict so tightly that I cannot breathe.

I wonder if he hates me. I wonder if he looks at me now and feels the same disgust and disappointment my parents must feel.

When I cannot bring myself to confront that idea, what else can I do? The only thing I can think of, and the course of action that I predictably take, is to simply throw myself back into other matters. Namely, my never-ending quest to find out the truth behind Oscar's disappearance, and the ghosts of Whisperwood.

My first task, I decide, will be to sit down and pen letters. Of course, I haven't the addresses with which to post them, and without William's help, I haven't the faintest idea of how to go about obtaining them, but—one problem at a time.

The first letter I write is to Oscar. Of course, I'm positive that he isn't at home to receive it, but it seems an obvious step that I should not overlook. The missive I pen is simple: Hello, how are you, we miss you at school, we hope you're doing well. Nothing to draw any suspicion, but full invitation and even the expectancy for him to respond.

The next letter is to Oscar's mother. This one I plan to send a week after the first, and it runs along the lines of that I've yet to receive correspondence back from Oscar, if he's come home, if she's heard from him, and that I consider him to be a dear friend of mine and I'm merely checking in to make sure that he's doing well with hopes of hearing from him soon.

The letters that will follow those are ten in total. Names William and I found in the records room that night, each perished under suspicious circumstances, and each note is almost the same. *Hello, we are looking to put together a commemorative book in honour of students lost at Whisperwood; would you mind telling me a bit about your son so that his story can be included?*

I spend nearly a week on these letters, putting in my best effort to make them look as neatly written as possible and to word them in a way that seems proper, educated, and kind. I hope to command some respect and a sense of ease, after all, so these families will see fit to write me back. That is, if I'm able to acquire addresses. If those addresses are current and correct. If the parents themselves are even still living. Some of them would be quite old by now.

When the letters are done, I'm still at a loss as to how to go about getting back into the records room. I could ask William, and it's something I contemplate for only a second before my nerves and cowardice kick that idea clear out the window. Perhaps an opportunity will appear to me in which I will be able to get the key on my own with minimal risk. That's the best I can hope for, right? I must wait until then.

In the meantime, I can resume looking for the tunnels. Which means it's back to wandering about the grounds like a fool. At this point, I'm not even looking for something suspicious or in areas that seem likely to hold hidden entrances. I'm going inch by inch and making certain no stone is unturned.

The first few days, my searches are much like any of the ones with William. That is to say, unsuccessful. It's only on the third day that I make headway, and that has little to do with any detective skills on my part, but rather...

A boy.

Different and yet very much the same as the one I've seen before. I spot him after drill, as I'm heading back to the dorm, and he lingers just out of the corner of my gaze, and though he is a fair distance off, I can tell by the colour of his skin and the state of his clothes alone that he is not amongst the living.

I linger on the path, watching him watching me, our gazes locked and the hair along the back of my neck beginning to stand on end.

Then he turns, takes a few steps, and vanishes.

I straighten up. Such brief glimpses are not so rare anymore. I catch sight of them from the corner of my gaze almost daily. But rarely this early—the sun is just now setting—and rarely still there when I turn to look.

I shake off the chill that's settled over me and resume my trek to the dorms, only to realise he's appeared again. Further off from where he was before. Again, he stares at me when I lift my eyes to meet his. And again, he recognizes this, turns, takes a few steps, and disappears.

Does he want me to follow him? What a dangerous and foolish prospect—who in their right mind would follow a dead man anywhere?—but at the same time, I cannot deny the sense of excitement and hopefulness bubbling up inside me. If anyone were to know where the tunnels are, it would be one of the spirits. Perhaps he's aware of what I'm looking for, perhaps he wants to help me, perhaps he, too, wants the truth to come to light and—

Perhaps I will lose sight of him entirely if I keep allowing my thoughts to run away from me. He's gone only a matter of seconds before he flickers into view again, further off still, so I zero in my focus and jog across the field towards the line of trees to follow while maintaining a safe distance, because I have no interest in venturing *too* close.

We play this game for a while, he and I. He appears, moves, disappears, and I try to keep up. Through the trees and into the woods, until the school has vanished behind us altogether. I'm so intent on this, on keeping in motion and hopefully bringing myself closer to my goal, that I lose thought of all else. Even as the sky grows dark and the air becomes chilly, I pay none of it any mind. There's just enough moonlight filtering in through the trees to keep me headed in the right direction.

Then I hear the bells. Ten in total. Signalling curfew. Damn it all.

I haven't a clue how far from the dorms this boy has led me, but I'm sure that even if I were to run full-speed, I wouldn't come close to making it to my room in time. Shit.

Not that I've ever minded being out after hours, and I don't particularly mind now, except that it occurs to me I've been stumbling through the woods in the dark. Alone. Not something I've dared to do before, and certainly never on my own. I always had William.

I give it another ten or fifteen minutes, but the boy does not grace me with his presence again. Cursing quietly, bemoaning that this seems to have been another opportunity lost, I begin to make my way back through the forest. Nothing to be done for it now. All I can do is try to sneak back into Gawain Hall without being noticed, and hopefully I'll be able to find my way back to this spot at a later point in time.

By some grace of God, the forest thins and eventually deposits me back into the fields with the dorm in sight. I let out a relieved breath, stealing a look around before jogging to the door. Everything is quiet and still as I slip soundlessly inside, thinking that I've made it, and all will be well.

No sooner has my foot touched the bottom of the first flight of stairs that my luck runs out.

"What do you think you're doing?"

It's not a friendly voice that greets me. I could not be so fortunate. I close my eyes, not having to turn around to envision the way Charles Simmons is sneering in delight to have caught me breaking the rules. Lovely. "I had hoped to run away and join the circus, but alas, their applications were closed."

"Shame, that. You would have been a wonderful addition to their freak show."

I want to roll my eyes. Instead, I slowly turn around to unflinchingly meet his gaze. "Quite. If you'll excuse me, I believe I should be in my room."

Charles is in his night clothes and a robe, a candlestick in hand and a pleased smile plastered on his obnoxious face. "You should've been in your room forty-five minutes ago, and yet here you are. Do you know what that means?"

I wonder. Trouble is really the last thing I need right now—the welts on my back have only just begun to not cause me pain—but my tongue will not stay still. I loathe this man almost as much as I loathe the headmaster. "I cannot say I know, but I'll wager a guess. Is it a jerk or a suck?"

He laughs at that, damn him. "You keep dreaming, Spencer. You're nowhere near my mark."

"Of course. I'm probably too old. Are first years more appealing to your tastes?"

His smile is tight, cold. "Maybe you should ask *dear William* what my tastes are."

What he's insinuating makes my stomach roll, and if he's determined to make me doubt William, he's going to be sorely disappointed. But, God, I want to hit him. It would be worth any punishment I would receive. "I would consider your next words very carefully."

His smile widens a notch. "To your room, Mr. Spencer. You know the punishment for nightwandering. Since it's a first offense, I'll let you off easy. Stand out 'til the prefects do their morning rounds and think about what you've done and why you ought not to do it again."

"What a terrifying punishment," I mutter. Standing out is the simplest of reprimands, one I've seen plenty of my dorm-mates perform. One only needs to stand outside their room in the hall with nothing to occupy themselves. It means I'll be foregoing sleep for the duration of the night. More important still is the fact that the hallways aren't the most pleasant of places after dark. If Charles has any knowledge of my asking around about ghosts, then maybe this punishment is on purpose.

Charles tails me all the way up to my room, where he gives my shoulder a push to turn me around and put my back to the door. "I suppose you know the rules," he drawls. "No moving, no sitting, no singing or talking until you've been dismissed in the morning. Disobey, and it will mean an instant trip to the headmaster's office, and I'm sure you wouldn't want that again."

My back aches at the thought. "Have a lovely night, Simmons."

"Not as wonderful as yours, I'm certain," he responds before he heads down the hall, back to whatever hole he crawled out of.

When he's out of sight, I heave a sigh and slump back against the door. I have hours upon hours before Virgil or Augustus will come to relieve me. Not that I know if Charles will actually check on me to make certain I'm still standing here, but knowing my luck…

I'm in for a long night. Not even just one of boredom, exhaustion, and sore legs, but because it takes only an hour before the noises begin.

Whispers I cannot quite catch, scratching at the walls in the darkness, just out of sight, quiet sighs, groans, and crying in the distance. At least I have no worries about falling asleep, because any time I think that I might, something moves just at the corner of my gaze and has me jerking my head to look. My heart spends the entire night galloping a mile a minute.

Come morning, I'm so exhausted that I can barely see straight, and every inch of my body is stiff and aches from tension. Virgil strolls down the hall bright and early, before the sun is even up, and startles at the sight of me.

"Mr. Spencer, were you caught out of your room last night?"

My eyes burn with tiredness and I cannot even muster a cheeky smile or witty retort. "It would seem that way."

He clicks his tongue, opens his booklet, and scribbles something down in it. My name, the date, and my offense, I'd imagine. It'll go into the headmaster's book and then in my record. "You've been having a bit of a time of it lately, it would seem."

"Mm."

"Is there something bothering you?"

I blink slowly at him, surprised by the concern. "Thank you, but I'm well."

He presses his lips together, nods briefly, and gestures at my door to dismiss me before he resumes his patrol down the hall. With a relieved sigh, I retreat into my room, peeling out of my clothing as I go and collapsing into bed, fully nude, and burying my face into a pillow. I get no more than forty-five minutes of sleep before the morning bells are chiming and I'm forced back up.

I don't remember washing or getting dressed; the cold water does nothing to alert me. Breakfast and my morning classes go by in a similarly blurry fashion, with me in a daze and retaining nothing of our lessons. Hopefully classes aren't covering anything important today.

The only thing that sticks out to me is lunch. Even then it's only because Preston catches me before I can have a seat. "Can we talk for a moment, just the two of us?"

I nod dumbly, wondering if he'd be offended if I slept through our chat.

We have a seat away from our usual spot, although I catch Benjamin and Edwin's glances in our direction and wonder if they have any idea what I'm being cornered about. I begin to serve food onto my plate; I didn't have dinner and I ate little at breakfast. A proper meal might help.

Preston watches me for a few moments, mouth drawn, before asking, "What's going on with you?"

"What do you mean?"

"Don't play dumb with me. I heard you and Simmons last night, you know. What were you doing out so late?"

I wonder just how much he heard, but—his door is in the same hallway as my own, and so he must have only caught the tail end of our conversation.

Sighing, I run my hands over my face. "I lost track of time, is all."

"Until after curfew? What were you doing?"

"Just wandering the grounds. I was restless."

The pull of his brows suggests he doesn't believe me in the slightest. I cannot blame him. I wouldn't believe me, either.

"Look, I'm going to be honest with you. I haven't the foggiest idea what's gotten into you lately, or if you're dealing with something. I know Frances' departure has been hard. We're all feeling that loss. Just know you aren't alone, all right?"

I stare at him, unsure of what to say.

"Don't give me that look. I mean it. Me and the lads—we're your friends, too. And maybe we aren't as important as Frances or Esher or whatever, but we've got your back. You can come to any of us, and if there's something we can do to help; that's what friends are for, right?"

My chest aches. Things haven't really been the same since Oscar left, have they? And that's been my fault. Preston and Benjamin and Edwin have still been there, hurting over the loss of a friend, too, and I've been...well, anywhere else. With William, and then all on my own. Turning my back on them even if it wasn't my intention to do so. I've been a shit friend.

"I'm sorry," I say, and I mean it. I cannot tell him everything that's going on. I wouldn't even know where to begin. "You're right. I suppose I've rather shut myself off since Oscar left. I'm going to try to do better, because even if I've been an arse, you're my friends and I'm quite fond of you. I'll try to snap out of...whatever this is. I give you my word."

Preston studies me a moment before he relaxes, seeming to decide that's a good enough answer for him. "That'd be good. It's not the same without you, you know? Rugby's boring with just them little ones." He inclines his head towards Benjamin and Edwin who both are, in fact, built quite small and not much of the rugby-playing variety.

"Well, I think I would fall asleep on the field if I tried to play today, but what about tomorrow?"

That's enough to make his smile widen. "That would be great. After classes?"

"After classes," I agree.

14

As promised, and after a proper night's sleep, I devote the next day doing my best to engage more with my friends. I arrive at breakfast bright-eyed and bushy-tailed, intent on being my usual chatty and carefree self. And Rugby, yes, because I did promise.

My heart, however, is not in it.

I've far too much experience going through the motions of pretending I'm fine when I'm not. There is simply too much on my mind, from Oscar to William to ghosts to—

Yes. *That*, too.

I try desperately not to think of *that*, of *him*. I do my best to keep busy even if it means repeating the same routine every day, like the aimless wandering in search of the tunnels, or the trips to the library to look through the same books again and again—but memories of home still seep through the cracks. For a time, before things went so horribly wrong here, I had almost convinced myself that everything of *him* had been sufficiently buried, chased away by the soothing feel of William's kisses and touch.

Now that I'm alone, now that the memories have been forced to the surface, I cannot help but reflect on them.

Sometimes I still scrub at my skin extra hard when I wash, as though it will rid me of the lingering remnants of an unwanted touch. Sometimes I meet someone's gaze in the hall and I'm positive that they *know*. Sometimes, nightmares wrest me from a deep sleep.

Like tonight.

I'm upright in bed before I'm even fully awake, heart lodged in my throat. Swimming in the first few moments of disorientation, I'm certain I'm not alone. That a familiar, deep, unwanted voice is murmuring familiar refrains against my ear.

No.

Just a dream.

I'm alone in my room. At school. Far from a home that no longer exists.

My breathing slowly returns to normal, and it's in that newfound silence that I realise while I may be alone in my room, I am not alone in entirety. Someone is moving about.

I remain immobile, straining to make sense of what I'm hearing. Footsteps? Quiet, not like the heavy thumping that I tend to hear when the halls are active with the undead, and I'm not sure if they're coming closer to my room or I'm imagining things.

A moment later, though, I become aware that the steps are indeed approaching. Pausing, just outside my door, then a slow creak, and I realise...

The door is opening.

William, is my first thought. Though it was far more common for me to sneak into his room, it wasn't unheard of for him to visit me from time to time. Who else would it be? What would prompt a visit from him now, when we've not spoken a word since that night?

"William? Is that you?"

No response. Silence and tension build in the air and in my body as I begin to think it isn't William after all.

Then I hear it. Or...I think I hear it. So brief that it's the softest whisper, but I'm so unbelievably certain the voice belongs to Oscar.

"You have to..."

The words are lost to the ether before the sentence can be finished, but it's enough to have me pitching forwards out of bed and hurrying to the door to stick my head into the hall.

Nothing. Nothing to see, and nothing to hear except the heavy thrumming of my own heart.

Unwilling to give up so easily, I step fully out into the corridor. "Oscar?" I whisper. "Oscar, is that you? Are you here?"

It doesn't matter how many times I call to him. I'm left not knowing what's just happened and feeling undeniably distraught. For however brief a second, I thought I had found him and was filled with such excitement—and I could cry with the frustration of having it ripped from me again.

Back in my room, the door clicks quietly closed behind me. I crawl into bed and pull the blanket up to my chin. I foresee a lot of tossing and turning for the rest of the night. Regardless, I force my eyes closed, concentrating on steady breathing that sometimes helps me to drift off.

A ruined effort as an icy hand clamps over my mouth.

Eyes flying open, what I see should not in any way be possible for a multitude of reasons, but there is a dead boy sitting upon my chest.

His dark hair hangs in stringy, limp wet strands, freezing water dripping from his person; I can feel it sinking through my clothing. His milky eyes bore into mine, wide and emotionless, and his mouth scarcely moves as he whispers, "We have to be quiet."

Being quiet is the opposite of what I want to do. It's the opposite of what I plan to do, for that matter. I have every intention of opening my mouth and screaming past the boy's clammy fingers in hopes that I'll draw the attention of the whole damned dorm.

No sound comes from my mouth.

I cannot even get it to open.

I want my lips to part, and so they should. A boy of this size should not be able to silence me.

He seems to realise what I'm trying to do because his fingers dig into my cheeks bruisingly hard and he leans closer. "We have to be quiet."

I don't understand how a boy significantly smaller than myself has the capability of immobilizing me. "We have to be very, very quiet," he rasps, followed by a wet cough as though trying to breathe around waterlogged lungs. "We cannot let him hear us. We have to be quiet, be quiet. Don't make a sound, don't move…"

I cannot breathe, with the weight bearing down on my chest, with the hand over my face. I cannot move, cannot turn my head to try to suck in air, and I don't know what more he wants from me because I'm being utterly silent because I cannot even breathe *to* make a sound.

"We have to be silent. Quiet, quiet, quiet… We have to—"

The door opens again. Not the same slow creak as before but flung wide as though by a burst of wind, and I am distinctly aware that the room has suddenly plummeted to ridiculously low temperatures and a musty, damp odour fills my nostrils, unpleasant and unfamiliar.

I don't know if it's the sudden noise that frightens him, but the boy vanishes. I gasp in large gulps of air. With my regained capability to move, I bolt upright and paw at my face to wipe away the feeling of that hand on my skin.

My heart will never settle again. I swiftly dismiss the idea of rushing out of here and up to William's room, desperate to be held and comforted. I could also go wake one of my friends, but would they believe a word of it? They would surely try to reassure me, if nothing else.

But can I be reassured? I don't think it possible right now. I have no faith these encounters will stop. They've only grown in frequency the more I learn about the school, while everyone else remains so blissfully, wilfully ignorant.

I dwell on that for a time, contemplating what it could mean. If I continue and these interactions have escalated to the point where I'm now being attacked, could I end up another name in the Whisperwood cemetery? Or would the headmaster mark me as a runaway, never to be found?

Such ideas should scare me, I know. The feeling of icy fingers against my skin should frighten me into choosing a safer path, but I cannot. Whatever risks may come attached, I made a promise to Oscar to find him and to bring light to whatever has happened, and I cannot turn my back on that.

I cannot turn my back on *him*.

It takes me a few days to regain my bearings after the incident in my room, to stop feeling so jumpy at every sound, every presence. When I emerge from the other side of my fear, I'm more determined than ever in my quest for answers. If the dead hope to scare me into silence, then they've failed miserably. I've reached a place I cannot turn back from.

It's this newfound determination that leads me to my next course of action. It's one that I've toyed with since my meeting with the headmaster, but one I put off for a variety of reasons. Dread, perhaps. Nerves.

I'm going to see Mr. Hart again.

This time, I do not plan on being so polite.

After classes have concluded for the day, I knock lightly on his half-open door and step in without waiting for invitation. "Mr. Hart," I greet as I approach his desk, where he appears to be grading papers. "Do you have a moment?"

He doesn't look up from his writing. "Of course. Did you need help with today's work?"

The idea is absurd and not worth an answer; English is my strongest subject, after all. Instead, I place a book atop the stack of papers he's reading. *Pendennis.* The book Oscar never would have left behind. I have a hunch as to who gifted it to him, and when Mr. Hart's gaze snaps quickly to me, wide and surprised, I know my gut feeling was spot-on.

"Where did you get this...?"

I have no reason to lie. "It was hidden beneath Oscar's mattress. This is why I know he didn't leave Whisperwood of his own accord. He told me that book was given to him by someone special, and it was one of his most prized possessions. He *never* would have left without it."

Mr. Hart's eyes drop back to the book as he picks it up and opens it. He runs a hand across the worn pages, a heavy sadness working its way into his expression. "I've already told you, Mr. Spencer..."

"The headmaster said Oscar ran away in light of being expelled for his involvement with a teacher," I say. I place my hands upon the edge of the desk and lean forward. "And do you know what I think of that? I think it was you."

"Then you think incorrectly," he quickly shoots back, and his tone is uncharacteristically cold. "I have no interest in sitting here and listening to this—"

"And I have no interest in being spoon-fed more lies," I snap, my temper rearing its ugly head. I have every reason to believe that this man, in some form or another, is responsible for whatever foul thing has become of my best mate. I don't give a damn about his feelings. "The night of the dance, you asked after Oscar. You were downright nervous when I told you I'd not seen him."

"I have no—"

"What about when William and I came to visit you? I saw that flower on your mantel. The paper one. Oscar used to make them to send home to his sister."

"James..."

"That isn't even covering the state you were in after he vanished," I continue, refusing to be interrupted. "You looked as though you'd not slept in a week. What happened, Mr. Hart? Did Oscar decide all those beatings from the headmaster weren't worth it anymore? Did he want to end things with you and you became enraged? Or were you the one who wanted things to end? With suspicions mounting, did you worry Oscar would sell you out to the headmaster and you'd lose your job? Easier to get rid of him and then—"

Mr. Hart lunges out of his seat, hands slamming flat upon his desk. "I would *never* hurt that boy!" he snarls, far more force behind that simple phrase than I thought a man so soft-spoken to be capable of.

Startled by the outburst and the fierceness behind it, I pull back. A movement which seems to make Mr. Hart reel himself in, because he takes a deep breath, straightens, and slides a hand back through his normally kempt hair.

"I will admit, I was very fond of Oscar. He was a brilliant student with a wonderful heart, and I hated that he suffered from such loneliness in coming from a family that did not appear to care for him at all."

I swallow hard. "So, you two—?"

He lifts his eyes to mine, filled with weariness and a touch of regret. "I did begin to suspect that Oscar's affections towards me were heading in an inappropriate direction. I hesitated to tell anyone for fear of how it would be perceived or the repercussions he might face. I didn't want him punished, and I thought I would be capable of firmly establishing boundaries between us on my own. I wanted to be a mentor to him. A friend."

"Then when the headmaster began punishing him..."

"I have little knowledge of that. I know more from the headmaster than from Oscar. King questioned all of Oscar's teachers, stating he'd received proof from a reliable source that Oscar was involved with a member of the teaching staff, but he had no hints at to which one." He sighs. "I suspected I was the teacher in question. When I questioned Oscar, he was quite adamant he didn't want to discuss it."

And Oscar wouldn't have given up Mr. Hart's name to the headmaster, not if he could protect him. That's the sort of person he is. What proof did King have, I wonder? Something that showed Oscar's guilt but didn't directly point the finger at Mr. Hart?

Do I believe him? The doubt must be evident on my face because he continues, "I have no proof to offer you that any of your suspicions are unfounded. I have only my word, and I don't expect that to mean much to you. However, I *will* say it as many times as I must: I had nothing to do with Oscar's disappearance, nor do I have any knowledge about it beyond what you know." He sinks back down into his chair, slumping back tiredly. "I wish to God that I did. I wish that I could produce him fine and well, but I'm as lost as you are. I apologize for that."

I hate that he sounds so damned sincere. I hate the way he looks at me, as though he's hurting from this loss as much as I am, that he had no means of stopping whatever happened.

I hate it, I realise, because I *wanted* to be able to blame him. It would be easy, wouldn't it? Case closed, book shut, chapter over. Mr. Hart would have been the perfect villain and I would have had my answers.

"Mr. Hart, I…"

"Jonathan?" comes a voice. We both look up to see Mr. McLachlan standing in the doorway, frowning. More at me than anything. "Is everything all right?"

Mr. Hart seems to relax a little, though his smile is forced. "Fine, Graham."

"I didn't mean to interrupt."

"I was just about to leave," I assure him. "Thank you for the homework help, Mr. Hart. I think I understand now."

Without waiting for a response, I scoop up Oscar's book, slip past Mr. McLachlan and out of the class and then the building, eager to get back to my own room. I think I need to be alone for a bit to try to process the conversation I've just had, and what this means for what I should do next.

For as much as I wanted Mr. Hart to be the culprit, there is also a part of me that desperately latches onto the idea he's being truthful. It makes things harder and I'm practically back to square one.

But it would be good for Oscar to not have been betrayed by someone he cared for, someone he looked up to. I can be grateful, if nothing else, that such a horrible thing didn't happen to him. But it still means I'm at a loss as to what I should do now, which is equal parts frustrating and depressing.

Definitely depressing, yes.

It isn't even about my own peace of mind, though that is also a factor. There are so many things tugging at my brain; what if Oscar is being held somewhere and my inability to figure things out is keeping him there? What if he *was* being kept somewhere and my inability to figure things out resulted in something horrible happening to him because I didn't get to him in time?

What if his spirit, if that's all he is now, cannot find peace until I find answers?

The idea that Oscar could be dead rolls over me in one large, nauseating wave. To think that such a bright and lovely soul is forever stuck wandering the halls of Whisperwood, just another face to scare boys who wander out after dark.

I cannot seem to quiet my mind. I think about trying to work on my poetry, to perhaps go out and socialise with Preston and the others as I'd been trying to do, but I cannot bring myself to be around anyone right now. Instead, I mentally re-enact the last few conversations Oscar and I had, my conversation with the headmaster, with Mr. Hart, even with Mr. McLachlan. There is something I'm missing. There has to be. Somewhere I should be looking, questions that I should be asking, and…

I don't know.

I honestly don't know.

It makes me feel like the biggest failure and sends me spiralling into a fit of despair because, well, what *have* I been able to do right lately? I've been a disappointment to my family, who may never want anything to do with me again,

I've driven away the boy who may very well be the love of my life, and I cannot figure out how to help my best mate.

I feel, quite honestly, like staying in bed and never getting up again.

16

The third day I skip dinner, Benjamin brings me a few sneaked goodies. I thank him sincerely, but they don't look the least bit appetizing. He watches me with a calculated concern that only Benjamin can achieve and says, "We're worried about you, you know. You've not been yourself."

I don't move from where I'm lying on my bed, not even changed out of today's drill clothes. It feels like too much effort. "Must be homesick," I lie with a reassuring smile. "I promise, I'll be fine."

"Hm. You and Esher appear to be not on speaking terms."

Ah. Yes. They would notice that, wouldn't they? I had hoped it would be something they didn't bring up to me. Skipped meals aside, I've been trying my damndest to pretend to be normal. To be full of smiles and jokes around my friends, like I promised Preston I would.

"Things are fine," I insist, and my tone is firm enough that Benjamin knows to leave well enough alone. Only for half a moment does he look as though he might prod further, but then he smiles faintly and nods once.

"We're here if you need us," he says before departing.

The door clicks shut. I sigh, running my hands over my face and thinking that I really am not deserving of the people in my life.

I WOULD BE lying if I said I didn't desperately want to approach William. It's so commonplace, so familiar by now, that every time I leave class, every time I sit down for a meal and he isn't at my side, I feel a piece of me is missing. I cannot sleep most nights, wondering if he's all right, if the ghosts are frightening him into unrest, if Charles or anyone else is giving him grief. He sits all alone at meals again, tucked away at the far end of the table, just like he did when I first saw him.

It doesn't keep me from keeping an eye on him, though. Even if not as overtly as I originally did. I'm good at being sneaky, or perhaps William simply isn't paying me enough attention to notice how much I'm watching him.

I notice when he isn't feeling well. The listless way he picked at his breakfast this morning, the distant manner in which he answers Mr. Keys when called upon in Latin. It isn't like William to be distracted in class.

He's notably absent at lunch and comes into maths with seconds to spare, where he earns a disapproving frown from Mr. McLachlan. A further oddity occurs when the teacher passes back a graded assignment; he stops before William's desk, and his voice is low but not quiet enough that I cannot hear. "This is the first time I've ever seen you with such a dismal grade, Mr. Esher. Are you well?"

William stares down at the marks upon his paper, and his only response is a mute nod and a murmured apology.

Is he sick, I wonder? Is he overly medicated? It wouldn't be the first time he's done that, but it would be the first time he's allowed it to get in the way of his studies.

An hour into class, Mr. McLachlan calls on him and at first, William doesn't respond, his head down, eyes closed. With a sigh, Mr. McLachlan repeats, "*Esher*. Rise and shine."

He startles, cheeks flushed, though I'm not certain if that's from his not feeling well or from the chorus of quiet snickers about the room. "Yes, sir."

"The board." Mr. McLachlan nods towards the equation written upon it. "Solve for us, if you would."

Normally, this would be a moment for William to shine. Never has he had any difficulty completing anything an instructor throws at him.

Today, however, he slides slowly from his chair, and within the first few steps I'm aware that something is off. It's the way he moves, the way he extends a hand towards the corner of Mr. McLachlan's desk to guide himself, the way his steps slow to a stop and—

Every bit of colour drains from his face as his legs buckle, and he crumples to the floor.

I don't recall leaping from my seat to get to him, but there I am at his side, sliding an arm beneath him to draw him up while Mr. McLachlan crouches across from me, worry writ across his face.

"William," I say urgently, comforted only when his eyelids lift, and he focuses blearily on me. He appears startled as he comes to, and slowly the colour begins to return to his cheeks and lips, although he's broken out into a cold sweat. His glasses are askew, and he reaches up to adjust them out of habit. "What...?"

"You fainted," Mr. McLachlan says, and I'm surprised at the gentleness in his voice. "Come. On your feet."

Together we help him up, and only then do I notice that most of the class is standing with their necks craned to get a look at what's going on. I try to position myself between them and him. He is not some spectacle to be gawked at.

"I'm sorry," he mumbles, keeping his head down in embarrassment. "I wasn't... I haven't been feeling well."

"I can see that." Mr. McLachlan draws back only when he seems certain William's legs won't give out on him again. "He seems to be running a fever. Mr. Spencer, can you help him back to his room, get him settled, and call Doctor Mitchell to have a look at him?"

William grabs hold of my arm at the mention of a doctor. I nod, placing a hand against the small of William's back and gently coaxing him out of the classroom.

He goes along with me easily enough, seeming steadier on his feet the longer we walk, and it is a bit of a trek from the school to the dorm. The cold air has him shivering violently, and I wish I had anything of substance to offer him beyond wrapping an arm about his shoulders and holding him to my side.

Neither of us says a word. What would I even say, after having not spoken to him for weeks?

William is exhausted by the time we reach Gawain Hall. He pauses at the bottom of the first set of stairs, bracing himself before beginning the arduous trip up one flight and then the next. Only once inside his room does he pull away from my support, and he collapses into bed without so much as removing his shoes and coat.

I linger in the doorway, debating if I should at least get him out of those things, or if my help would be unappreciated. "Do you need your medicine?"

"No," he sighs, sinking back into the mattress with his eyes closed. "None left."

It's unlike him to let his supply run out. "I'm certain Doctor Mitchell will give you more. I'll go track him down." As I turn away, William reaches for me.

"*No*, no. Don't. I'm not— I won't take it."

I pause and slowly shut the door with a frown. "What? Why not?"

He focuses his gaze upon me tiredly but doesn't answer.

"William. Why aren't you taking your medicine anymore?"

He swallows hard and looks away. "Because you were right."

A wave of guilt washes over me. "Don't be ridiculous. I lashed out at you because I was angry."

"No, you were right," he repeats, removing his glasses and setting them aside on his dresser. "Look at me. I'm a wreck. I don't even know how to function or who I am without it."

I never would have thought that; my concern has always been the high dosages William takes without care, the way it affects his ability to think clearly. I've heard of instances of a person taking too much and not waking again, and that is a fear I harbour over William, as well.

"I've taken it for years," he continues softly. "At first, Mother gave it to me because I was such an anxious child. Then I began to take it on my own. I don't honestly remember what sort of person I was before, and I..." He exhales, running his hands over his tired face. "You are far too precious to me, James. I don't want to engage in anything that makes me a hindrance to you. I don't want to disappoint you."

My eyes widen. The ache that floods my chest is one that I cannot begin to describe. "Why would you care what someone like me thinks?"

William looks to me again, this time with a quietly perplexed frown. "Someone like you? James, you heard every horrible rumour about me from every boy in school, and yet there you were, refusing to let me alone. You looked at me as though I were a person worth caring for. *That's* the type of person you are, and that's why I know you never would have done what you did to your home without good cause. I believe that with all my heart."

My throat constricts. I look down, trying to blink away the tears that rush forth. "Yes. Well. My parents certainly didn't feel that way."

In my periphery, I see him scoot aside, wanting me to join him. "I'm hardly your parents, but what does that mean?"

I don't move, however. I don't even look at William; I cannot bring myself to. It's all I can do not to bolt from the room or try to change the subject, to laugh it all off. But it's my choice to speak of this now, I decide. I have control over it, and William is watching me so openly and gently that I feel he needs to know. *I* need him to know.

"My uncle was raping me."

William is silent as the weight of those words settle over the room like a blanket of snow. He sits up slowly. "What...?"

I lean back against the door, needing something to physically support me. "When my aunt died of illness, we took in him and his two daughters. They were quite lovely, but he was nothing but a drunk who acted as though the world owed him on account of his loss. He never gave me any reason for his actions beyond 'family takes care of family.' Perhaps I was a safer bet than his own daughters. It took me longer than I care to admit to tell my parents what was transpiring."

"And...?"

"They told me I was being foolish. Father even insinuated that I was acting out of jealousy because there were other children in the house."

He only looks away for a moment, thinking, and I wonder if things are clicking into place for him now. "Then... The fire? That was revenge?"

"After all this time, I still don't honestly know," I admit quietly, lifting a pained, tired gaze to his face. "I was so desperate for *something* to change. I didn't want anyone to die; please understand that. I just wanted it to stop. Perhaps it was my way of coping with my own grief at the loss of everything I felt he was taking from me, I don't know. It wasn't right, but I just didn't..."

The words catch in my throat. I remember the kitchen around me beginning to burn while every member of the household slept. I remember stepping outside and watching still from the road as the building went up in flames, as my family scurried out in their nightclothes, our servants on their heels.

I had felt nothing but a dim level of satisfaction—up until I saw my uncle emerging from the building.

Maybe I'm lying. Maybe I *had* hoped that one single person would have stayed asleep in his bed until he woke with the flesh being burned from his bones.

William pitches himself forward, getting to his knees at the edge of the bed and leaning across the distance to grab my hand. I allow him to pull me closer, onto the bed, into his arms, where he wraps me in a tight embrace and whispers in my ear, "Darling, I believe you."

A shudder courses through me. I bury my face against his shoulder, biting back every emotion I'm feeling, and yet my voice still comes out laced with tremors. "I'm so sorry. I should have told you."

"You owe me no apologies." William cradles me against him, lying back and wrapping his smaller figure around mine, as though he might somehow shield me from the rest of the world by doing so. "This isn't your fault."

I don't think I knew how badly I wanted to hear that up until now. For someone to tell me they believe me, and that it isn't some sort of overreaction on my part. That the excuses my uncle fed to me were not, in fact, justified at all. In hindsight, I feel almost ridiculous for thinking William would react any other way. Then again, I never thought my parents would turn their backs on me when I needed them most, either.

William holds me close and tight for the better part of an hour, simply stroking my hair and face, rubbing my back. He doesn't say anything and that's all right; he doesn't need to. I am comfortable. Safe. Once I've calmed, I'm incredibly worn out but feeling better than I have in a long while, and eventually I press a warm kiss against William's throat and murmur a *thank you* against his flushed skin. He makes the softest of pleased sounds in response and asks, "Do you want to stay?"

I pull back just enough to meet his gaze. "I do. I would feel better keeping an eye on you. You look miserable."

"I'm fine," William insists. "I just…need to ride this out."

Is it really so easy? Not that I would have any idea. "If there's anything I can do, I hope you'll tell me," I murmur, ducking my head to kiss him on the mouth. William gingerly touches my cheek.

When he draws away, he looks so exhausted and not quite in his right mind, but he has a smile upon his face. "Ah. I almost forgot, I have something for you."

"Do you?"

"Top drawer there." A nod directs me towards his dresser.

Curious, I slide out of bed, pulling open the drawer. There on the top, above neatly folded socks and undergarments, are a few large sheets of paper, rolled and tied with string. I pull them out, lose the ties, and unroll them atop the dresser. "Are these…drafts of the school?"

William rolls onto his side, watching me through half-lidded eyes. "Put them next to one another. What do you notice?"

I do as instructed, scanning over one map—which looks significantly older, ink worn in places and the parchment yellowed—and the other, which is dated in one corner just a few years ago. I study the labels of each room, take notice of the stairwells and where the breaks in lines signify doorways.

It takes me a minute, but when I see it, my eyes widen. "There are doors missing on the newer map."

"Exactly. I only procured those yesterday, so I've not had a chance to investigate, but doors don't simply disappear."

This is an incredible find, and one that has my hopes soaring for the first time in a while. I turn to him. "Where did you get these?"

He shrugs. "The records room. I figured there had to be something of use beyond the student files, so..."

"You broke in," I say, incredulous.

"Breaking in is such a coarse way of wording it. I merely begged the key from May again."

Oh, what a ridiculous and perfect man he is.

"We'll investigate and see what's become of those doors now, if they've not been sealed up." Just not any time soon, I think. Not if William is feeling so miserable. I'll not drag him around in this state.

Although, he seems to have other ideas. "Tomorrow?"

I give him a long look and decide it isn't a battle I want to fight right now. That's a bridge we will cross if his condition has not improved by then. Nodding, I roll the maps back up and lay them atop the dresser. Shedding my shoes and everything above the waist, I crawl into bed once more to curl myself around William.

He sighs, and I feel his lips ghosting little kisses along my throat in a way that makes me shiver pleasantly. "For now, try to get some rest. I can tell by your face you've been sleeping poorly."

True, but I think that I'll sleep just fine tonight. It's still early, and the bell has just rung for dinner, but rest sounds far more appealing. "Sweet dreams, dear William."

William drifts off to sleep surprisingly quickly, but I lie awake and listen to the sound of his breathing. Lying so close to me like this, I'm all too aware of how impossibly hot to the touch he is. Worrisome. But he sleeps soundly and, eventually, I follow suit.

For a while, I get some good, solid sleep. Only awhile, though, because the last thing either of us needs is to get caught like this. Which means when I wake several hours past curfew, I reluctantly untangle myself from William and slide out of bed. I'm used to him not stirring an inch when I do so, but normally that's because he's too medicated to be aware of me. This, though, is different. He truly isn't feeling well.

I lean down, smoothing his hair back and kissing his forehead. Then I gather my clothes, slip back into my shirt, and hurry downstairs to my own room.

There, I strip down completely and change into my night clothes. Despite a few hours of sleep already, I'm grateful to be able to collapse into bed and close my eyes. Even after all this time, I still find myself listening for the sound of Oscar's breathing across the room. My chest hurts and, God, I hope those maps lead me to the answer I've been looking for.

17

Come morning, I dress quickly and dart upstairs to William's room. He's not budged an inch, and it takes me giving his shoulder a shake and saying his name to rouse him. His fever doesn't appear to have broken, but despite my protests, he drags himself from bed and sets about getting ready.

While he does so, I pull out the maps to go over them at his table, using a pen and ink to circle any differences. There are only two I've noticed thus far. One is a door on the second floor that appears to lead to a very small supply closet-shaped room, and I don't think it's quite what we're after. The other is located on the ground floor, off of the kitchens. The original map doesn't show that it opens into other rooms, but rather, to a set of stairs.

Exactly what we're looking for.

I glance up, mouth open to tell William what I've found, and see him braced against his washing table, head bowed, water dripping from his face and hair. I push back my seat to get up. "William?"

"I'm all right," he says quickly, reaching for his towel to dry himself off. He hasn't bothered to shave, which is so unlike him that it might be more worrisome than anything else thus far.

If he's determined to go to class, there's little I can do to stop him. Little I can do but watch as he pushes his breakfast around his plate, taking no more than a few bites, and he sits listlessly through Latin and I'm just waiting for the moment where he passes out again.

When he has to go on his own to his next few lessons, I find myself squirming through my own classes, fretting over his well-being. Come dinner, when he's looking worse enough and announces to me that he doesn't feel like eating, I think I need to be more insistent that he seek some help. He's scarcely touched his meals all day, and his skin is still scalding to the touch when I catch him by the arm and press the back of my hand to his clammy forehead.

"I really think you ought to let Doctor Mitchell look over you."

William recoils at the suggestion, shaking off my hand. "He'll only insist on giving me laudanum to treat my symptoms."

"You're getting worse," I press. "Maybe he'll have other ideas. You can tell him you don't want to take it."

His jaw clenches, and the look he gives me is both anxious and defiant. "I don't *want* to, James."

I have no interest in pushing William into doing anything he doesn't want to do, but... "I'm sorry, but I'm worried about you."

He sighs, rubbing the back of his neck. "I don't trust Doctor Mitchell. How many students fell 'ill' and then vanished while he was supposedly caring for them? Not to mention, isn't he the one who told King you were nosing about?"

That's a fair enough argument. "May I stay with you for a bit tonight?"

William's expression appears to soften. "I suppose. How can I say no to that face?"

I smile. "It *is* a very sweet face, isn't it?"

He steals a quick touch to my cheek. "It is. Now go on, go fetch yourself some dinner. I'll be fine on my own for a spell."

I would feel better if he'd come with me, or would at least ask me to bring him something back. Perhaps I'll sneak some things out of the dining hall with me.

As it so happens, I manage to tuck away a couple of rolls and smuggle a few tea sandwiches wrapped in a napkin away from the dinner table. It isn't much, and not particularly the healthiest of meals, but it's better than the whole lot of nothing he's feasted on today. I keep my meal short, eager to get back to him.

When I do, the first thing I notice upon entering the room is that the window is wide open, sending a shiver straight down my spine. "It's freezing in here."

The second thing I notice is that William does not so much as stir at my entrance. The most I get out of him is a soft noise when I approach the bed and reach out to touch his forehead.

Christ, he's burning up.

"Sweetheart, are you all right?"

William lets out a sigh, leaning into my cool hand. "Fine," he mumbles, blindly reaching for me as though to drag me down beside him. I do allow myself to sit upon the edge of the mattress, abandoning the stolen snacks onto his dresser.

"Your fever is getting worse, William. Do you want a cool cloth?" When he relinquishes his hold on my sleeve and nods, I crawl right back to my feet and go to his wash table, where the basin is still full of cold, seemingly clean water. I dunk a square of linen into it, wring it out, and return to William to gingerly wipe down his face and then settle the folded, damp cloth across his forehead. A plaintive noise escapes William's mouth at first, but he doesn't fuss at me beyond that.

There must be *something* I can do. It kills me to see him like this, helpless and miserable. Short of going to Doctor Mitchell, all I know to do is to keep him comfortable. I lie down beside him, and William promptly curls up against me, face buried against my chest. If it brings him any comfort, I'm happy to hold him and stroke his hair back from his face, occasionally rising to re-wet the cloth, and allow him to rest.

Eventually, of course, I have to go back to my own room, something I'm far more reluctant about than I've been any other night. I dampen the cloth one last time to lay it across William's forehead, bend down to kiss his cheek, tuck him in, close the window at least most of the way, and let myself out. William doesn't move an inch at any of this.

A few steps down the hall, I become aware that I'm not alone.

I come to an abrupt halt, face to face with a figure at the top of the stairs, and my heart lodges into my throat and steals my breath.

Then the figure lifts the candlestick in his hand and light washes across his frowning face.

"Spencer? What are you doing out?"

Virgil. But of course. When it rains, it pours, and I'm not certain if this is better or worse than encountering a ghost. I cannot even bring myself to care overly much about getting into trouble right now. "Just heading to my room."

He heaves a sigh, moving down the hall towards me. "Two hours after curfew? You know what that means."

"Then write me up and I'll stand on my head outside of my room again or whatever."

That makes his eyebrows shoot up and his mouth downturn. "Someone's in a foul temper. Something bothering you?"

"William is unwell," I say, figuring I'm not divulging any secrets with that. Plenty of people have seen as much over the last two days.

Virgil hmms, glancing from me to the door a few feet behind me. "Feeling unwell enough to have company in his room this late?" It isn't an accusatory tone, really; merely curious.

"It would seem that way."

"Has Doctor Mitchell been to see him?"

My jaw tightens. "William has no interest in seeing the good doctor."

"Why is that?" He steps around me and goes to William's door, lifting his free hand to knock.

"I would appreciate it if you didn't wake him," I say quickly, and he lowers his hand. "I'm also not certain why that's your business. He simply doesn't want to."

"I heard he fainted in class the other day." He casts a glance my way. "If he doesn't wish to be seen by Doctor Mitchell, then perhaps I can be of assistance."

I raise an eyebrow. "Are you a doctor?"

"My father is. I've worked alongside him since I was a child."

I study Virgil for a long moment. I've never quite been able to get a read on him, but he's never been unkind, exactly. And rather than doling out a punishment to me, he's offering to help. That ought to count for something. I finally relent by nodding towards the door. "He's been sleeping most of the evening."

Virgil pokes his head into the room before stepping inside, and I follow after him, unwilling to allow anyone I don't fully know or trust be left alone with William. While Virgil moves to his bedside, I linger nearby, arms crossed, to silently observe.

He picks up William's hand, pressing fingers to his wrist, feels his face, lifts his eyelids. He even attempts to gently wake him, to which William only makes the quietest of sounds in response. When he pulls back, it's to look about the room. "I've heard rumour he partakes of opium on a regular basis. Is that true?"

My gaze snaps to him. "Not anymore."

That appears to get Virgil's attention because he turns to me, frowning deeply. "When did he stop? Recently?"

William and I weren't exactly speaking, so... "It's been a few days, I believe."

Virgil sighs. "And he stopped abruptly? Do you know what sort of dosage he was taking?"

"I cannot say that I ever asked him. It seemed a rather private thing."

"You need to take him to Doctor Mitchell, Spencer."

"I've told you that isn't going to happen. If you have other suggestions, I'm listening."

Virgil's look is an unimpressed one, but it is not unkind. "Last summer, a woman came into my father's clinic, the wife of a merchant. At first glance, she simply displayed symptoms for a bad cold and stress."

"Fascinating story."

"And then she admitted she had been taking regular doses of laudanum, exceeding the recommended amount. When she attempted to stop abruptly, it caused many complications. She died after a convulsive fit two days later."

He may as well have doused me in cold water. "What?"

"The medical community has known for ages about the physical dependence of this stuff. The more one takes, the more their body relies on it to function normally."

"And when they stop?"

Virgil ticks them off on his fingers. "Cold-like symptoms, for starters. Fevers, insomnia, aches and pains, nervousness, agitation, nausea... In the worst of cases, fits, severe dehydration, and heart problems. Why do you think they've begun cracking down on the accessibility of opium-based medications? There's a reason they label it as poison." He turns to William. "Father said it would have been wiser had his patient been weaned off the medicine, allowing her body to adjust without subjecting her to the side-effects of withdrawal."

I brace a hand against William's wash table, trying to breathe, trying not to panic as this situation has just grown far worse than I had imagined. "Do you think that would work? Would he be all right? How slow would I need to wean him off it?"

Virgil holds up a hand. "Those would be questions better suited for a doctor. I'm afraid any suggestion of mine would only be a guess."

"It would be better than my guess," I plead.

He frowns, and I worry he's going to again direct me to Doctor Mitchell, but— "My assumption is that Esher was taking a much higher dose than prescribed. So, give him only the standard dosage, just to take the edge off. It won't fix the problem completely, and he may be bed-bound for a bit, but it should help. Just keep the bottle away from him so he doesn't try to take any when you aren't looking. Taper him off slowly and, God willing, he'll be fine."

My mind is racing a mile a minute. How do I even get my hands on this stuff without going to the doctor? I have no way to reach town on my own. "Thank you, Appleton. I'll see to it."

"Should you need me, I trust you know where to find me."

I duck my head, falling silent. After Virgil takes his leave, I check on William once more before retreating to my room, ever more anxious about leaving him alone.

18

Sleep, of course, does not come easily. The few times I doze off, I begin to dream of waking and finding William dead in his bed. William, hollow-eyed and pale skinned, just like the ghosts wandering the school. I had no idea that William's attempt to cease his medication would be so grave a matter, and I could shake him for either not looking into it beforehand, or simply not informing me of the risks.

I must figure out a way to obtain a bottle of laudanum myself. Doctor Mitchell would have some in stock, no doubt; it's used to treat everything from colds to nervous fits to nausea. But if I've learned anything about Doctor Mitchell, it's that he takes his job seriously and would probably notice if such a thing turned up missing.

William got his supply from one of the maids, May, who would purchase it during her bi-weekly trips into town for supplies. William would leave the funds inside the trinket box in the common room, and May would swap it for the laudanum. How neither of them has been caught after all this time, I haven't the foggiest idea, but I suppose it's now my turn to give it a try.

All I know about May is her name, not a thing about what she looks like or what, exactly, her job entails. However, logic says she would be someone who has reason to come into the dorms, and thus has easy access to the common room. Which doesn't narrow it down terribly much but gives me a starting point. There are servants who deliver our fresh bath water just outside our bedroom doors each morning, servants who scrub the floors and banisters, servants who empty the chamber pots once the students have gone to class.

This is precisely why I wake with the sun come morning and make quick work of dressing. Before even popping upstairs to check on William, I venture through Gawain Hall, in search of whoever might be working.

The first member of staff I encounter is an older woman, grey-haired but clear-eyed. She pauses in the middle of scooping the ash from the common room fireplace, wiping her soot-covered hands on her apron.

I pause in the doorway, hands behind my back and a smile upon my face. "Good morning."

"Mornin'," she greets, almost cautiously. "Bit early for you boys to be up, isn't it?"

"Quite. I couldn't sleep. I wonder, might you be able to tell me if one of your girls, May, is around?"

Her brows pinch together. "Has she done somethin' wrong?"

"No, no, not at all. In fact, she found something of mine I'd lost and saw fit to return it; I wanted to thank her personally."

The old woman appears to relax. "Ah. Well, she'd be scrubbin' down the bathroom right about now, I'd reckon."

I tip my head in her direction, thank her, and scoot out of the common room to head downstairs.

For the most part, our bathing regime is simply a good wash in our own rooms. Now and again, it isn't enough, or one simply prefers the comfort of a full, proper bath. Should the servants have to cart water in to fill tubs for every student in school, they'd never have any time to rest.

Inside the bathroom—which is, frankly, just one large room with a row of tubs and wide windows, all of which are open—I spot a woman on all fours, vigorously scrubbing at the floor. I step inside, stealing a proper look around to ensure we're truly alone.

"May?"

The girl sits back on her haunches and lifts her head, startling me by the fact she cannot possibly be older than myself. "Sir?"

I have the right person, then. Excellent. I advance further into the room, hands folded behind my back, careful to keep my voice down so no passer-by happens to overhear. "I understand you're familiar with one of the other third-year students. William Esher?"

May presses her lips tightly together, a touch of nervousness flashing across her eyes. "I'm afraid I don't know many of the students by names."

That's not exactly a denial. I stop just before her, crouching down and attempting my best, most disarming smile. "I'm a friend of William's, and I would like to request your assistance in obtaining a bottle of laudanum."

She looks me over. "For you?"

"Well..."

"Because Mr. Esher came to me not a few days back and told me I was not to get any more for him, no matter if he changed his mind later."

Damn him. "It's not for William," I say easily. "Although I can surely match whatever he was paying you for your services."

"Never felt right about doing it before," she admits, shoving the brush into her bucket and swiftly rising to her feet. "Didn't feel good about it, see."

"It would only be for a while," I quickly counter, standing up, unable to help the edge of desperation in my voice. "I assure you, this is not a long-term agreement."

May glances behind me, as though afraid this might be some kind of trick, or we're being listened in on. "You know how we do the exchange?"

"The trinket box in the common room of Gawain Hall, yes."

"All right. Two shillings. Thursday evenings. I'll do the swap then."

Two shillings is doable, albeit steep for a bottle that would cost me perhaps a quarter of that were I to have a way into town on my own. "Thank you, Miss."

It's a bittersweet victory. Yes, I will be able to obtain William's medicine for him, but it's only Wednesday morning, which means he's going to have to suffer until tomorrow night, and who knows what time that will be?

I just need him to hang on a little bit longer.

WHEN MR. MCLACHLAN requests me to stay after class, I'm unsurprised and don't need to inquire as to why.

"Is Mr. Esher still unwell?" he asks, watching me in that careful way of his that I never quite know what to do with.

"He attempted getting through the day yesterday, but I'm afraid he lost that battle this morning. I urged him to stay in bed."

"A wise decision. Has Doctor Mitchell been to see him?"

"He has opted out of seeing the good doctor." I hug my books to my chest. "I don't feel inclined to fight him on it. He's certain, with rest, he'll feel better in no time."

I don't think he likes that answer, not with the way his shoulders square and he looks at me intently. "He should be seeing a professional and not trying to make such judgments on his own, especially in his state."

My gaze lowers. I could brush it off, of course, and with any other teacher, I just might. Perhaps I hold some bitterness towards Mr. McLachlan, though, because I'm still certain he knows more than he is willing to admit regarding Oscar's disappearance. "With the number of boys who have mysteriously died while under the doctor's care, I stand by William's lack of confidence in him."

Ah, I said one of those things again. It doesn't quite turn the conversation awkward, but there is a certain edge of tension there that wasn't before. Mr. McLachlan sighs. "For what it's worth, I don't believe that Doctor Mitchell had anything to do with things like that. And I feel that, given

William's health hasn't been the best as of late, you might want to be wary that his stubbornness doesn't exacerbate his condition."

I meet his gaze without flinching and, in all sincerity, I say, "I would never let anything happen to William. I'm quite assured he'll feel better soon and, if he doesn't, I will do whatever is needed to make certain he's properly looked after."

Mr. McLachlan studies me wordlessly for a moment, as though he's trying to assess me, before he nods and straightens up. "I'll see to it that his school work is gathered up from his teachers, so he doesn't fall behind."

I'm grateful he has ceased arguing, and I'm more than ready to get out of here and check in on William; it hasn't been easy being away from him all day. "Thank you, sir. Nothing says speedy recovery like a bunch of missed schoolwork."

19

As agreed, I leave payment in the box Thursday afternoon, and spend the remainder of the evening with William until curfew requires me to retreat to my room. Then I spend hours pacing, listening to sounds from out in the halls, anxious and impatient and thinking that should any spirits see fit to get in my way tonight, I will be most displeased.

My exhaustion gets the better of me for a time, and I fall asleep until sometime in the middle of the night. Thankfully, it's a light sleep, and footsteps in the hall cause me to startle awake and suck in a sharp breath. After throwing on a robe, I creep silently down the hall. Inside the trinket box is a familiar amber bottle of laudanum. *Thank the heavens.*

I make quick work of going upstairs to William's room. My breath is held for a few seconds as I ease the door shut and get a candle lit, until William slowly opens his eyes and turns his head towards me. Tired and distant, but alive, and that's the important part.

"It's just me." I move to his bedside, extending a hand to check for fever—which has yet to break. "How are you feeling?"

He leans into my hand, likely because my fingers are chilled. "I'm just fine," he mumbles.

"You're still very warm." I rise to my feet to fetch him a cold, wet cloth. "Were you able to get any sleep?"

"I alternate between not being able to sleep at all and not being able to keep my eyes open," he admits.

Once I've soaked a cloth in the cold, fresh water from his wash bowl, I return to sit beside him and begin to cleanse his face and neck. "I think I know what will help."

His eyes have drifted shut again and he only makes an inquiring sound.

"Your medicine. Before you protest, I don't mean going back on it entirely. I've been looking into it, and physicians suggest a slow withdrawal process from opium-based products. We need to wean you off of it." I don't mention the physician in question is Virgil and his father; I doubt that would instil confidence. The sharp look of betrayal he casts my way is unsurprising but makes me flinch inwardly all the same. "*Please* trust me, William. We will get you through this, just in a safer way. I'll be right here with you, to make certain you only take what you need."

His mouth turns down and he tips his head away from me, embarrassment edging into his features. "If you think it's a good idea."

Oh, what a relief. I pluck the bottle from my pocket and remove the cork. "Thank you for humouring me."

William makes a soft noise, and the sound of the uncorking catches his attention. I give him only a meagre few drops, as recommended on the bottle. It also suggests mixing it with something to improve the taste, but I've yet to see William do such a thing. Probably too inconvenient to manage when he's been sneaking it around school.

The effects will not be immediate, I know. William lays back, and I suppose he must not be *too* cross with me because he shifts closer to lay his head in my lap with a tired sigh. I set the bottle aside, making note not to leave it in here unsupervised, and run my hands through his hair to push it back from his feverish face. "My poor sweetheart. Hopefully you'll be feeling better soon."

For a while, not terribly far off from an hour, William only lies there silently. I almost think he's fallen asleep except for, eventually, he murmurs, "What an utter failure I am." His voice has that familiar, slightly blurred quality to it, so I imagine the laudanum has begun to kick in.

A frown tugs at my face. "What's that supposed to mean?"

"I did this in order not to burden you further, yet here you are tending to me." He sighs. "It was like this last time, too."

I resume stroking his hair. "Last time? Did you try to quit before?"

He rolls onto his side and presses his face against my stomach. "Tried. Simmons insisted I couldn't do it. He was right."

That's a bit of a surprise. "Simmons?"

"Mm. He was my prefect, remember? He caught me retrieving it from the drop-off location one night. Threatened to report me to the headmaster, of course, unless I did what he asked. I attempted to quit."

Every single instance I've witnessed of Charles Simmons lording over William, crowding into his personal space and making him uncomfortable, comes to mind. The stirrings of anger begin to bubble inside me. "What happened then?"

William opens his mouth, inhales slowly. "...Nothing. Nevermind."

My brows furrow with worry. "No, no, don't do that. No more secrets, remember?" Which is highly unfair, I suppose; it's not like I was forthcoming with my own secrets until I had to be.

He hesitates. "I did favours for him, and he kept my secret. So when I attempted to quit, he was displeased."

"Favours such as cleaning his room?" I watch him with a sinking sensation in the pit of my stomach. My conversation with Charles the night he caught me outside replays in my head. The things he insinuated then...

He does not look at me. "You know better."

"William..."

"Please don't make me say it. It's not something I'm proud of."

My chest hurts. I don't need him to say it, no. I know precisely what kind of favours a piece of filth like Charles Simmons might demand to blackmail someone, and for as much as I want to hear the details so that I know precisely what I'm going to murder him for later, I also know that to force William to share them would be cruel. God, my blood is boiling. I want to march up to his room right this instant and cave his face in.

I resist the urge because right here, right now, William needs me. I want to reassure him that I think no less of him, that it was not his fault. If he had tried to quit, someone should have been there to help, not to discourage him and take advantage.

"Come here." I coax him into sitting up so that I can gather him into my arms. William comes to me easily and without protest, tucking his face against the curve of my neck.

"I'm so sorry," he mumbles. "I meant to tell you. I just…"

"I know. You owe me no apologies, all right? You've nothing to be sorry for."

William's lashes lower. His eyes are glazed, and I think this conversation would be going very differently were he not medicated, and perhaps, just this once, it's a good thing, because it makes him more honest. "It's really all right? I'm still good?"

I really am going to kill Charles. With my bare hands, and with great pleasure.

I take his face between my palms and press my mouth gently to his. "You are absolutely perfect. I adore you more than I could ever say."

He sighs warmly against my lips, and I think it has been some time since he has seemed so at ease, despite the heavy conversation. "It hasn't happened, you know. Since you and I. I made certain of that." Which might explain why Charles has been particularly obnoxious in the past many weeks. Even if something had happened, I'm not certain my feelings on the matter would be any different.

My thumbs glide across his cheekbones. "I'm going to snap his neck, you know."

"No, you won't. You'd be arrested, and then I would be all alone."

"I would have to make certain no one knows it's me."

He whimpers softly when I kiss him again. "Instead, perhaps you could just sleep here with me tonight."

"Of course you'd ask me the one thing I cannot resist." Given everything, it's a dangerous situation to place ourselves in, but I can hardly tell him no when he specifically requests to have me near. Besides, how many dangerous situations has he stepped into on my behalf?

I shift away from him only long enough to slide out of my robe, snuff out the candle, and return to his side, where he's laid down and waiting for me. I curl myself around him protectively.

"There will come a day where we can sleep all night like this without fear of being discovered," he says.

The mere thought of it brings a smile to my face. I kiss the side of his neck. "Such sweet promises, dear William. I'll hold you to that."

20

I know that I shouldn't make the journey into the tunnels alone. If William knew I had even begun to entertain the idea, he'd strangle me with his bare hands. I should wait until he's feeling better.

Yet, his recovery is slow. He seems to be feeling more like himself with each passing day, but he's still some way off from being able to run around and deal with ghosts. As much as he's ever ready to deal with ghosts, anyway. Without a doctor and more knowledge of the subject, who knows who long it will be? I feel I've waited so long already, spent so much time going in circles with no progress, and now to finally have something of substance that might lead me closer to finding out the truth of this school...

Ultimately, though, it comes back to William. I cannot rid myself of the image of that ghost atop me that one night, suffocating me. They're able to physically harm us, although I haven't the foggiest idea why they would want to or if that was even its intention, and thus I'm afraid for William. Putting myself in danger is one thing, but if harm were to come to William because of my pursuits, I would never be able to live with myself.

Mind made up, I head out one evening after checking on William and ensuring he's settled into bed for the night. Once he's sleeping soundly, I slip out the door, closing it quietly behind me. Ordinarily this would be the part where I go back to my own room, but not this time.

Deep breaths, James.

This is going to be very different than my normal night-time explorations, sneaking back and forth between our two rooms. For one thing, I'm alone. For another, I'll be venturing out of the dorms, and the last time I did it—following that spirit through the woods—it was a rather frightening endeavour. If I get caught by someone, it likely won't end as nicely as Virgil giving me a disapproving look and sending me to bed or being made to spend the night standing out in the hall.

I keep as quiet and careful as I can. I have a candlestick with me, but don't light it just yet, hoping I'll be able to go unnoticed by anyone who might be out and about.

I've almost made it out of the dorms when footsteps put me on alert. Clamping a hand over my mouth, I flatten myself back against the wall. It isn't Virgil or Augustus; it's far too late for them to be doing a check. They need to sleep, too. Who would be out this late, if not a ghost?

Charles Simmons steps into view.

What is he doing? I'm certain he'll see me if he just turns his head a little further to the left, but he seems to have something on his mind, because he marches down the hall, towards the dorm exit. I wonder where he's getting to this late, but honestly, if it doesn't involve William, then Charles can throw himself off a bloody cliff for all I care.

After I've heard the front door open and shut, I wait a few minutes longer to ensure the coast is clear. Even when I follow him, ducking outside, I expect to spot him, but he's nowhere to be seen. Doesn't bode well, and it might be smarter to give up for tonight knowing he's wandering about.

No, I'll not allow the threat of him to derail my plans.

Not wanting to waste any more time, I head straight for the school. Having studied the map intensively, I believe I'm looking for an old storage room of sorts, a room that no one would think to bother with.

The school is immensely unsettling in the dark, more so now that I'm tackling it alone and don't have William's presence to distract me. According to the building map, the lone room that appeared on the old version but not the new is off of the scullery, and thus difficult to access during the day. Even if I stay out too late, I risk encountering one of the early-rising maids or cooks.

Down the darkened halls, following the paths I know only from having memorised the maps, I find my way into the empty scullery. The door in question is at the far side of the wall, blocked by crates of flour and potatoes and various other foodstuffs. With effort, I manage to drag some of the crates away just enough to access the door, which then opens with an aching creak.

Sighing in relief, I squeeze inside, descending the aged wooden steps. I have no choice but to light my candle now that I'm without windows to let in any moonlight. I give my vision a chance to adjust before looking around. As I suspected, this place appears to have been a storage room, once upon a time. Even now it's littered with old furniture and empty crates and boxes and spiderwebs.

But a storage room is all it seems to be. I see no other doors, and I make it a point to run my hands along the wall as I search just to make sure. When that yields nothing, I turn my attention to the floor instead. It's there, towards the back corner of the room, that I spot the edge of a hatch peeking out from beneath an old armoire. A hatch means something below the basement, and that something could be exactly what I'm looking for.

I set the candle atop a nearby crate so that I can brace my hands and shoulder against the side of the armoire and push with all my might. It groans across the wooden floor, slowly but surely, until I've relocated it far enough that it's no longer obscuring my path. The hatch itself is latched shut, and the rusted metal clasp requires some fussing with to get it loose, so I can heave it open. Below me now is a ladder, which leads down far beyond what I'm capable of seeing, even with the help of my candle when I hold it out. A smell of damp earthiness wafts up to greet me.

This is it. This is what I've been searching for.

Perhaps it *is* better I came on my own, because I can imagine the heart attack William would be having right about now. I'm not certain I could get him to entertain the idea of descending into that darkness even with a promise of all the kisses in the world. I suppose I couldn't blame him for that, but truthfully, the rush of excitement I feel for having actually found something outweighs any fear or hesitation I might otherwise have. At least for now.

All that's left is for me to begin the climb down, which requires some skill in order to bring the candle with me, unwilling to snuff it out even for a moment, and I'm careful to mind my footing on the creaking ladder rungs.

The further I go, the colder it becomes. Not simply in the way I would expect from being underground, either, although I cannot precisely place why or how it's different. The hair along the back of my neck stands on end, and no number of woollen layers are enough to keep me warm.

I climb until I can no longer see the top of the ladder. Nothing above nor below. After what feels like forever, my feet touch solid ground once more and I'm both relieved and not, because when I look around, I determine this is definitely not an inviting place. The smell, I realise, is reminiscent of the boy in my room, when I woke to find his hands clamped down upon my mouth.

The tunnel is narrow and musty, and it's not as though I can see far in either direction; the candle's light only carries so far, and I swear I can almost make out shapes, dancing in the darkness, just faint enough that it could be my eyes playing tricks on me.

I put thought into crawling right back up the ladder. Is this really the smartest idea? Would this be a plan better executed during the day, if I could figure out how to get past the staff? If something were to happen to me here, how long would it be before someone found me?

Who would care for William in my absence?

The crying distracts me from my thoughts. That, in and of itself, isn't strange. I've grown so used to it in the dorms. On its own, it would not even be enough to draw me away from my current dilemma, but the longer I listen, the more it sounds like—

Oscar.

All thoughts of leaving are immediately abandoned. I scramble down the tunnel, towards the sound of that voice, not caring about what I might find or what unnatural thing I may disturb in the process. If Oscar is down here, if he's in trouble, if he's *alive*, I need to find him immediately.

I rush further into the darkness, yet the voice seems to be getting softer, always just out of reach. The panic surges up inside me, making me call recklessly out to him.

When I reach a fork in the tunnel, the sound has vanished completely. I want to cry in frustration. I want to throw my candle. I want to—I don't know. It's difficult to think beyond the overwhelming surge of emotion at having felt *so close* for a moment. I force myself to stop and take a moment to breathe in order to calm myself.

While standing there, I come to realise that though the crying may have ceased, the tunnel is not silent. There's another sound, soft enough that I cannot even quite make out what it is beyond that it sounds pained.

I've come this far, and I might as well see what awaits me. The sound comes from the right fork in the tunnel, so that's the way I proceed, but slower to be more aware of my surroundings. I can almost hear William's voice in my head, lecturing that we ought to go back. Oh, he's going to let me have it when I get out of here.

Eventually the tunnel leads me to what at first appears to be a dead end, but as I near, I spot another ladder off to one side, not unlike the one I originally came down. Is it possible I got turned around and returned to where I started? That doesn't seem likely.

Wonderful. Just what I wanted to do was to put more walls and floors between myself and safety. But that's exactly what I do. Right up the ladder, where the scent begins to change. It smells like mould, or rot. Like something very, very old.

The hatch at the top opens into the end of a long, narrow, pitch-black hallway lined with doors. I'm in the school again. At least, I think I am. Everything in this hall is reminiscent of the rest of the building, from the arched ceilings to the dado railing and wallpaper, although the place reeks of dust and dirt. I sincerely doubt any maid has been here to clean in some time, if ever. I approach the first door and give it a try, and then the second, and the third, and not a one of them is unlocked.

I shiver, wondering if the darkness is beginning to grow thicker or if my fear is making me imagine things. Even the air feels heavier here, and my sense of unease is beginning to overpower my desire for answers. I want to be done here. I want to go back to William.

The hall dead ends with one last door, differing from all the others only because there emanates a faint flicker of light from beneath it. And, from within, the sound that I can now pinpoint as a boy whimpering, and the distinct rattling of chains. The sound of my own breathing is impossibly loud as I move towards it, slowly, carefully trying the knob. This time, it turns with a timid *click*, and allows me to pull it open just enough to peer inside.

I don't fully grasp what I'm seeing. I must be imagining things, and if I rub at my eyes, the sight before me will vanish.

This time when the distorted whimpering hits my ears, I can see the boy it comes from. His gaunt, emaciated form dangles by his wrists from chains latched to the ceiling, his feet only just scraping the floor. The wavering light from candles on the wall is just enough to illuminate the bruises on his shoulders, back, and the backs of his thighs, all where his uniform has been shredded, and the blood smeared across his face and a swollen eye.

He's dead. A spirit not unlike all the others.

But he is not the worst of it.

No, that award goes to the thing that shuffles slowly across the room. A man. I think. Whatever it is, whatever is was once upon a time, is unrecognizable now. The husk of a body looms over everything, not an inch of its flesh untouched by burns and disfigurements. He looks like someone set alight, and then put out after their skin has half melted from their bones.

I forget how to move, how to breathe, even as I'm internally screaming at my legs to get me the hell out of here. Before I can make my body cooperate, the creature lifts his hand, holding onto what appears to be an old cat o' nine tails. I understand what he's about to do and my mouth opens before I can stop it.

"No!"

The second the word leaves my throat, my eyes widen. In what world was that a brilliant idea? He does stop before striking, yes, but only to turn in my direction. As he begins to walk towards the door—and me—it dawns on me the grave mistake I've made.

I tear away from the door, scrambling back, tripping over my own feet as I rush down the hall the direction I came. Behind me, the door flies open with such ferocity that it takes my breath away, and I refuse to look back again.

I hit the hatch at the end with the sensation of breath on the back of my neck and drop down through it so quickly that I nearly lose my grip on the rungs. I slip upon nearing the bottom.

As I land on my side, the candle does, too, snuffing out and plunging me into darkness.

I lurch to my feet and plant my hands against the nearest wall and begin to inch myself down the way I think I'm supposed to be going.

I may not be able to see anything, but I can *hear* them.

Whispers. Groans. Shifting and scratching and sobbing.

All around me, closer and closer, until I'm certain I will scream just to drown them out.

A hand grasps at my trouser leg as I attempt to pick up my pace. And then another hand. And a third. Grabbing at my clothes, my feet, my ankles, until I trip over myself, hitting the ground hard enough that the air is slammed from my lungs and I'm gasping in pain.

When I try to get up, however—

A hand grabs a fistful of my hair and I'm shoved onto my back, a sudden, intense pressure bearing down onto my chest. I cannot see a thing, but the smell of burning flesh floods my sinuses, makes me choke on a cry for help. Fingers wrap about my throat, rendering me both voiceless and breathless.

The edges of my vision begin to darken. I have most certainly botched all of this.

I will die in this place.

No one will ever find me.

Please forgive me, William.

A brilliant, warm light flashes before my eyes, illuminating the burned and grotesque face of my attacker.

And then he's gone.

The pressure vanishes from my chest, the grip on my neck relinquishing its hold, and I can finally suck in a huge lungful of air while trying to come to sorts with what is going on. As my vision clears and I regain some of my hearing, another face appears over mine, this one familiar and a brilliant beacon of hope as he begins to drag me to my feet.

William shouts, "*Run!*" and I don't hesitate to obey.

How or why he's there, I haven't a clue. I wrap my fingers tightly around his as he hauls me to my feet and proceeds to drag me down the tunnel. The sound of our steps echoes deafeningly in the narrow passageways, drowned only by the furious roar of the creature a few steps behind us. I do not dare look back. It's all I can do to run alongside William, to trust that he knows where he's going.

My lungs scream in protest, a cramp beginning to develop in my leg. Yet as we round a bend and moonlight pours into the space around us, I see we're headed right for an opening that spills us out into the chilly night.

We find ourselves outside, amongst trees and shrubs and melting snow, and we collapse to the ground while gasping for air. When I finally spare a look back, I see no sign of anything, and the enraged shrieks of the monster in the darkness have faded.

We're safe. At least for the moment.

Which means William and I turn our attention to one another. I'm trembling all over, mostly from fear, and he looks to be in about the same shape. He reaches for me, touching my face.

"Are you all right?"

Some of his hair clings to his face, and I can tell just by looking at him that he's still fending off a fever. Worry overtakes me. "What are you doing here? You're supposed to be resting!"

William scowls, taking my face in his hands and looking me over. Cold fingertips touch to my throat, and I wonder if he sees bruises there, because he whimpers. "You bloody fool! Why did you go without me?"

I have the grace to look as apologetic as I feel. "I'm sorry. You've been feeling so unwell, I didn't want to risk anything happening to you."

"If something had happened to *you*, I…" he begins to say, voice heated, as though he's waging an internal war on whether he's angry or relieved that I'm all right. A deep breath drawn, he leans in, resting his forehead against mine. "You're safe. That's all that matters."

"How in the world did you know where to find me?"

William's eyes widen. "You didn't see him?"

"See *who*?"

He sits up straighter, turning to look all around us while a slow frown tugs at his brows. "The ghost. I woke to one in my room, and he led me straight to you."

I balk at that. "*You* followed a ghost across school grounds?"

"Well, yes." He averts his gaze. "Call it a gut feeling."

"You're bloody brilliant, do you know that? You saved my life."

William shakes his head. "Don't. I don't want to think— You're all right. Let's get back to the dorms before that thing decides to follow."

For as much as I want to lie right where we are and rest, that does sound to be a wise idea. I rise to my feet, helping William to his. Now that the excitement is beginning to fade, I can see he's grown shaky and in need of the assistance.

The lantern he scoops up from the ground is still lit, by some miracle, and it guides our way through the trees back towards the school. As it turns out, the tunnel entrance we escaped from is located about a quarter mile behind the cemetery.

Throughout the entire walk, I catch glimpses from the corner of my gaze. Faces and figures lingering at my periphery, and I think William sees them, too, because now and again his head will jerk to one side to look. Unnerving as it is, no one appears to be bothering us. Small favours. It's a sensation that continues all the way into the dorms and up into William's room.

It is not until we've secured ourselves safely behind his door, jammed shut, that I heave a sigh of relief and lean into William, dropping my head to rest upon his shoulder as the exhaustion settles in. William sets the lantern aside on his wash table, attention fully upon me, arms about me as his hands stroke over my sweat-soaked hair. "You're all right," he whispers. "But so help me God, if you ever frighten me like that again…"

"I'm sorry. I had no idea it would go so poorly." I'm not certain what I thought would happen, but certainly, I hadn't expected to encounter what I did. William leans in to kiss me solidly upon the mouth, and I think it might be a reassurance for himself in as much as it is for me that everything is all right.

When he pulls back, he drops his hands to the front of my rumpled and dirty coat to push it back off my shoulders. We do need to get out of our filthy clothes, I think. "What did you see in there?"

I would rather forget it, truthfully, but that would hardly be beneficial. Never mind that I have no idea *what* I saw. I draw in a deep breath and, as William busies himself undressing me, I recall to him how I entered the tunnels, my trek through them. Most importantly, the hallway in which I encountered the ghost.

William remains silent while I speak, brows furrowed. I'm exhausted enough that I scarcely notice he's stripped me down to my undergarments, and I'll finish the removal of those on my own.

"A burned man. What do you suppose it means?"

"That someone wasn't very good at cooking."

William gives me an unimpressed look.

"No? Wrong answer?"

"You're impossible." He presses a palm to my chest, above my heart, and leans in to kiss me softly.

"The truth is that I haven't an idea what it means. It cannot be anything good."

"We've scoured every inch of that library, questioned students, searched the school. So then, what would our next step be?"

I watch him slide off his shirt. "The staff is all we have left."

"You truly think they're going to tell us anything? We'll be reported to the headmaster again in no time."

"It's the only option I have left. There has to be someone we can speak to."

"You said you cornered Mr. Hart already, and he's the one who was close with Oscar." He pauses as he considers. "Mr. Hart and Mr. McLachlan seem to be friendly, don't they? And he appeared sincerely concerned over Frances' disappearance."

True, I think. He also wasn't very forthcoming with information before. To get him to talk, I may have to press further and tell him some of what we've discovered.

"It's worth a try." I find the tail end of my sentence stuttering to a stop as I watch William remove his clothes, stripping down completely, which is a very new thing. We've seen each other in various stages of undress by now, but not fully, if I think about it, and it is distracting, to say the least. He's thin and elegant, a bit on the skinny side, which I think may be attributed to his poor health these last several weeks. He scarcely eats, after all, and he does little in the way of exercise.

He fetches two nightshirts, turning to offer one out to me, and I take it while navigating my eyes back up to his face. "Scandalous. What would your mother say?"

He scoffs, slipping the other shirt over his head, much to my disappointment. "Would you like me to sleep in nothing?"

I feign a gasp of disapproval. "We'd need to get you to church."

"While naked?" he muses, turning back the blankets and slipping beneath them.

I laugh as I strip down the rest of my own clothes, pull on the borrowed nightshirt, and then permit myself to join him in bed. "I'm going to say a prayer for your sinful soul, dear William."

"By all means."

I bury my face against his throat and breathe in deep. Admittedly, we're both in need of a wash, but the scent is still unmistakably William beneath the dirt and sweat we've accumulated tonight. "Dear Lord, please forgive this harlot…"

He chuckles, warm and soft, and the subtle movement of him shifting one of his bare legs against mine makes my breath hitch. Is it the near-death experience that has me so very aware of his presence tonight, and the fact that he's wearing nothing beneath his nightgown?

Any thoughts about what he might feel like beneath that fabric are quickly extinguished when I realise William's breathing has evened out, and when I draw back enough to look at him, he is good and well asleep. All for the best; we need our rest. The way William has curled up around me, tangling our legs together and wrapping an arm about my middle, must have to do with having been so frightened tonight.

I'd be lying if I said it didn't make me hold onto him a bit tighter, too.

21

The next day is surprisingly dull in contrast to that miserable night. At least, until after morning announcements when the mail is distributed, and I'm left staring dumbly at an envelope that is placed in my hand, unable to fathom who would write to me.

It must be a mistake. Not once have I received a letter in my time at Whisperwood, despite the number that I've sent out. There is no mistaking my mother's achingly familiar handwriting upon the envelope, however.

"What do you have there?" Preston asks, startling me as he leans over my shoulder in an attempt at friendly nosiness. "A letter from home? Or from a sweetheart, perhaps?"

I shove the letter between the pages of my English book. Embarrassment is not the reason, of course, but considering I've heard nothing from them the entire school year, well... It's a personal matter, and not one I feel inclined to share with anyone. I offer my most charming smile at Preston. "Don't be silly. Why would you write to me when we're both here?"

He laughs it off, and it won't be until later, when I can sneak away between class and lunch and am unlikely to be disturbed, that I will pull the envelope out and stare at it some more. I cannot imagine what Mother has to say to me. I cannot imagine it would be anything good. I almost wish I could bring myself to throw the letter into the nearest fireplace and pretend I never got it.

Hardly a realistic option, of course. For better or worse, I must read it. Some part of me is even hopeful for a miracle, that I'll find something kind and encouraging within, some glimmer of hope in what has otherwise been a nightmare. They would have heard of my good marks, though whether or not the headmaster will have written home about my "indiscretions," I don't know. Perhaps time and distance alone will have softened them towards me.

With hands that slightly quake with nerves, I carefully open the envelope and slide out the letter, unfolding it to read. Only a single sheet, headed with, *Our Dearest James.*

Mother tells me they have indeed been told of my good performance at Whisperwood, and to continue with the good progress. She says they have been faring well, although she's recovering from a slight cold. The factory is doing well, business is steady.

Honestly, it's quite bland when it's all said and done, though it's not harsh in tone, and I try to soak up that simple fact as I read over my mother's words. I'm glad they're doing well. I'm glad they're thinking of me. I'm glad they're not disappointed in anything I've done—that they know of, anyway—since I left home.

The last paragraph is what causes my stomach to lurch.

> *Of course, we anticipate your return home for the summer upon completion of the term. However, should you put serious thought into the matter and decide to remain at Whisperwood, we would understand. We have only just moved into the new house and, amongst the chaos, I fear it would not be very restful for you. Your cousins are still attempting to settle.*

If my cousins are there, then my uncle is, too.

Of course. Nothing has really changed at all, has it?

They may have softened in tone towards me since the last we spoke, but the message is much the same. I don't know what I thought would happen, why I bothered to hope. Six people in the house would be entirely too much, wouldn't it? By at least one, I'd say, and that one-person-too-many is still me.

THE LETTER LEAVES me in something of a foul mood, which may not be the best thing for approaching Mr. McLachlan at the end of the day. I linger as students hurry out of his class. William remained in bed today at my behest; although his fever has mostly vanished, I think one last day of rest will do him well. Maybe wanting to speak to our teacher alone is a part of my insistence, as well. I've dragged William into enough of this.

Once the class has emptied, I rise to my feet. Mr. McLachlan doesn't seem surprised to see me still there, and he gathers a stack of papers from his desk and offers them out. It takes me a moment to realise it's the school work he promised to get for William.

"Send Mr. Esher my regards. I trust he's on the mend?"

"He is, sir, thank you." I tuck the papers into one of my books. "I was also hoping to speak to you, if I may."

He eyes me somewhat warily. Fair enough, given the last time I wanted to talk to him and how well that went over, and I do wonder if Mr. Hart told him of our recent discussion. "Of course."

I've battled with this all day. What to say, how much to divulge. Too much and he might go straight to the headmaster. Too little and he might brush me off. Mr. McLachlan is truly my last hope for any answers because he displayed at least some concern over Oscar's sudden disappearance from school. I must remind myself of that.

Breathing deep, I place my things atop one of the empty desks. "Have you ever heard of the tunnels beneath the school?"

He squints. "That's an odd question. To my knowledge, there are no tunnels beneath the school. What purpose would they serve?"

"I don't know, but I've found them, so I know they exist."

His eyes snap to my face, thick brows knitting together. "Pardon?"

I wring my hands together. "Please, hear me out. I've been seeing things, sir. Ghosts in the dorms, across the property. It was those spirits that led me to the tunnels, and into a part of the school I don't believe anyone has seen in a very long time."

"Mr. Spencer..."

"I know what I've seen. And *you* know the stories. Surely, you've heard about what boys have seen in the darkness, in all the years you've worked here. Haven't you?"

His mouth twitches, displeased. "This is not a conversation we should be having right now."

"If not now, then *when?*"

"Never," he says sharply. Then he sighs, voice softer, and extends a hand to place it upon my shoulder. "Listen to me. I *have* heard the stories, and in a building as old as this, it's understandable boys would see and hear things. I'm begging you to just keep your head down until graduation. Then you will be able to leave this place and never have to look back, and none of this will matter."

I draw away from his grasp. "It *will* matter, because Oscar will still be gone! It's all tied together somehow. I *know* it. You asked me yourself if I thought he left Whisperwood of his own accord or not, and I'm positive he did not. I think you know it, too."

Hesitation flashes across Mr. McLachlan's tired face, and he runs a hand back over his head with a heavy sigh. I think I have him. Almost. So close. But then—

"This isn't something I can help you with. I'm sorry."

My expression hardens. How foolish was I to hope for anything different? He was no help before; what would have changed now? "Of course."

I snatch my things from the desk and turn to leave, angry enough that I could not care less if he decides to bring what I've said in confidence to light of the headmaster. A decision I will inevitably regret later.

Only a few feet from the door, Mr. McLachlan calls to me and I stop, but do not turn.

"What would you have me do? What is it you think I can help with?"

I swallow back the furious lump in my throat. "You have more leeway to investigate than I do. *You* can speak with the headmaster without fear of being beaten bloody or expelled. Look at the history of students who've died here in the past. Look at the date and manner of deaths compared to their history of punishments." I turn to him. "You're good friends with Mr. Hart, so I imagine you know why Oscar was supposedly expelled."

"I do," he admits.

"You know that Mr. Hart is the one the headmaster suspects Oscar was involved with."

"I know that, too."

"Yet Mr. Hart wasn't reprimanded, and Oscar wasn't outright expelled. So what 'proof' did King have that anything at all was amiss?"

He folds his arms across his chest, chest rising and falling with a heavy sigh. "We don't know," he says, and when I give him a dubious look, "I mean it. Jonathan—Mr. Hart—and I have been curious about that, too. King has not seen fit to release that information."

"Then if you want to help, you could find out."

"I'd be risking my own job to dig around into an issue that may not be an issue at all."

"But you *know* that it *is* an issue, don't you?"

He opens his mouth, closes it again, and merely watches me wordlessly.

"I've no one else to go to, sir," I say quietly. "I'm at a loss, but I *will* find out what happened to my friend. With or without your help."

I leave the conversation and the room. Perhaps I won't change his mind here and now, but I hope, at the very least, I've given him something to think about.

22

I spend the evening assisting William with the influx of missed assignments he's determined to complete, despite having the entire weekend to do so. Saturday, I have to take my leave of him to tend to laundry duty—something he's able to get out of only because I work double-time to cover for him. Upon completing my chores, I return to find him napping at his table, head upon his arms, papers spread about. I coax him awake so that we might go and fetch lunch together. He still displays more fatigue than I would like, but overall, his condition is steadily improving. I shall have to think of a way to thank Virgil.

The rest of the day I spend poring over my own books. With only a week remaining in the term, I think it prudent to study for final exams. It's some miracle my grades haven't slipped more than they have in the past few weeks. William offers to assist me, but he has his hands full sorting through the work he's missed, and so I take myself to my room to work on things alone.

Hunched over books and notes late into the night, I find myself periodically distracted. For a while, I read some of Oscar's copy of *Pendennis*.

It's nearing curfew when I hear voices outside. Nothing of importance at first, and then louder, out of place, the sound of shouting across the grounds. Frowning, I push back my chair and step over to peer out my open window. A few boys have gathered below. My eyes follow where they're looking, to a group off in the distance, emerging from the woods. It's difficult to tell from here, but they appear to be in police uniform. Their hats make me think so. What would police be doing in the woods here, this time of night?

Already, my stomach is turning. I draw back, reach for my coat, and then hurry downstairs to join the group of onlookers, who are whispering amongst themselves. Benjamin, Preston, and Edwin are near the forefront, and I step up alongside them.

"What's happened?"

"Not sure," Edwin says. "The police showed up a bit ago and they've just come back from the woods."

"Are they carrying something?" Benjamin frowns, lifting a hand to point.

From this distance, it's hard to tell at first. Then the moonlight hits just right, catching a glimmer of white on the stretcher two of the officers are carrying between them.

A body.

They've found a body.

Despite feeling as though my legs are about to give out from under me, they pitch me forward, hurtling across the grass towards the officers and the faculty awaiting them near the courtyard. I dimly hear Preston call to me and ignore it. It does not matter. It does not matter at all.

They've draped the body in a sheet, but I can make out the shape of him beneath it, one bare foot sticking out at the end, an arm dangling over the edge of the stretcher, a pale hand covered in dirt, fingertips grazing the ground when their footsteps dip the stretcher too low to the ground.

I jog closer, reaching, wanting to pull the sheet back, just wanting—*needing*—to see his face to confirm what I already know.

An officer catches me before I can, pushing me back. "Hey, now."

"Is that him?" I ask, voice cracking. "Is that Oscar? Let me see him. Let me see him!"

I wrench away from the man, desperate for an answer. William rushes up behind me, slipping around in front of me, hands to my chest. "James, please, calm down—" And, when I proceed to shove past him because he's hardly strong enough to restrain me, he calls for Preston.

Two pairs of arms secure me from behind, halting my progression, and I realise Virgil and Preston have hold of me and are speaking my name, and it does not matter.

"Please, let me see him!" I beg, even as I strain against them, even as the police are carrying Oscar towards their carriage.

They're going to take him away, and I will never see him again.

I was too late.

I was supposed to help him, and I was too late.

The body is loaded into the back of the carriage, and some of the officers linger, speaking quietly with the members of staff. The headmaster is not present, but Mr. Hart and Mr. McLachlan are. Mr. Hart's face has gone as white as the sheet Oscar's body was wrapped in, and I see his trembling hands covering his mouth, and Mr. McLachlan holding onto him so that he does not crumple to the ground.

"Stop them!" I beg, greeted only by Mr. McLachlan's shocked gaze and Mr. Hart's distraught, glassy-eyed stare.

William sounds near tears as he moves in front of me again, helping Virgil and Preston to redirect my attention. "*Please.* If you get yourself into trouble now, we'll never know what happened."

I'm going to be sick. It's all I can do to watch as the police slide into their saddles and upon the carriage, as they begin to leave, taking Oscar away. Only as they get down the driveway do Preston and Virgil ease their grip enough for me to yank free. I've half a mind to chase down the death carriage, but instead I turn to my teachers, and suddenly every ounce of anger I have is focused on them.

"You know who is responsible for this," I hiss. "You *know*, and if you don't do something about it, you are just as much to blame!"

Virgil reaches for me again and I shove his arm away, so angry I can hardly see straight, and I stumble as I spin around to storm away. The others are at my heels; Benjamin is calling to me. It does not matter.

I just need…

I just want…

Distance.

I need to move. To get away. I need air, but I feel no matter how deeply I breathe, I am suffocating.

I flee to my room before anyone can stop me. Only William dares to follow, and he may be the only one I would permit to do so.

Still, he steps in behind me with caution, easing the door shut and leaning against it as he watches me begin to pace the short length of the room, not knowing what to do with myself. I yank off my jacket and unbutton the top few fastens of my shirt, feeling too stifled, too constricted.

King had something to do with this. I *know* he did. I don't know how or why, I don't know if it has anything to do with the ghosts of Whisperwood, but he is behind Oscar's death.

"That *bastard*."

"James..." William moves closer, brushing a hand against my arm and drawing me to a standstill. "We'll find the proof we need to bring him to justice. I promise. We will figure it out."

My vision blurs as I turn to him. "I didn't *want* to find proof of wrongdoing at this cost. I was supposed to save Oscar."

His expression softens, heartache plain as day upon his face. "Darling, you did everything you could. You did far more than anyone else."

"I didn't do *enough*."

William puts his arms around me, drawing me to him. The split second he touches me, holds me, the tears rush forth and I bury my face against his shoulder, clinging to him in return. "What does any of it matter now?"

"It matters because *you* matter," he insists. "Because you are *good*, James. You are good and kind and wonderful, and people love you. Frances included."

I want to believe those words. I always have, ever since Mother and Father used to tell me what a good child I was. "I couldn't help him. I haven't been able to help anyone. Nothing I do now is going to bring him back."

William draws in a deep breath. "You cannot bring him back, no, but I believe you can still help him. Delivering justice may prevent Oscar from spending eternity here, wandering the grounds like all the others."

A cold, sinking feeling settles over me. Could Oscar be trapped here somewhere, traversing the hallways at night, restless and in pain, reliving whatever miserable last moments he experienced? "You truly think he could be here?"

The way he averts his eyes makes my stomach twist itself into knots. "I know that he is."

"What does that mean?"

William's refusal to look at me does not bode well. "The night I followed you into the tunnels, I told you one of the spirits appeared."

Mutely, I nod, but say nothing, simply awaiting his ability to speak further.

"It was Oscar. Oscar led me to you, to save you."

"Did...did he speak to you?"

"No, not a word. I woke to him standing in my doorway, and I followed him into the tunnels through the opening we escaped from."

Slowly, I sink onto my bed. "But, then why didn't you tell me?"

William stares at his hands, and I can practically see the guilt and shame bearing down on him. Softly, he replies, "It's a very difficult thing to do, looking into the eyes of someone you care for and stripping away their hope."

Does he think I will be angry with him for hiding this? I suppose I could be, but I'm not. I don't like it, certainly, but realistically speaking I cannot say I wouldn't have done the same thing in his shoes. "I see."

"I'm so sorry, James. I'd hoped that perhaps I was wrong. But he brought me to you, and I wouldn't be surprised if he's been watching over you all this time."

I swallow thickly. "Why do you think he hasn't visited me?"

"I cannot say I know." He brings a hand up to stroke my hair back from my face. "It could be he was worried it would upset you. Or perhaps it's beyond him. None of the spirits we've encountered have been terribly good at communicating."

"You don't think it's because I let him down?"

"Absolutely not," he sharply insists. "I don't for a moment believe that. You shouldn't, either; you know that isn't in his nature."

I duck my head, attempting to reconcile how certain William sounds with my own overwhelming grief and guilt. He coaxes my face up after a moment, so that he can lean down to press a warm, gentle kiss upon my mouth. "Everything is going to be all right."

"I want to believe that."

"I wouldn't lie to you."

That much I believe. Yes, William and I have had a nasty history of withholding information from one another, but he has never lied to me.

He leans in, resting his forehead against mine. "Would you like me to stay here with you tonight?"

Yes. No. I don't know. I want William near, and yet I need to be alone. I force myself to breathe in despite how fiercely my chest aches, eyelids dropping shut. "I think I need to be alone for a spell, if that's all right with you."

I'm grateful William doesn't look wounded by my request. He only lightly smiles, kisses me once more—lingering, wonderfully so—and sliding from the bed. "You know where to find me should you change your mind."

After William departs and I close the door behind him, I let my forehead fall to rest against the worn wood. A part of me longs to go after him, to tell him that I don't care about the rules and just want him near. What am I to do with all this silence and emptiness?

I don't, though, because the other part of me does want exactly that. Solitude. To be alone in my grief, to be able to sink into it without interruption. I don't want to think about anyone else right now. I need to think this through.

When I finally move to go to bed, I head not for my own bed, but for Oscar's. Untouched for so long, and I realise now that it never mattered how dark things became, or what evidence I found that pointed to something sinister, I never gave up hope I would find him alive and well.

I never stopped thinking I would one day fall asleep again after wishing him a good night, to the sound of his quiet snoring across the room.

Now I know such things will never happen and I fall onto his bed, burying my face against blankets that have been long since washed, struggling to contain the ache in my chest. I feel as though I cannot breathe. Whatever has happened to me in the past, I haven't known the pain of loss like this. What do I do with it?

What about Preston, Benjamin, Edwin, and everyone else who cared for Oscar? It was cruel of me to storm off as I did, but they have one another, I remind myself. Absently, I wonder how Mr. Hart is faring. What is he thinking right now? He appeared so devastated. Will he be able to sleep tonight, or will misery keep him awake? Somehow, I think it will. If he had any means of preventing this, I pray to God it eats away at him.

For that matter, was there something *I* could have done differently? I refer back to every moment I thought to say something to Oscar, to inquire further when he brushed aside my concerns. Could I have badgered him into telling me the full truth? If he had, would I have been able to do anything about it? Could anyone have?

Logically, I know this isn't my fault. It isn't the fault of anyone except whatever bastard killed him, and yet—of course I blame myself. I could have pushed harder, been less wrapped up with ghosts and William and myself.

I draw in a shuddering breath and roll onto my back. Though I thought I had finally finished crying for the evening, my vision blurs all over again and I swallow back a sob. I swipe at my eyes and pull myself up to sitting, leaving the bed only long enough to fetch from the table Oscar's copy of *Pendennis*. I've no interest in reading right now, but it's the only thing of Oscar's I have. I flip through it, fingers tracing slowly over dog-eared pages that show more wear than others. How many times did he read this, I wonder? One of his most prized possessions. I should have asked him about it.

His smiling face comes to mind. The way he'd seemed so full of hope and promise and excitement. How quickly he'd put me at ease when I first arrived at Whisperwood, and how good of a friend he'd been in the weeks that followed. Even when dealing with his own demons, he was still there when

I truly needed him. Without hesitation, without judgment. Truly, at his core, Oscar was a good man.

I never deserved him.

I'm not sure anyone did.

I curl back up on the bed, bringing the book with me, hugging it to my chest. My eyes squeeze shut to stop the flow of tears. Behind my closed eyelids, I see Oscar's lifeless hand from beneath the sheet.

"I'm sorry," I find myself saying in a barely audible whisper to an empty room. I don't know if he's there, if he can hear me, but he showed himself to William, didn't he? So maybe he's listening, maybe...

"I'm so, so sorry, Oscar. I'm sorry I didn't figure things out sooner. I'm sorry I couldn't help you. You were bloody amazing, do you know that? One of the kindest, most brilliant people I've had the pleasure of calling my friend.

"You deserved so much better than this. You deserved a happy ending. I will find out what happened, and I will make certain those responsible pay for it. I'll kill them with my bare hands, if I must."

I say it, and I mean it. I don't care what I must do or who I must cross and what I have to risk—I am more resolved than ever that I will see this through to the end. For everything Oscar gave me in the time that I knew him, for his friendship, I owe him that much. I owe him rest and peace, if such things exist for him. I cannot bear the thought of him being stuck in this school for eternity, trapped as those other boys have been.

I cannot let him become just another ghost story.

Nothing but silence greets my outpouring of emotion. I don't know if I truly expected him to appear, to answer me in some way, but it hurts nonetheless. So selfish to want to see him for my own reassurances, to ease my own guilty conscience.

I wonder if I will ever grow up.

23

Eventually, I will need to pick myself back up.

I made a promise, not only to Oscar but to myself as well, and I've no intention of letting anyone down again. Sooner or later, I must get back into the swing of things, and I will need to be more driven than ever.

But not in the days that follow.

No, for the next several days, depression consumes me.

Every day is a battle of forcing myself out of bed and going through the motions. Meals, school, sleep. I give the bare minimum that is required of me and nothing more, because I feel I have so little left to give. Were it not for William, I think I may spend every day sleeping.

Thursday, I slog my way through classes, sensing William watching me throughout maths in that carefully worried manner of his. He has been a constant shadow since that night, saying little, but there as silent reassurance that I'm not alone.

He isn't watching, though, when Mr. McLachlan passes out our graded assignments, and when I discover a folded note between the pieces of paper. I glance about, ensuring no one else has taken notice, and tuck it safely away.

Despite my curiosity, I don't take it back out to read it until William and I are walking back from dinner.

Cemetery at 7 is all it reads, in handwriting that is a touch messy, and the handwriting of the seven is familiar. I've seen Mr. McLachlan write it on the chalkboard hundreds of times. It's six now, only an hour until then.

Wordless, I offer the note out to William, who takes it with an inquisitive noise and reads it over with a frown. I ask, "Are you coming?"

He hands it back. "Silly question."

THE SUN HAS just about set, and the cemetery is not a place I want to be at night. William fidgets at my side, clutching tightly at the lantern we've brought along. The cemetery gate stands open wide, signalling that Mr. McLachlan has already arrived.

He isn't difficult to spot, standing before a grave at the far back of the fenced in area. We head straight to him, stopping a few feet away as I say, "An odd place to ask someone for an assignation."

Mr. McLachlan scoffs, not immediately turning to regard us. "Good thing this is not one, then." He nods to the grave at his feet, wanting me to have a look. I step up beside him. The headstone is ancient, the name decimated and only the date of death truly legible.

"What is this?"

"This is the grave of Nicolaus Mordaunt. I wonder if either of you have encountered that name during your poking about in the library?"

William and I exchange looks before he says, "It doesn't sound familiar, no."

"The original headmaster, when Whisperwood opened in the sixteen-hundreds."

An interesting titbit of information, but I'm not sure what he wants me to do with it, so I merely raise an eyebrow and wait for him to continue.

"The history of the school is sketchy on details," Mr. McLachlan says. "But what I've gleaned is that he was not a kind man. It may only be a rumour, but it's said he was locked in the gardener's pavilion and killed when students set fire to it."

That catches both of our attention. My shoulders square. "He burned to death?"

"So I've heard." Finally, he turns to look at us. "When I began here, it was under the leadership of a different headmaster. After he passed, King took over. He was strict. Keener on corporal punishment, yes, but not ultimately a poor leader.

"The staff noticed when he began to change. He took things a step too far sometimes, yet he was still within his rights to do so and no laws were broken, so what could we do? But the number of student deaths these last two decades has steadily climbed and, I'll admit, I've found it suspicious."

"You don't seem to think it was simply the job getting to him. Perhaps something to do with the ghosts?"

"I am not a superstitious man, Spencer." He sighs, slipping off his spectacles to clean them. "At first, I did believe King was merely growing too comfortable with his position of power. Truly, we've had no evidence to link him to any of these deaths that would suggest otherwise, and I can hardly request he be investigated based off a gut feeling alone."

"Why are you telling us any of this?" William asks. "Why now?"

Mr. McLachlan pauses, staring down at his glasses. "Because perhaps you two can piece together what I cannot. And because I located the 'proof' King had that led him to punishing Oscar Frances in the first place."

My eyes grow wide as my heart skips a beat. "What?"

He returns the glasses to his face and slides a piece of paper from his coat pocket. It takes everything I have not to snatch it from him. "The headmaster was in possession of a letter, penned by Oscar. I have no idea how he came by it."

"How did you...?"

"Very, very carefully. I located it in his file in the headmaster's office while King was off school grounds."

"Has Mr. Hart read it?"

"No. And at least for now, I would prefer to keep it that way. Later, perhaps. When all of this has been resolved."

I swallow hard past the lump in my throat. The second Mr. McLachlan offers the letter out to me, I take it and draw it to my chest. "May I keep this?"

"It's yours," he agrees. "I'm afraid it's only a copy. Had I taken the original, I worried he would notice."

A smart move, and I'd expect nothing less from someone like Mr. McLachlan. My fingers itch to open the letter and read it, but for the moment, I refrain. Instead, I lift my chin to look him in the eye. "Do you think the headmaster killed Oscar?"

He pockets his hands, and I notice how tired he looks. I've often thought about what this has meant for Mr. Hart, but now I wonder what it has meant for Mr. McLachlan, as well. Did he know about the close relationship Oscar and Mr. Hart had formed? Has he been trying to navigate the dangerous waters of whatever is happening at Whisperwood, too, while keeping his friend safe? "If I said that I don't believe it's out of the realm of possibility, what then?"

"Then something has to be done. He cannot be allowed to get away with this."

"The police are already performing an inquiry into Frances' death."

A bitter laugh escapes my lips. "When have the police ever cared about the death of some supposedly ill-behaved, poor boy?"

The way he sighs suggests he agrees with that assessment. "I am doing all I can."

This is information I wish he'd come to me with far sooner, but better late than never. He didn't have to offer me this at all. When I say, "Thank you, sir," I mean it with the utmost sincerity.

He nods once, curtly, and turns away from us, returning his hands into his pockets. "Go on now. It's late. And please, be safe."

WE TAKE OUR leave, and I'm so focused on the letter inside my coat that the shadows and figures at the outskirts of my vision are an afterthought to me. They keep their distance, and I almost wonder if they're curious, too. If getting a step closer to the truth somehow pleases them. The only ghostly face I've any interest in seeing is Oscar's, but it's noticeably absent amongst them.

Retreating swiftly to William's room, we crowd together on his bed, sitting hip-to-hip, as I shakily unfold the letter to read it. It's written hastily in Mr. McLachlan's scrawl, and so it feels disjointed, seeing Oscar's words in someone else's hand.

> *This is a letter I have no intention of ever giving you, but I fear my heart will burst if I do not put into words all the things I've wanted to say to you for some time now. I regret that I am not well-versed in phrasing things beautifully, I haven't a knack for such things, and so I will say it plainly that I think of you from the moment I wake in the morning until the moment I sleep at night. Never has anyone occupied my thoughts so completely.*
>
> *It began so subtly at first. A smile, a kind word. Something I am not accustomed to outside*

my small circle of friends. You had no real reason to reach out to me as you did, and for that, I am eternally grateful. You have been a mentor and a friend. Yet, surely, were I to express to you the extent of my feelings, the way that my heart skips a beat when you look at me, you may disregard it as merely a childish infatuation, unworthy of more than a laugh and a dismissal.

Or perhaps you wouldn't. Perhaps you would surprise me, as you always do, and the feelings would be mutual. I have dreamt of that, honestly.

But there is no happy ending in sight for such a thing. Either I confess, and you reject me, and I am left picking up the pieces of my heart... Or I confess, and you should accept me, and the life we would be forced to live would be one of secrecy and torment. Costing you your job for the sake of my whims? I am not sure I've reached that level of selfishness yet.

And so for now, I keep these words to myself, and perhaps, come graduation, I may have grown brave enough, selfish enough, to share them with you. Until then, you have my respect and my love. And all of my heart.

Yours,
Oscar

For a brief moment, my eyes blur, and I have to blink back the tears. When did he write this, I wonder? Was it one of the many times I sat in bed, reading, while he sat hunched over at the table, head bowed and scribbling away? How it hurts to know this secret he carted around with him was one he felt he couldn't confide in his friends. In a sense, I feel as though I'm betraying his trust by reading it now.

William sits back a little as he finishes reading. "If he wrote this with no intention of sending it, where did the headmaster get it?"

"I don't know," I murmur. "Perhaps he had it on his person. Perhaps he dropped it." How foolish and careless, though. Surely Oscar was smarter than to carry around such a thing where anyone might have come across it. It would have been safest tossed into the fireplace or, if he truly insisted upon keeping it, tucked beneath his mattress alongside *Pendennis*.

William rests his hand upon my thigh, and I feel his worried gaze upon me. I've been wallowing all week in this guilt and pain, and while I don't believe it will be over just yet, I think...

It's time to pick myself back up.

24

I remain with William until after curfew, reading and re-reading Oscar's letter again and again even as William dozes with his head upon my shoulder. Written in Mr. McLachlan's writing, I feel as though I'm missing some of the impact. As though seeing it written properly, in Oscar's hand, would fill in some missing part of the puzzle.

It occurs to me well after curfew that I've neglected to get William his dosage of medicine, and although he's currently napping, I know he'll wake utterly miserable if we were to skip it. Gently I prod him awake, and we slide from bed to sneak downstairs to fetch it from my room.

The moment we reach the first-floor hallway, I know something is wrong. My door is slightly ajar, and the memory of waking to my opening door and a ghost upon my chest washes over me in a nauseating fashion.

"Wait," I whisper, intending for William to remain where he is, but of course he grabs hold of my sleeve and keeps directly behind me. Slowly, step by step, we approach my room, and the door creaks quietly as I push it open.

Inside, Charles Simmons is seated upon Oscar's bed, and he flashes me a smile so sickeningly sweet that I instantly wish any number of ghosts would show up instead.

My blood runs cold. "What are you doing in my room?"

Charles stands, and I see he's holding the letters I wrote to Oscar, his mother, and the numerous families of the deceased students. Also in his hand is William's bottle of laudanum, dangerously low, and all we have until May heads back into town again. "What are you doing *not* in your room at this hour?" he says cheerfully. "I dropped by and thought I'd allow myself in to wait for you."

William grips tightly at my arm, and it may be the only thing that keeps me from launching across the room and punching Charles in his smug, stupid face. "You've no right to go through my things, Simmons. Put them down and get out."

"I think not. As your housemaster, I have every right to go through whatever I please." He lifts the letters and bottle with an eyebrow raised. "The headmaster will be quite interested to see these things, you know. Prying into personal affairs of students, smuggling drugs onto school grounds..."

"You know damned well that's mine," William interjects.

Charles sneers. "Really? That would be a shame, seeing as you and I had a deal and you've been shit at keeping up your end of the bargain."

William inches around me. "I've been tapering off. I'm quitting, and I'm just about there. So, please, give those over. We've done nothing wrong."

For half a moment, Charles eyes William's outstretched hand as though he just might be considering it. Then the door creaks behind us, and our attention is swiftly diverted. The three of us fall silent, turning to look, but only darkness seeps in from the hall.

"Who's there?" Charles demands. "One of your friends?"

I shake my head mutely. Charles shoves past us, none too gently pushing William into the wall as he steps out into the hallway. He looks right and then left; I see him scowling before he says, "You there!"

Without even stepping into the hallway, I know what I'm going to see. Not a student. At least, not a current one. All the same, I follow Charles with William flanking my side, and spot the boy seated at the end of the corridor.

His back is to us. He's barefoot, donning only a nightshirt. His long hair reminds me momentarily of Benjamin's, all curls, hanging limp and wet against his neck and shoulders. Every inch of him is sopping wet, in fact; water puddles around him, and the odour of something musty and waterlogged fills my nose, making it hard to breathe.

"You there," Charles snaps again, taking a few steps closer. But even he seems to pause, undoubtedly sensing, just as we do, that something is terribly wrong.

This time, the boy responds to being called to. He turns slowly, and his eyes are rolled back into his head, blue lips parted. He coughs, choking on the water that begins to pour from his mouth.

"Back into the room," I whisper urgently, extending a hand towards the knob, contemplating if I have time to shove William inside first to get him out of harm's way.

Everything happens all at once. Charles whirls, intending to follow my instructions, and the ghost lets out a low, bone-shattering bellow, like the sound of a siren beneath water. It rattles me to my core, freezes me to the spot, even as the boy drops onto all fours and charges towards us in a most inhuman fashion.

Charles scrambles straight back, forcing William and I to do the same lest he trip over us, and the ghost is on him in seconds. He hits the floor on his back and the boy grabs Charles' face between his bony hands and bows over him.

Prone and helpless, Charles seems incapable of moving, frozen in place, not unlike I had been weeks ago in my room. Water pours forth from the creature's open mouth, washing over Charles, making him sputter and choke and gasp for breath.

We need to get out of here.

I need to get William to safety.

But Charles and the boy now block our way to my door, and if we were to run for the stairs, I fear the sudden movement would attract his attention.

"Slow," I whisper. "Very slow."

William clings to me as we inch, step by step, backs to the wall, away from the drowning Charles and the dead boy.

Soon, Charles has gone deathly still, and a creaking floorboard beneath our feet has the boy's head snapping up in our direction. We stop moving, breaths held, as though it will somehow dissuade him from paying us any mind.

The boy rises to his feet. He begins down the hall towards us, making no sound, movements crooked and disjointed like a poorly constructed marionette. Unlike with Charles, he does not lunge, and I hope—I pray—if we remain still, he will crawl back into whatever hole he crawled out of.

He stops in front of us. I see nothing but the whites of his eyes, shrivelled and milky. Water has stopped pouring from his mouth, and his tongue and teeth are black as ink and his breath smells like a stagnant pool in the heat of summer. I press my back further into the wall, as though I might get it to swallow us whole and deposit us safely on the other side.

But the creature only regards me for a moment before moving on to William. He lifts a hand, bony fingers touching William's face while a low, guttural sound escapes his lips. It's trying to speak, but the words don't come out.

I cannot stand there idly. If he chooses to turn violent, if he lashes out at William, I will not have time to protect him. The moment the creature leans in towards him, the moment William squeezes his eyes shut in fear, the words burst forth before I can stop them.

"Leave him alone!"

William sucks in a breath. The boy's head snaps in my direction, letting out another deafening scream that rattles my bones.

He does not have the chance to attack. A nearby door is thrown open and two boys look out into the hall, followed by another door, and then another. I've screamed loudly enough to be heard, and if I have woken the whole bloody dorm, I shall be grateful for it. The door across from us opens, and candlelight floods the corridor.

The ghost has vanished.

All around us, sleepy-eyed students are stumbling out to see what the commotion is about. From the far end of the hall, Preston and Benjamin emerge, catching sight of William and me with their eyes widening in concern. Several boys rush straight to Charles, forming a circle around his prone figure.

"What's going on?" the lad across the way asks. "Are you all right?"

William is a shaking mess. I desperately want to usher him away into my room, away from the stares and questions that are undoubtedly about to follow. "We're..."

"What in the hell?"

Never have I been so grateful to hear Virgil's voice or to see our two prefects rounding the corner, candles in hand, although Augustus keeps behind Virgil as though he isn't prepared to deal with whatever is happening.

Virgil casts only a glance at me as he whisks past, going straight to kneel at Charles' side while snapping at the others to give him space. He shoves the candlestick into someone else's hand, leaning over Charles and checking him over. Fingers to his wrist, lifting his eyelids. There is no hesitation—although a good deal of displeasure—as he tilts Charles' chin back, bows over him, and covers Charles' mouth with his own.

It takes only a moment. A few breaths in, and then Charles jerks to life, eyes flying wide. Virgil rolls him swiftly to his side, where he proceeds to hack and cough up lungfuls of water. Trembling and disoriented, but alive. I'm uncertain how I feel about that.

Augustus has dropped to one knee on Charles' other side, observing, a hand outstretched and just shy of touching his shoulder. "Simmons? Simmons, can you hear me?"

Charles swallows in several deep breaths. Still, his eyes are wide and wild, and as soon as he's coherent enough to do so, he snaps an arm out, fisting a hand into the front of Augustus' nightshirt. "The creature...the creature was here, and it tried to kill me and *he said they wouldn't hurt me!*"

He said? Who? Did Charles know about the spirits before tonight? I have to bite down upon my lower lip to keep from asking those questions aloud with a hall full of other people.

Startled, Augustus rears back, attempting to pry the fingers from his shirt. "Creature? What creature?"

"He's delusional." Virgil grabs hold of one of Charles' arms and orders him up. The pair of them get Charles to his feet, though he looks ready to collapse again at any second. Virgil turns towards two nearby boys. "You there, help Augustus get him to Doctor Mitchell's immediately. The rest of you, if you saw nothing, return to your rooms. You've exams tomorrow."

The hallway begins to clear. I think to steal William away upstairs, except from the corner of my gaze, I notice Virgil has retrieved my letters and William's laudanum from where they lay on the floor near Charles, and I freeze. Long enough for Virgil to turn, lock eyes on us, and point to my bedroom. What's worse, he follows us into it, and I think we're about to have a none too pleasant tongue lashing about whatever he thinks has happened.

I ease William down to the edge of my mattress, where he's still attempting to gather his bearings. With our prefect present, I can hardly draw him into my arms to properly comfort him.

Virgil shuts the door before turning to us. One look at William likely tells him he's not in much shape for speaking right now, so he focuses instead on me.

"What in the bloody hell happened?"

My throat is impossibly dry. "I don't know," I say, because a lie will not come to me fast enough and the truth isn't believable.

Virgil's gaze is steely, although it's a touch more difficult to see him as imposing when he's standing there in his night clothes and his hair a mess from sleep. "I hear shouting in the middle of the night, find our housemaster drowned and unconscious in the hallway and babbling nonsense about monsters, and you 'don't know'?"

William places a hand over mine atop my leg. He wants me to keep quiet, but then again, he knows nothing about how Virgil helped me with him while he was ill. I'm not certain that I trust him implicitly, but I trust him enough to cautiously venture a wager on him. "And if I said his babbling was not nonsense?"

Virgil crosses his arms across his chest. "Your question does not answer my question."

"No, but your answer to mine will make a difference on how I respond to yours."

His jaw clenches, eyes flicking from me to William and back again, silently evaluating. "You don't get to be a prefect who wanders the halls in the dead of night without hearing and seeing things, Spencer."

I could laugh with the relief that statement brings me. "You've heard them? You've *seen* them? And you've never thought to tell anyone else?"

That earns a scoff from him. "Now *there's* a way to get my position promptly revoked. Now answer me. What happened?"

"We found Charles in my room, going through my belongings. He took a few things, claiming he was taking them to the headmaster."

Virgil holds up the letters and bottle. "These?"

William bites his lip, looking as though he wants to leap off the bed to grab for the laudanum. By some grace of God, Virgil steps forwards and offers them out, and William takes them gratefully. "Thank you."

Virgil nods once and returns his attention to me. "How did that turn into...whatever that was?"

I've not truly spoken aloud of this to anyone but William. Even Oscar only got bits and pieces, and he was long gone before the worst of it all began to happen. The words are cottony on my tongue as I try to force them out. "It was one of the spirits. We encountered it in the hall, and it attacked Simmons."

"With...water?"

"He must have drowned," William says quietly. We both look at him curiously. "The ghost. Perhaps he was a victim of drowning. So, he did the same thing to Charles."

"I noticed there was no other water anywhere in the hall," I add, having observed as much while Virgil was occupied resuscitating Charles.

Virgil helps himself to a seat upon Oscar's bed across from us, hunching forward, elbows upon his knees as he heaves a sigh. "I have come across things a number of times this year. It seems to have increased these last few weeks. They never stay long; always a flicker in the corner of my vision. But they have always been harmless. Never have I thought they were capable of doing more than giving someone a scare."

"Consider yourself lucky, then. They've left bruises on dear William, and I woke to another spirit suffocating me one night."

William's shoulders stiffen. "What? You didn't tell me that."

Oh. No. I suppose I didn't. "It covered my mouth and kept telling me I needed to be quiet. Then the door flew open and it seemed to have been frightened away."

"That isn't comforting," Virgil mutters.

"Not at all."

William wrings his hands together. "We've been at a standstill attempting to find out what's made them so active, and we think it has to do with Oscar Frances."

"Frances?" Virgil's brows furrow.

"His death was no accident," I say quietly.

"How do you know?"

I could delve into all the things we know, but I'm not yet certain how much I can trust him. Even now, as always, Virgil is not someone I have a good read on. "We have our reasons for thinking as much."

He runs a hand over his face tiredly, and I think about how we do, in fact, have our final exams tomorrow and we're going to be absolutely exhausted. "You speak as though you have some sort of plan to sort this all out."

"Not yet," I admit reluctantly.

He ducks his head into a nod, rising to his feet. "Esher should remain here with you tonight, so the two of you are not alone." He gestures to Oscar's bed, as though there's any way in hell William would sleep anywhere other than beside me. Unless he isn't aware about the two of us, but I think him to be far more intelligent than that. "Try to get some rest. If necessary, this discussion can be continued tomorrow after I've spoken with Simmons."

What will Charles say, I wonder? Especially after his hysteria has passed and he's regained his ability to think clearly? How will any of this be explained—a man drowning and no body of water to be found?

I stand as well, wondering if I ought to offer to walk him back to his room. But I've no interest in being caught out in the halls alone, nor do I wish to leave William behind. Besides, if Virgil has been so fortunate thus far to not be attacked, perhaps the spirits have no interest in bothering him. "Thank you, Virgil."

"I've hardly done anything worth being thanked for." He glances at me from the corner of his gaze momentarily, likely on account of me using his given name. He retrieves his candle and relights it using one of mine atop my dresser, steps to the door, bids us good night, and leaves. I shut and chair-jam the door behind him, listening to the sound of his fading steps.

I leave the lone candle burning, thinking it best to keep a bit of light in the room, although I do relocate the candlestick to the windowsill close by the bed. The letters I stash beneath my mattress, thinking that I shall have to find a way to mail them, or feed them to the fire before Charles can come digging for them again. William's laudanum I open long enough to give him his dosage—he's no longer trembling, but I can tell he's in dire need of it—before tucking it amongst my socks and undergarments in a dresser drawer.

William watches me as I begin the process of undressing. There's an air of tense exhaustion in the room, and I think we're both so tired of all this that speaking of it feels like a chore in and of itself. "You aren't returning home for summer, are you?"

I take a deep breath. Truly, I had not wanted William to worry about me being here alone, but I have no interest in lying to him, either. "My family has recently relocated into a new house, and my uncle is still with them."

His eyes narrow a fraction, a flash of anger pulling at his mouth, gone as quickly as it appeared. "That is utterly ridiculous, and you cannot possibly stay here alone."

"It'll give me the chance to do some more searching." Despite that I am, in all honestly, afraid where any of this is going to lead.

"Then I'm staying with you."

"William…" I turn to him, and the intensity in which he meets my eyes makes me falter in whatever it was I had intended to say.

"I will *not* leave you, James."

"You are utterly impossible, do you know that?"

"You would do no less for me. Look, Frances was your closest friend, and I imagine he only tolerated my presence for your sake. I understand that well and fully. However, this has become my fight, too. We've come this far together, and we shall finish it together. Once this has been solved, you will leave Whisperwood and come home with me. Do you understand?"

A small smile edges into my face, unable to help myself at his stubborn insistence. "Of course, dear William. I understand." For that, for *him*, I am eternally grateful.

25

The school bells chime as they have every day before, but the sun seems a little brighter when I wake to it shining upon William's face.

Never before have I opened my eyes to him in the morning. He isn't immediately roused by the bells, meaning I have a few moments of studying him in the morning glow. I slide my fingers along his jaw, up to his forehead, to sweep back some of his tousled hair. Where I would normally be slipping out of bed as quietly as possible so as not to disturb him, I'm now blessed with the most blissful task of leaning in to kiss him awake. Even barely conscious, his mouth reacts to mine. He smiles, stretching out slowly, winding an arm about my middle beneath the covers. My bed is smaller than his, making it impossible to have distance between us even if we wanted to.

I want this to be my reality every morning for the rest of time.

"Good morning, darling," I whisper against his mouth. In response, he makes a soft noise, and catches my bottom lip briefly between his teeth, coaxing a chuckle from me in the process. "It's time to get up."

"Must we?"

"I'm afraid so. But, look, it's the last day of term."

This is both a blessing and a curse. I'm in no way mentally prepared to handle our exams today, and I doubt William is, either. Once it's done, we will be free for the next month. Whatever that month entails, I don't pretend to know. Yet somehow, waking next to William has put me in a far better mindset to prepare for whatever is to come.

It's with great reluctance we rise from the bed and begin our day together. It was only a few months ago that Oscar was the one fighting me for the mirror and washbowl in the mornings while we bantered about. Mornings with William are softer. Quieter. He washes and shaves and does his hair with practised ease, and I enjoy watching him do these things so much that I don't even try to nudge my way in to steal the mirror from him. Instead, I strip down and ready myself while he dresses.

It feels a touch scandalous leaving the room together, and I have to remind myself we were given express permission for him to stay with me. Still, I've no interest in attracting more attention to us. I cannot begin to imagine what rumours might be floating around about what happened last night.

The dining hall seems louder than normal when we arrive. It could be attributed to exam day excitement, everyone ready and eager to get home for holiday. I think of Mother's letter in my room. I shall have to write to inform her I won't be returning. Not now. Maybe not ever. Dramatic of me, perhaps, but my relationship with my family is a mountain I have not had a chance to scale with everything that has been going on here.

We take our usual seats, and we get no further than saying good morning to our friends before Virgil arrives and takes up the chair to my left, the one previously only ever occupied by Oscar. Certainly, as he has always sat several spots down, it's unusual, and has the lot of us falling silent and turning our attention to him.

"Good morning," Benjamin finally says, always the first to go out of his way to be friendly.

"Morning," Virgil agrees, beginning to serve food onto his plate from the platters before us. He looks, I think, as though he hasn't slept much or well. "I thought it prudent to inform you that Charles Simmons will be leaving Whisperwood this afternoon."

William's head snaps up. My eyebrows lift.

"Is he all right?" Preston asks.

Virgil skewers a sausage with his fork, takes a small bite, and the pause makes me want to shake him. "I informed staff that he had a fit last night in the halls. He spent hours babbling nonsensically to the point where Doctor Mitchell felt it necessary to drug him so he would sleep. He'll be departing this afternoon to be committed until he begins making sense again, however long that may be, I don't believe he will be allowed back as an apprentice."

None of us breathes a word, perhaps unsure what the correct response to this news should be. Manners suggest we ought to express regret for his poor mental state but I, for one, cannot find it in me to do so.

Then, to my right, William lets out a laugh. Soft at first, and then again, louder, until he has to bow his head and put a hand to his mouth to try to hold it back. The others watch him in stunned silence. Although the reasoning is clear enough to me, I touch a hand to his leg beneath the table in hopes to settle him. He does after a few moments, clearing his throat and keeping his gaze lowered with a mumbled apology. Still, I can see the smile tugging at his mouth, and I cannot say I blame him.

EXAMS GO BETTER than expected. That is to say, I'll be shocked if I haven't utterly botched my Latin test, aced English, and did passable in history and maths. My eyes are burning from a lack of sleep and stress, and I don't have it in me to be energetic after the last lesson of the day lets out and the other boys are rushing to their rooms to begin packing.

Instead, I fall into step alongside William, and we enjoy the remaining few hours of daylight walking the grounds together. We head to the stables, because although William doesn't enjoy riding, he does enjoy meandering from stall to stall, stroking the horses' noses and leaving little braids in their manes.

He's been quiet today, I've noticed. Not unpleasantly so; he hasn't seemed to be in a poor temper. Just...quiet.

Withdrawn. Idly I worry he's feeling unwell again, but when pressed he assures me that isn't the case.

On our way back from the equestrian centre, a carriage passes by on the main road. At a glance, I think it might be Charles I spot inside, leaving the property.

Good riddance.

We enjoy a final meal with our friends, and I find a sense of melancholy settling over me, as though this is, truly, the last time we will have this moment. Am I afraid of what the future holds? Of what will happen should our ghost hunting endeavours turn deadly? What's worse, what if something were to happen to William while I escape unscathed? I steal looks at him throughout dinner, the fear in my chest growing denser and deeper.

"Come sit with us by the fire awhile, would you?" Benjamin asks on our way back to the dorms. I can hardly refuse him such a request on their last night here, no matter how tired I am.

The common room is, for the most part, void of anyone but our group. Others are too busy packing and getting into bed early, eager to wake and leave come morning. William takes a seat upon the floor near the fire while I occupy my usual chair, sparing a look towards the seat Oscar most frequented. None of us have sat in it since. I wonder if it's a conscious decision on our parts, or if we simply know not to occupy the space of someone we've lost.

From the moment I get settled, however, I notice I'm being observed. Preston, Benjamin, and Edwin are exchanging looks, clearly waiting to say something, and I try not to sigh.

"Come on, out with it."

Preston takes a deep breath. "All right. Well. We wanted to ask you—*both* of you—what in the hell is going on."

My gaze flicks to William, who has his focus upon the fire and hardly seems to have heard a word. "I'm not certain what you mean."

"Don't insult us by playing stupid." Preston frowns. "For weeks, I've summed up your behaviour to grief over Frances—Lord knows we're all struggling with that—but then last night, and you asking around about the ghosts. What's happening?"

I try not to squirm in my seat so nervously. "You and Benjamin made it clear you don't believe anything supernatural is happening here, and so I hardly see a reason to bring up the topic again."

Benjamin shakes his head. "We're listening. Truly, we are."

"Whatever it is you're going through, we need to know in order to help you."

I drum my fingers upon the arm of the chair, relocating my attention to the fire, and to William. "That's a very long story, I'm afraid."

"We have time to hear it," Edwin says.

What do I say? How much do I tell them? It seems cruel to leave them in the dark when they're directly asking, when I've already divulged information to both Virgil and Mr. McLachlan.

With great uncertainty, I begin to recount to them everything of importance that's occurred at Whisperwood. I tell them of Oscar's run-in with the headmaster, but I leave out the part of the letter for now, not wanting to betray that secret of Oscar's more than I already have. What he held in his heart was for him only, and no one should be privy to that even in death.

I tell them of the ghost who attacked me in my room, of the one I followed into the woods. I speak of our search for the tunnels and what I encountered within them. Through it all, they listen and watch, interjecting only for clarification. To their credit, no one scoffs, no one turns their nose up at what is undoubtedly an incredulous story.

When I'm done, they remain silent still, absorbing the information I've just thrown at them.

"You think King murdered Frances?" Benjamin asks.

"Yes. No. I don't know. I've put a great deal of thought into that. King is an old man; I hardly think he'd be physically capable of harming a student unless he caught them unaware. Not to mention, moving Oscar's body after the fact, all by himself?"

"Then, an accomplice?" Edwin asks.

"I've thought that, too. Doctor Mitchell, perhaps. Hell, I wouldn't cross Simmons off the list. He's played loyal servant to King a number of times already this year, and I suspect it was him who ratted Oscar out to the headmaster in the first place."

Preston scoffs. "Well, he's out of the picture."

"What happens now, then?" Benjamin looks to Preston, as though relying on him for an answer to that.

He shrugs. "If we had more time, I would write to my aunt, see if she has any ideas, but…"

I look between them, a flicker of relief and hope striking within me. "You believe me now?"

"I believe you," Preston agrees. "And I'm fairly certain Benji never doubted you."

"He was certainly adamant enough about ghosts not existing," I point out, not without a touch of bitterness. Benjamin has the grace to look ashamed of that.

"I won't get into my own feelings on the matter. Just know that I'm sorry. I think I'd just hoped you were wrong. I didn't want you to have reason to be afraid."

As brushed aside as I'd felt, I cannot say I ever thought any of them had ill intentions in discouraging me from pursuing silly ghost stories. "It's over and done with now. All is forgiven."

"Then—" Benjamin pauses as he glances to William, and the frown on his face immediately draws my attention, as well. "Are you all right, Esher?"

William is watching the flames in an almost trance-like state. More than that, his expression is slack and vacant, and he's sitting closely enough to the fire that I cannot imagine it's comfortable.

"William," I call, scooting to the end of my seat. "*William.*"

His spine straightens, and he inhales sharply. "What? Sorry, I was..."

"Are you all right?"

He shakes his head and picks himself up from the floor. There's something in his movements, an uncoordinated sluggishness, that is too reminiscent of his earlier days of being ill. "Excuse me a moment. I think I need to step outside and get some air."

I've already risen to my feet in concern as he begins to cross the room, and I recognize the signs he displayed that day in Mr. McLachlan's class. The way the colour drains from his face, the way he reaches to brace himself on whatever he can find, and then—

I dive for him, managing only just to catch him beneath his arms as his legs give out. The others are promptly out of their seats and rush to help me lay him down. The first thing I notice upon touching his face is that he's covered in sweat and burning hotter than I have ever seen a person get.

Fear surges bright and vicious in the pit of my stomach. "Someone, go fetch Virgil!"

Edwin promptly flees the room to do as instructed while Benjamin makes quick work of undoing William's tie and the top few buttons of his collar and shirt. "Christ, he's scalding."

"William." I pat his cheek, stroking back his hair, anxiously awaiting the opening of his eyes. That day in maths, he was only out for a matter of moments before coming to again, but the seconds are ticking by into minutes, and he is still unresponsive. Panic lodges itself in my throat, makes it difficult to talk. "William, sweetheart, please, you need to open your eyes."

What is only a minute or two seems to take forever before Edwin returns with Virgil, who rushes straight to our side and crouches. He scarcely needs to touch William's forehead before he says, "Let's get him downstairs. Fill one of the baths immediately; we need this fever down."

Preston, Edwin, and Benjamin rush ahead. Virgil assists me lifting William from the floor and transporting him, taking care in going down the spiral staircase to the ground floor. A few boys we pass in the halls crane their necks to watch, met immediately with Virgil's sharp reproach that sends them scurrying back to their rooms.

Into the bathing room we go, where the others have already gotten enough buckets of water transported from the faucets into the tub to fill it halfway. Virgil and I get William out of his jacket and shoes and waistcoat before we ease him into the tub. Almost immediately, poor William gasps, grabbing hold of my arm and trying to claw his way out of the icy water like a drowned cat. It pains me to have to grab hold of him and shove him back down, and it requires Virgil and I both to keep him pinned there while the others continue running back and forth across the room with bucket after bucket.

Yet for his struggling—and now, his fierce trembling—William doesn't properly open his eyes, nor does he speak; he only lets out the most pitiful of sounds that shred my heart to pieces.

"It's all right," I croon, wincing as he has a painfully tight grip upon my bicep. I bring my free hand up, smoothing back his hair, letting the rivulets of water slide down his flushed face. "Deep breaths, darling. Deep breaths. We just need to get your fever down."

William shakes so fiercely I'm terrified we're somehow hurting him further, but Virgil's watchful eye on him is confident and sure, and I must trust him as someone who has far more experience in this than I.

Minutes tick by. Occasionally, one of the boys scoops some of the water back out to replace it with fresh, cold water. My own shirt—Virgil's, too—is sopping wet all up the sleeves and down the front, and I cannot feel my fingers anymore.

Eventually, slowly, William eases his grip enough that we can draw back, though it's not as though I venture far. I continue petting his hair, whispering to him, hoping that even unconscious my voice might somehow reach him.

Virgil rocks back onto his heels with a sigh. "What in the hell happened this time?"

"No idea," Preston says. "He got up, and then down he went."

"He's been feeling better. I haven't a clue what came over him so fast," I add.

"Has he complained of stomach pains?"

"Not at all."

"Breathing problems?"

I shake my head. "Sometimes the weather causes him distress, but, no, not recently."

Virgil frowns as he stands, wiping his damp hands against the thighs of his trousers. "We'll give him a little bit longer in there, but we don't want him to get too cold, either. Watch him a few minutes. I'm going to fetch a blanket."

"He's going to need some dry clothes," Edwin points out.

I let out a breath. "Go to his room. Just fetch one of his nightshirts and see if Virgil needs help. There are spare blankets beneath William's bed."

Edwin nods and slips out briskly, leaving me alone with William, Benjamin, and Preston. I sigh, bowing until my forehead rests against the cool lip of the tub. Nothing has scared me quite like this, and still my heart is galloping wild.

Neither of them speaks, permitting us to sit in silence for a while, for which I'm grateful. Eventually I draw away, in dire need of stretching my legs, which have begun to develop a horrible ache from crouching on the hard floor. I grant myself a moment to step into the hall and around the doorframe, just out of sight, shoving a hand back through my hair and reassuring myself that everything will be all right.

Preston accompanies me. "All right?"

"All right," I tiredly agree.

"You're positive we shouldn't fetch Doctor Mitchell?"

"William would murder me if we did." Though I'll admit, the idea has crossed my mind. Virgil is an invaluable asset, true, but asking him to act as our doctor when he hasn't the formal training is unfair, and puts him into a horrible position should something go wrong.

Nothing will go wrong, I sharply reprimand myself. *William will be fine.*

From in the room, I hear the sloshing of water and suspect Benjamin is swapping out warm for cold again.

Except then I hear, "Esher!" and Benjamin's voice sounds equal parts confused and concerned. Preston and I exchange a brief look before we're hurrying back into the room.

William is no longer in the tub. Which makes no sense in any world because he had been unconscious, and Benjamin would never be capable of lifting him alone. Instead, William is very much standing on his own, poised before the windows that overlook the grounds. Benjamin stands several feet away, looking as though he was in the process of approaching but stopped for some unknown reason.

A wave of relief washes over me. He's conscious again and standing on his own; that's good. Yet as I cross the room to go to him, a new sensation crawls across my skin. Something unsettling and wrong. I halt a foot or so behind him, and the moonlight catches on his face, granting me a look at his reflection in the glass panes of the windows, and my heart stops.

His eyes. Something is wrong with his eyes.

"William." I speak soft and uncertain, fear not prohibiting me from reaching to him, touching his arm and attempting to turn him to me. He does so without fuss, but the direness of the situation hits harder the moment I can see his face, and the milky white of his eyes.

I am staring into the face of a dead man standing before me, and that should not be possible.

Even more impossible still is that William steps forward, towards me at first and then around me. He shuffles for the door in uncoordinated, sluggish steps that remind me far too much of the creature that attacked Charles.

Preston steps into the doorway, blocking William's path, and William stops, staring directly at nothing and simply... waiting.

"What is he doing?" Benjamin whispers.

I don't know, but I don't believe it's William we're dealing with right now.

"Let him pass," I say. "Let's see where he wishes to go."

Preston seems relieved and more than happy to move out of the way. William advances the moment he does, disappearing around the corner, and the three of us swiftly follow. I instruct Benjamin to hurry upstairs and inform Virgil, lest they return and find us all gone.

The halls have emptied now, and it isn't far before we reach the front door. William opens it and ventures outside. I fear being out in the cold will exacerbate his condition. He walks bare-footed out into the wet grass, seeming not the least bit bothered, and yet I'm already being chilled to the bone through my wet shirt and so I cannot imagine how it isn't bothering him.

It's a slow walk; William—or whatever has control of William—either is in no big hurry or hasn't the capability of hurrying. He leads us across the grounds, behind Gawain Hall, and the further we go the more my heart sinks because

I know where he's taking us. The only thing so far back on the grounds is the cemetery.

Thankfully, he doesn't go directly to the gates, but stops twenty or thirty feet away from them, and then lifts a hand and points. That's it. He stands and he points, unmoving, unblinking.

I move in front of William. From over his shoulder, I see Benjamin and the others jogging our way. Backup is good, and Edwin has a blanket in hand. I cup William's face, which has gone from unbearably hot to deathly cold, in my hands. "Darling, can you hear me? We need to get you back inside. We've seen what you wanted to show us." For however little sense it makes to me. I would rather have William back than have a ghost utilizing him like some sort of puppet.

Those must have been the magic words. William blinks once, twice, again, and his eyes clear back to their familiar blue, and the colour returns to his face. He begins to crumple, but my close proximity allows me to get my arms around him so that he can steady himself before he hits the ground.

I cannot help the whimper that escapes my mouth. "Oh, thank God. Are you all right?"

He clutches at me, disoriented as he casts a look around. "Yes? What's happened?"

"You passed out with a horrible fever, and then you got up and led us out here."

Edwin, who has stopped several feet away, lingers until Benjamin snatches the blanket from him and hurries over to unfurl it and get it around William's shoulders. William straightens up slowly, gaining his bearings back and tugging the blanket securely about himself as the cold seems to be registering.

"I...I don't remember any of that."

"Let's get him back inside before we get him sicker," Virgil says, and that sounds like a grand idea to me.

By the time we've ushered William inside, upstairs and into my room, he's walking just fine on his own. Most importantly, his fever has vanished, and he appears to be perfectly coherent and no worse for wear. I do promptly urge him to get out of his sopping wet clothes and into one of my nightshirts. He begins this process looking mildly embarrassed to be doing so with an audience, and with me insisting on helping him.

I should be more aware of the others, of the fact that I'm hovering too close to William, fussing over him too much, but I cannot help it. He gave me a terrible fright, and the fact that he remembers none of it is alarming in and of itself.

"So, we think one of the spirits, what, possessed him?" Edwin asks. He's been eyeing William like he has the plague since we came in, and it's starting to irritate me.

"To show us the cemetery," Virgil adds. While the other three have taken a seat upon Oscar's bed, Virgil has sat in one of the chairs at the small table, which is still scattered with papers and books from my exam studying. "What's so special about the cemetery?"

"We know at least some of the ghosts' bodies are buried there," William says. Now that he's properly dressed, I wrap the blanket back around his shoulders, ignoring the muttering he does under his breath that I'm worrying too much. I direct him into my bed beneath the covers and have a seat on the edge.

I add, "The original headmaster of the school is interred there, as well."

"The one you said burned to death?" Benjamin asks.

"From what I've heard, yes. I suspect he's the creature I encountered in the tunnels. He looked like charred remains, and he seemed afraid of fire."

"If the other spirits are afraid of him, then it'd make sense for them to try to lead us to where he's buried," says Preston. All of us turn our attention to him, waiting to see why, precisely, he thinks that makes sense. The sudden looks make him smile a little embarrassedly. "My aunt—the medium, remember—she would say when an evil spirit is restless, cremating the remains and scattering the ashes keeps it from being able to manifest itself. Used to think she was a bit batty, but…"

"That's completely mad," Edwin grumbles.

Burning the remains. It *does* sound insane, but what about this entire thing hasn't? I'm also neglecting to see any other options. But my friends will be leaving tomorrow to go home, and this might be too much for even dear William to stomach doing.

William sighs. "The new dilemma we're presented with, then, is how to dig up a grave on school grounds without getting caught."

I look askance at him, both grateful and surprised. "You would help me dig up a grave?"

"I'm almost offended you should ask me that. Haven't I helped with everything else thus far?"

A smile pulls at my mouth, and I reach out to rest a hand atop one of his. To hell with who bears witness to it. If they don't know there lingers something between William and I by now, then they're utterly blind.

"After tomorrow, the school will be empty," Virgil says. "Even most of the faculty and staff will be leaving. Really, there will only be a bare skeleton crew and a scant few students left."

"What of the headmaster?"

"Hard to say. But, you know, he typically leaves in the evenings anyway, so if nothing else…"

"It grants me some time to do this." At night, which is not at all preferable. Being so alone on school grounds with King and the ghosts that seem to be growing more and more restless and dangerous? If I am going to attempt to take Preston's advice, it will need to happen sooner rather than later. At least we've been blessed with Charles' absence; one less thing to worry about.

I run my hands over my face. "It's getting late, and the lot of you have travelling to do tomorrow. Please, go and get some rest."

They reluctantly look to each other before getting to their feet. As I escort them out the room, Benjamin and Preston linger, and Preston asks, "Are you sure you'll be all right on your own?"

"I'm not alone. I have William with me."

Preston laughs softly. "I meant someone to look after *you*, not the other way around."

I smile, and it isn't insincere. "You'd be surprised how much he looks after me."

After they've gone, I close the door, leaning against it and breathing in deep.

I startle at a hand against my back, turning to William as he peers, concerned, into my face. He looks so drastically different than he did a mere two hours ago; his cheeks are rosy, and his eyes are bright. Healthy and alert like I have not known him to be since—well, maybe since ever, if I'm truthful. It's as though he was never ill to begin with.

"Are you well?" he softly inquires.

The smile on my face this time is gentler. "We will end all of this, and then I will be."

"You're not planning on doing anything without me, are you?"

"I'm not certain this is something I *can* do alone," I admit, turning towards him and taking both of his hands in my own.

William leans in, resting his head against my shoulder. "A good thing you won't be alone then, hm?"

I press my cheek against his head with a sigh. "A very good thing."

We linger there for a moment before William presses his lips to my neck and pulls back. "Come now. Let's get some rest. I anticipate tomorrow is going to be a very long day."

Have we had a day recently that *hasn't* felt long? I give his hand a squeeze and release it, so that William can crawl back into bed and I can get changed before joining him.

William curls neatly up at my side in a position that has become familiar and comfortable to me. He draws the blankets up around us and rests his hand upon my chest, over my heart, and kisses my mouth with such gentleness that it melts away much of the night's tension.

"I love you," he whispers against my lips. "You know that, don't you?"

Oh, the way my heart stumbles over a beat. "Do you?"

"With all my heart," he says, and I wish he would smile at me like that forever. "You and I, we are going to solve all of this, leave this miserable school, and spend the rest of our lives getting to wake up beside each other."

I gaze at him adoringly. This ridiculous man never ceases to amaze me with the things he says and does. I push myself up, pressing William back onto the bed, leaning over him and bowing down to kiss him solidly. "I love you," I murmur. "More than I can begin to say, my darling William."

He makes the softest of sounds, a blend between a sigh and a whimper, putting his arms around me to hold me right where I am. "Say that to me always."

The subtle way he shifts beneath me has me going still, pulse kicking up a notch. This might ordinarily be the point wherein I pull away and lie down, simply hold him while we fall asleep. Yet instead, I find myself settling atop of him, able to feel the lines of his body against my own through the fabric of our nightshirts, and immensely enjoying the way it makes him shudder. "The *darling William* part?"

His breath has hitched in his throat, and his hips arch, searching for further friction from mine. "That, too. But the *I love you* bit is quite nice."

"I love you," I say again, thinking I'm happy to repeat it as often as he wishes to hear it. Just to be able to finally speak the words aloud, to have him speak them to me... I'm suddenly desperate to have my hands all over him and find myself tugging up his nightshirt to splay my fingers out over his ribs and up over his chest.

For the first time, it's William who stops me. "James, if you're doing this because you're concerned about what awaits us tomorrow..."

I draw back enough to peer down at him. "I'm so tired of my life being determined by everyone else. I want to do what I want to do. And this is something I've wanted to do for quite some time."

His expression softens, and he strokes his fingers down the length of my jaw. "Well, far be it for me to protest."

"I didn't think that you would."

William takes a moment to slip out of his nightshirt, and before I can quite comprehend what's happened, we've both shed our clothes, and William has his mouth against my neck, my collarbone, his hands skimming down my sides and around to my back. He mumbles another *I love you* into the curve of my throat that makes me shiver.

I'm not certain I could express to him the way that makes me feel. I kiss him instead, deep and full of want, wishing to convey to him all the things that no amount of poetry in the world could convey. The way William clings to me, the sighs he makes against my mouth as his fingertips glide across my back as though he can still feel the remnants of my lashing, and the arch of his body as he rocks up against me...he's perfect. This ridiculously flawed, difficult, beautiful man is absolutely perfect and everything I could have wanted or needed. I could kick myself for having waited so long to do this, for every time that I wanted to touch him and refrained because I was afraid.

I don't know what awaits us tomorrow, but for tonight, I will think only of William and the press of his thighs against my sides and his hands in my hair, and I will hold onto my happiness.

26

Sleep comes surprisingly well. I choose to skip breakfast, preferring to lie there with my limbs tangled with William's, head against his chest and listening to the steady thrum of his heartbeat. From the halls comes the commotion of students hurriedly packing and leaving, and it dawns on me that this school holiday is very much different than the last.

For a month, the school will be void of life. Assuming we get through our endeavour, William and I, too, will be taking our leave to return to his family's home. I'd be lying if I tried to say it has not crossed my mind simply taking him and leaving now. To depart Whisperwood and, preferably, never return. Were it not for Oscar, maybe I could even talk myself into that, for William's sake if nothing else.

Not only that, but when everyone returns, it will be to begin the next school year. The lot of us will have moved into the fourth-year hall, and I will be given a new roommate. William and I will have to resort to sneaking around all over again, and my new roommate may not be as kind about covering for me. The thought makes me sigh heavily.

I doze off and on until William begins to stir. Even when he wakes, he says nothing, and he busies himself sliding his hands through my hair, trailing his fingertips down my neck and back in ways that make me shiver delightfully.

Eventually he says, "We should be getting up if you want to bid the others goodbye."

"Working on it," I mumble, tipping my head to leave a few open-mouthed kisses along his throat.

"Not productive." He sighs, head leaning back. "We've slept through breakfast."

"We have."

"Are you hungry?"

I cannot help but grin against his neck, nipping playfully at the skin there. "I think I just might be."

He laughs, soft and warm, and gives my shoulder a gentle shove. "Have I created a monster?"

I roll up onto an elbow and lean over him, catching his eyes with my own and sliding a hand up and over his chest, up to cup the side of his face. The manner in which I settle myself between his thighs makes him suck in a breath, long lashes lowering. "You just might have," I say, and lean in to kiss him deeply.

If everything goes wrong, if everything ends horribly, if this is the last day I spend in this school or on this earth, I want to go out remembering this. Us. Just as we are, and how I've found at least one perfect thing in my life.

27

William and I are able to catch lunch together, just barely. The meal selection is meagre compared to our usual, but there is enough to go around for those who are left. Preston and the others are absent, and I dread to think we've missed bidding them farewell. Though surely, they'd have come to my room to say goodbye.

Unless they didn't want to. Maybe after last night, they thought it too much. Too strange. Too dangerous.

I really don't want to broach the topic, thought I know it needs to be addressed. After he's finished eating, I turn to William. "I think we should do it tonight. The school will be empty, and the headmaster will likely be gone."

William breathes in deep and nods once. "I know. Why don't you head back to Gawain? Say goodbye to your friends. I'll join you shortly and we'll formulate a plan."

As loath as I am to let him out of my sight, I remind myself it's still daylight. I give him a small smile, a squeeze of his arm, and excuse myself from the table.

The weather smells thickly of rain. Unsurprising, as this time of year it's stranger to not have rain, and I think it may make digging tonight easier. A million concerns are cascading through my mind. We need shovels, for one. Is William physically up to digging up a grave? How long will it take? I cannot say I've ever had cause to dig such a hole before.

It also dawns on me that dear old Nicholas will not much like us disturbing his remains.

In the dorms, I steal a look into Preston and Benjamin's room. They aren't present, but their belongings are still packed and readied on their beds, so they clearly haven't left yet. When I cross down to my own room, the door is half-opened, and I hear their voices before I've stepped inside.

Benjamin, Preston, and Virgil are all waiting, and turn to look at me when I arrive. I smile easily. "What's all this? Come to give me teary goodbyes? I promise, we've only a few weeks before we'll be together again."

Preston pockets his hands. "Yes, well, about that. We aren't going home."

I blink, unsure I've heard him right. "Sorry?"

"We're staying to help," Benjamin says.

I stare at the two of them before turning my attention to Virgil, who only sighs and rolls his shoulders back into a shrug. "My family will forgive me if I'm a few days late in returning home."

A lump forms in my throat and I swallow hard. "You do realise the dangers of this."

"All the more reason you and Esher shouldn't embark on this alone," Benjamin says. "This is for Frances, too. He was our friend, and we owe it to him to find out the truth of what happened."

"I take it Edwin didn't agree with that."

Preston's smile is tight enough that I suspect he's not pleased about that. "Not all people are made sturdy enough to handle this sort of thing, I suppose."

It hardly matters. What does matter is that these three are incredible, and whatever tonight throws at us, I think together, we can overcome it. I feel guilty for ever having doubted them, and for having been so reluctant to trust Virgil after all the assistance he's provided. "Well, then, I don't suppose any of you have ever had to dig a grave?"

Preston says, "Not a grave, but plenty of holes. Put a shovel in my hands and I can manage."

"How long do you suspect it will take?"

"Depends on how deep the body was buried, and how much the rain has permeated the ground. Wet is easier to dig, but too wet means we'll be fighting against mud and water filling up around us."

"I was afraid of that."

"Two or three hours, if we switch off when one of us tires," Benjamin offers. "Once it goes deep enough, only one person will be capable of digging at a time."

I take a seat on my bed, elbows upon my knees. "That's manageable."

For the next forty-five minutes, we discuss our plan of action, our concerns, our thoughts. I've begun to worry about William's whereabouts when the door opens, and he steps in.

And with him, Mr. Hart and Mr. McLachlan.

We all stand abruptly, tension flooding over every one of us. William holds up a hand as though that simple gesture will calm me. "They're here to help."

Was this the reason he sent me back here alone? So he could approach them? It could have gone poorly, and I'm a touch annoyed he would have done such a thing without at least warning me. "Really." I turn my attention to the teachers. "You two are truly going to risk your jobs to help us desecrate a grave?"

Mr. Hart doesn't so much as flinch. "For Oscar, yes."

"We've known something was wrong for years," Mr. McLachlan says. "I told you as much. We knew, but we had no proof."

"Doing this is not necessarily going to lead us to any proof of anything," I point out. King will still likely not be held accountable. "Although it may open up more of a chance to find proof without fear of the ghost stopping us."

He folds his arms across his chest. "One step at a time. Besides, I should think you need our assistance. How else are you going to obtain shovels from the gardener's shed? And I imagine you don't know the headmaster's schedule."

He has a point, which only serves to make me give him a rather sullen look. I don't know if I can trust them, but I want to. Mr. McLachlan gave us the information about the original headmaster to begin with, and Mr. Hart…whatever the truth is about his feelings towards Oscar, I think he cared for him a great deal. I need to trust that will make him our ally in this.

"Any assistance would be appreciated."

Mr. McLachlan nods curtly. "Headmaster King has already departed for home. He said he suspected he would return tomorrow morning in order to handle some paperwork for next term."

"Tonight it is, then." I look to William, whose expression is tense in unease, but he is, as always, unfaltering in his resolve to stand by me. "We'll wait until just after dinner. That way, we have a chance to eat and gather our energy, and anyone who might still be here will be preoccupied. I cannot promise this will go well, or that it will even work."

"It will work," William assures me gently. "It has to."

28

By planning this for just after dinner, not only had I hoped to make sure the rest of the remaining school occupants were busy, but to take advantage of the little bit of daylight we would have. Those hopes are dashed when it begins to rain steadily, and the clouds have overtaken the sky and blocked out the sun, leaving everything in a mosaic of dark and dreary greys.

William, Benjamin, Preston, Virgil and I head to the cemetery, dressed in our thickest coats to protect against the elements. Mr. McLachlan and Mr. Hart meet us halfway there, three shovels and two axes in hand. Preston takes one shovel and I take another, and we say little as we begin the march towards the gates.

Upon arriving, we slow to a halt, peering through the towering iron bars into the rows of tombstones beyond. It's with a sinking sensation that I realise something is amiss, that a heavy presence lingers from within. William catches my arm, directing my gaze straight back to where, in the darkness, the barely visible outline of a humanoid figure looms. A flash of lightning overhead illuminates the familiar face of a charred, red-eyed creature.

"Dear Lord," Mr. McLachlan murmurs beside me, and I think that this is the first time he or Mr. Hart have seen this creature.

"What now?" Even Preston's voice wavers with an undercurrent of fear.

I wrack my brain for ideas. He needs to be drawn away. I turn to William. "The tunnels. I need to go into the tunnels and find those rooms again. Perhaps my presence there would draw it away."

His face pales, but he doesn't hesitate. "Fine, but I'm going with you."

"I remember the way, I think. I should—"

"I'm going with you," he repeats, hotly this time.

There really isn't time to argue, and it's a double-edged sword. If I bring William along, I risk him being hurt. If I leave him behind, I risk him being hurt here, and me not being present to look after him. I bite briefly at my lower lip. "As you wish."

I turn to the others. "William and I will lure it away. Once it's gone, start digging, quickly as you can."

"This is too dangerous," Benjamin whispers. "There has to be another way."

"If you've a better idea, I'm happy to hear it."

He lowers his gaze, and his silence suggests that, no, nothing better comes to mind. There's nothing more we can do to be more prepared than we are here and now, with an empty school and King gone and all of us here to band together.

God, I hope William was right. I hope Oscar is out there, looking out for us right now.

Preston says nothing but claps a hand tightly onto my shoulder. Virgil gives us a tight nod, mouth drawn thin, and Mr. McLachlan softly says, "Godspeed, boys."

I trade my shovel for an axe. It may come in handy should I encounter any locked doors like I did before. Armed with our lanterns, we begin the long walk toward—and into—the woods. Finding our way to the tunnels seems almost impossible. The landscape looks different without the snow, dismally disorienting in the dark. Even through layers of clothing, the chill seeps in. William visibly shudders.

We've been walking no more than five minutes when a voice calls our names from behind, and we turn to see a faint halo of lantern light and Mr. Hart navigating his way through the trees towards us.

"What's wrong?" William asks.

He stops, a bit winded from having hurried to catch up to us. "I'm coming with you."

I frown. "They need your help, sir."

He scoffs. "So many people aren't needed for digging up a grave. We've only three shovels. And sending the two of you off alone, I won't allow it. I wasn't there for Oscar when he needed someone to look after him, and I'll not make that mistake twice."

William and I exchange glances. Truly, I don't have a reason to tell him no. I still partly blame him for Oscar's disappearance, and if he wants to make amends for that, then far be it for me to refuse him. "Let's go. We're running out of this pitiful excuse for daylight."

We continue our trek, and it drags on long enough that I begin to grow nervous we'll not find the entrance again, up until Mr. Hart lets out a gasp and, upon turning to see where he's looking, I spot the source of his shock.

One of the dead students, amongst the trees, a hand lifted and pointing. He's scarcely visible amongst the gray backdrop of the forest, standing as still as he is.

I change course, heading towards him. He fades from view when we near, but another, different figure is off in the distance, hand raised to direct us. Another, and another, and I search their faces in desperate hope of seeing Oscar's, but he is not among them.

What awaits us at the end of their guiding path is the opening to the tunnels, a dark blemish against a small hillside, just barely tall enough for a man to step inside. Mr. Hart has to stoop a little to clear the overhang. It's difficult to tell for certain, but I wonder if this is what the ghost was trying to lead me to that night Charles caught me out past curfew. Had I ventured just a little longer, a little farther then, would I have found this entrance? I had not paid it any mind when William and I escaped this way, but now the familiarity is hard to dismiss.

The rain from outside has flooded into the tunnels, and I can only imagine at some point during this rainy season, the entire tunnel will flood and make traversing it nearly impossible.

Mr. Hart marvels as he looks around. "Where in the world did this come from?"

"Not something we've been able to figure out." I squint nervously into the darkness that lies ahead.

Mr. Hart lifts his lantern high and takes the lead, venturing into the corridors with us on his heels. Despite my confusion and disorientation the last time I was here, the tunnels are fairly straightforward. There's a deviation off to the right at some point, leading to, I believe, the entrance off the kitchens. We press straight ahead, a trail that eventually ends with the ladder I previously took into that unknown hallway.

It's there that I stop, head tipped back and heart racing. I recall what I witnessed before, the burned man delivering punishment upon that poor boy. Do all the spirits here endure such torture? Is that their fate, to be subjected to Nicholas Mordaunt for the rest of time?

That thought—the thought of Oscar being on the receiving end of that torment—sends me up the ladder without a moment more of hesitation.

Crawling into the hallway, I'm instantly aware that the ominous presence of last time is not as prevalent. Possibly because Mordaunt is busy guarding his grave.

I hope to change that.

Mr. Hart follows only after William does, and they both turn full circle, surveying the hall and its row of closed doors.

"None of the faculty knows about this?" William asks.

Mr. Hart shakes his head. "I haven't a clue where this even is. I've seen drafts of the school layout before, but never noticed anything like this."

"It wasn't included on any of them. Even the older drafts." Our maps are old, but certainly not the originals, and I've a feeling there's a reason why those weren't lying around for anyone to stumble upon. Perhaps Mordaunt wanted to ensure no one else knew about this part of the school.

Without hesitating, I begin down the long hall, grip tightening upon the handle of the axe. I pick the first one on the left. Locked. I heft the axe up high and bring it down into the wood near the knob as hard as I can. It splinters and cracks none too quietly. William and Mr. Hart jump. I repeat the action until the door gives completely and I can shove it open with one foot.

And then I move onto the next.

We want to get Mordaunt's attention, don't we?

I break them down in succession, until I've discarded my coat to avoid overheating. My shoulders burn in protest, and I have to stop to rest them and swipe the sweat from my forehead.

As I allow myself to recuperate, it gives me the opportunity to study the room of the door I've just kicked in. I stoop to pick up my own lantern and step inside for a better look.

At the far side of the room is a bed, not unlike the one in my own room, with a set of shackles latched to the iron frame, and a chamber pot crammed beneath. It's little more than a prison cell. I stop at the foot of the bed and touch the wall there, feeling the shallow grooves dug into the wood from years and years of someone desperate to claw their way to safety. Then my gaze drops to the mattress itself, and my breath is stolen away.

Clothing. Nothing I would look twice at any other day, except it's the familiarity of some of the fabric that catches my eye. Slowly, I place the lantern and axe on the floor, daring to pick up the waistcoat from the pile of bloodied rags.

The waistcoat I lent to Oscar the night of the ball, torn and bloodied.

I clamp a hand over my mouth to keep from crying out, tears blurring my vision. Was this how it ended for Oscar? Locked away in this miserable room, chained to the bed like some animal? Was he truly so close that I could have found him if I'd only...

I clutch the waistcoat to my chest, choking on the sound of a sob, wanting to call for William but unable to find my voice. Behind me, the floor creaks and I turn, desperate that William has come on his own and I can show him what I've discovered.

Instead, I am face to face with Mordaunt's scorching eyes.

The creature strikes me across the face with more force than a living man would be capable of. It knocks me clear off my feet. I collide with the ground hard enough the air is promptly displaced from my lungs. I choke in a breath. My nose fills with the scent of burning flesh and sends me into a fit of coughing.

Before I can attempt to get up, I'm met with a powerful, charred hand closing around my throat, and Mordaunt begins to haul me along, making it impossible for me to gain purchase on the floor in order to stand.

Out into the hallway it drags me, completely effortless in the action, and I see it's bringing me to the room at the end of the hall, whose door has opened wide and whose candles are burning bright. The same room I saw that poor boy's spirit being tortured in before. I cannot breathe around the smoke except to let out a single, strained cry.

It appears to be enough. Mr. Hart and William emerge from one of the other rooms. William's eyes go wide, and he damned near drops his lantern in his mad dash to get to me. But Mordaunt heaves me into the room. The door slams shut. I'm now separated from my companions.

Not good.

I cannot breathe, and the edges of my vision have begun to darken. I can only claw at the hand around my neck, chunks of burned flesh catching beneath my nails, and the feel of Mordaunt lifting me and cold steel clamping around my wrists.

It releases my throat, shackles and chains pulling taut, drawing my arms above my head. I'm left dangling with only my toes making contact with the floor. As my vision clears just enough, I can see the rows of tools lining the walls, better befitting a torture chamber than a school. Mordaunt has me strung up like a pig readied for butchering, and as he moves to the wall, I can hear the desperate voices of William and Mr. Hart from the other side of the door.

I pull against my restraints, which serves to do little beyond cutting painfully into my wrists. How many others stood in this place, just as I am, and how many died here? At its hands, at headmaster King's? The thought of it happening to anyone is horrid, but the thought of it happening to my best friend makes me sick to my stomach, and fury edges out the fear.

"Nicholas Mordaunt," I snarl. "That's your name, isn't it? You opened this school."

The creature stops, distracted, and turns to study me.

Speaking to it likely will do me no good but to buy some time, and if that's all I can do right now, then so be it. "How many have you murdered here? *Why?* Why are you doing any of this?"

From the wall, Mordaunt retrieves a cat o' nine tails and closes the gap between us, the smell of it filling my nose again, so overpowering I begin to hold my breath. It stops just before me, and its twisted mouth pulls back from blackened teeth in an ugly sneer. Then it leans in close, so unbearably close, so that I can see every detail of its shrivelled, piercing eyes and disfigured face, and hear the low, cracked sound of its voice when it speaks.

"Because...I...can."

There is nothing to brace me for the cat being brought down against my back. Nothing to stifle the scream of pain torn from my mouth. Because it is nothing like being beaten, nothing like taking a birching from the headmaster. There is no moment of reprieve to be had because the creature brings it across my skin again without pause.

Again

And again.

And again. Until I cannot see beyond the pain.

Again, until the moment wherein the door splinters wide open and the room floods with a most brilliant light amongst the shadows. Through my swimming vision and smoke, Mr. Hart's silhouette can be made out, axe clutched tightly. Around him steps William, and in his hands, he holds a long scrap of wood—from one of the broken doors, I'd wager— the end bound in sheet fabric and set aflame, granting him a far brighter light than any candle could offer.

And a much more effective weapon.

He marches forwards, thrusting his makeshift torch in the creature's direction. It recoils with a furious snarl.

With Mordaunt retreating to the corner of the room, William shouts, "Get him down!" He doesn't take his eyes off the creature, and as it begins to circle, so does William, keeping himself a steady barricade between it and me.

I cannot see Mr. Hart from my position, but I hear him moving behind me, searching the walls, and a relieved *Aha!* not a moment later. He rushes to my side, rising to jam the key into my shackles and releasing them. The sudden jostling sends pain shooting through my body anew, and he catches me so I don't immediately crumple to the floor.

"Are you all right? Can you walk?"

A shudder ricochets down my spine as I force myself to straighten up. Rather than answer his question, I grab William's free hand. "The other door," I manage. "We need to get it open." Going back the way we came, with Mordaunt currently between us and the hall, would be suicide. We cannot lead it back into the woods or anywhere near the cemetery. With any luck, Preston and the others will be making progress in their digging.

Please, Lord, let it be a shallow grave.

Mordaunt lingers by the exit, snarling. One by one the candles in the room proceed to die, plummeting us into darkness, save for the light of William's torch. It grows far darker than should be possible, a smoky, thick darkness that makes it difficult to breathe, and I can no longer see a single wall nor either door in the room. I drag William closer to me with one hand and Mr. Hart with the other—I can feel William's hand trembling in mine—attempting to keep us all within the small circle of safety the light offers.

"Straight back," Mr. Hart orders. "Towards the door."

Slowly, we make our way through the darkness, and I can feel the creature, *sense* it, just out of sight. An occasional flicker of smouldering red, a waft of burning flesh, fingers brushing dangerously close to my face, always out of the corner of my gaze.

Mr. Hart's hand finds the wall, and we inch left until he comes to the door. He grabs the doorknob, twists, and—"Locked."

Shit.

He wastes no time in lifting the axe to begin hacking away, but the process is difficult. We cannot put too much distance lest he be out of the protective circle of light that Mordaunt is still trying to figure out how to breach.

A look at William shows that the torch is on its last legs; it's begun to burn low, engulfing more of the wood than it should, and William's fingers are beginning to suffer the consequence.

"Give it here," I demand. He shoves me back behind him, unwilling to relinquish his hold.

The door caves after only a few strikes of the axe. Mr. Hart shoulders it open, grabs my arm, and shoves me through before reaching for William to do the same to him.

As we're herded through, William loses his battle with the torch. The flames lap across his hand and wrist. He cries out, forced to drop it and recoiling in pain. It's served its purpose. We're out of the darkness, spilled into a room filled with wide windows and moonlight, scuttling back and away from the door which we cannot, unfortunately, shut now that it's been broken, and a quick look around shows me where we are.

The headmaster's office.

I blink repeatedly to make certain I'm seeing things right. The same office I took a lashing in months ago. The same office Oscar came to again and again. The same office he may have entered and never left. At least, not through the same door.

It all clicks into place. How simple it would be for Mordaunt or King to render a student unconscious here and bring him through that hidden door into his own personal torture chamber? A boy gagged properly, perhaps even drugged, would never be able to cry for help. When he was done with them, he merely had to bring their remains through the tunnels and deposit their bodies into the woods. How he managed that alone, I don't know, but I flash back to the night I saw Charles Simmons slipping out of the dorm and I think I may have my answer.

I look to the windows, desperately wishing I could see the cemetery from here, to know if the others are still out there, if they're safe, if they're close to unearthing the body. Because where else can we go, what else can we do? How much further can we run before Mordaunt tires of giving chase and goes after them?

Smoke begins to billow in from the open doorway. Darkness has engulfed the torch William dropped, and any meagre hope I had that it may have set fire to the building itself is snuffed out as the light of it vanishes. The smoke smells of rot and decay, and with it comes that unearthly darkness that snakes its tendrils across the floor and walls, coating the windows and beginning to swallow our light whole.

From that darkness, Nicholas Mordaunt appears in the doorway with a hideous sneer.

Mr. Hart shoves us back behind him, arms outstretched. I hear him whispering the Lord's prayer beneath his breath.

We've no choice but to keep running. I push William towards the door, thinking if we can get outside, we might have a chance. We can lead it away from the school towards the first-year dorms, if necessary; a wide, open space with moonlight it cannot block out. I grab hold of the door and rip it open, positive we're so close to freedom—

I find myself face to face with King, and staring down the barrel of a revolver.

The sight of Maxwell King has me reeling back until my shoulder slams into Mr. Hart, who then whirls to see what's happened. We've become effectively trapped between the first headmaster of Whisperwood and the current. This does not bode well.

"You left," Mr. Hart says in shock. "Graham and I saw you."

"The point was to be seen," King agrees, stepping into the room and closing the door behind him. "I have to say, I'm *very* disappointed in you, Jonathan. I'm afraid this is going to affect your tenure."

Mr. Hart's expression turns cold. "Consider this my letter of resignation, you madman."

I wonder if I could move quickly enough, if I could grab his wrist, twist that gun from his grasp before he has a chance to pull the trigger. "How did you even know we were here?"

"This is my school. I know everything that goes on here," King chuckles. He still has the gun trained on me, and he jerks his chin in the direction of where we came. "Come now. All three of you, back into the other room."

"I'd sooner pitch myself out the window," I snarl.

His smile fades. "You know, I really should have dealt with you before I even bothered with Mr. Frances. Had I any idea you'd turn out to be such a thorn in my side…"

Fury rises like bile in the back of my throat, vicious and blinding. "It *was* you. You killed Oscar." Not Mordaunt, not Charles, but this flesh and blood human standing before me. He's the reason my best friend is gone. Whether he was influenced by Mordaunt or engaged of his own free will, I cannot say that I know nor care.

In that moment, Mordaunt does not matter. Neither does the gun in my face or anything else. I lunge for King with every intention of killing him with my bare hands if I get hold of him.

I don't make it more than a foot before Mordaunt intercepts, catching me by the throat and lifting me clear off the ground. He slams me to King's desk, sending a flurry of papers flying in all directions. The fingers digging into my neck render me motionless. From the corner of my gaze, I see William trying to rush towards me, stopped only by King shoving the revolver against his temple and instructing him to be still.

I strain against the burnt hand holding me in place. "Don't you *dare*."

"Hardly in a position to be making demands," King growls. "Jonathan, Mr. Esher, into the room, or I'll put a bullet in your fucking head."

"No, you won't," William says, his voice quaking.

King's expression darkens. "Is that a challenge?"

William speaks to King, but his eyes are locked on mine, as though seeking reassurance and courage. "You won't do it. You wanted the staff to think you'd left the grounds for the evening so that you could dispose of James and me, didn't you? You knew he'd be staying through holiday, you knew he was getting too close to the truth. But after all these years of being so careful not to get caught, to simply blow out our brains all over your office? Be a bit tricky to cover that one up." He slides his gaze over to King. God, I pray he's right. I'm praying King doesn't call his bluff and pull the trigger right now, just to prove him wrong.

Instead, King smiles.

That does not bode well, either.

He looks to Mordaunt and me, nothing but disgust upon his face. "...Kill him."

No sooner has he said those words than the creature's hand becomes a vice around my throat, no longer intending to hold me there, but intending to choke the very life from me. Its grip tightens so swiftly, so strongly, that I'm positive it will have snapped my neck before it suffocates me.

But the grip does not last long. William scarcely has a chance to cry my name before Mordaunt lets out the most unholy shriek and rips away from me as though he's been wounded. The sound shakes the building around us so violently that the paintings on the wall come loose, and books clatter from the shelves to the floor. I grip the edges of the desk while inhaling deeply, and William rushes to my side to help me up.

The creature grips its head, still screaming, so low and intense that it rattles me to my core, and even King has clamped his hands over his ears, eyes wide as he watches it thrash and struggle.

The body, I realise. *They've found the body.* Mordaunt is in pain, and if it's in pain, that means this just might be working after all.

King shouts above the sound, "What have you done?!"

I cannot help it; a sharp laugh bursts out of my chest, bitter and cold. "Must you ask? I thought you knew *everything.*"

Mordaunt's body bursts into flames, the light licking down every limb, chunks of fingers and arms and legs crumbling to ash, and the smell—

I remember standing in the kitchen of my home, striking a match and placing the flame to the curtains, watching numbly as it caught and spread. The brilliance of the firelight, how swiftly and silently it began to take over.

The smell, above all. The scent of burning.

Slowly, the darkness recoils. Shafts of moonlight begin to demand their way back in through the window, cutting through the smoke and, in the wake of their light, I see the first ghost.

The boy from the fields the night of the party. And then the boy who attacked me, and the boy who drowned Simmons.

Another, and another, every familiar face and several I've never seen, faces who guided us through the woods, the victims of Mordaunt and King and perhaps other headmasters in between. They watch from all the corners of the room, not daring to venture close but observing as Mordaunt is in its last throes, howling in pain.

King snarls furiously. He uncovers his ears, swinging the revolver around to William and me, and I am certain this time he fully intends to pull the trigger, and I haven't the time to react.

Another of the boys appears, a barrier between King and us, and the sudden sight of him has the old man startling and staggering back.

Mr. Hart takes the split second of time to lunge, grabbing hold of King's arm and wresting it up. The gun goes off, but the shot fires uselessly at the ceiling. King swears, and Mr. Hart twists the revolver from his grasp before stepping back. The barrel is now trained on the headmaster, although by the shaky way in which Mr. Hart fumbles with the revolver, I have a feeling he's never fired one in all his life. But King has been disarmed and appears too preoccupied with the ghost before him, and the others that have gathered, to care.

Mordaunt's remains continue to reduce to ashes, until there is nothing thing left but a thin layer of smoke and the remnants of burning flesh in the air. But it's gone, and I think that in its absence we have been joined by every victim of Whisperwood.

"What have you done?" King whispers.

The ghost before us snarls. In an instant, he stalks towards King, who presses himself back to the wall as though he wants to seep right through it. Without Mordaunt here, the ghosts are no longer afraid. He has no protection.

The boy thrusts a hand into the headmaster's chest. Although I cannot see it, I have a very clear image in my mind of cold, dead fingers wrapping around the old man's heart like a vice. King's eyes widen in terror, his mouth goes slack. He sinks to his knees with the ghostly hand still gripping his heart, squeezing the life out of him.

Finally, the ghost relinquishes his hold. King slumps to the floor, a vacant gaze staring forever off into nothing. A far kinder end for a man who did so much worse to others.

Mordaunt is destroyed. King is dead.

Somehow, by some grace of God, we are still alive.

William clings to my side. Mr. Hart has lowered the revolver, and I think to laugh, to ask him if he really knew how to work it well enough to shoot it. At least, until I see the look upon his face, the way his free hand slowly lifts to his mouth as he stares at the ghostly figure of the boy who saved us.

In that moment, I needn't see his face. I know who it is, because who else would have come to look after us? The name catches in my throat as I straighten and step towards him, with William still holding fast to my arm as though we need to hold one another up to remain standing.

"Oscar..."

At the sound of his name, he turns. His eyes are still as clear and bright as they've always been. I realise all of the ghosts are. No longer are they the faces of dead boys with contorted, tortured expressions, but the faces of boys who have been brought peace. They all look to us, full of tired smiles and relief. And, one by one, each of them is slowly heading for the door and vanishing from sight.

All except for Oscar, who remains behind while my voice has all but abandoned me. I want desperately to reach out and touch his shoulder, to beg for his forgiveness, and every word of it catches in my throat.

I wonder if he hears it all the same, because his head tilts and he smiles, warm and open and a little ridiculous, just as he did the day I first walked into our room and he bounded over to greet me. This is the smile I wish to hold dear in my memories for the rest of my life. This is how I want to remember Oscar. He turns to Mr. Hart then, who lets the revolver hit the floor as he steps closer.

"Oh," he says, so achingly soft and sad. "Dear boy. I am so, so sorry."

Oscar shakes his head, smiling still. Although he doesn't expressly speak, I can still feel what he's conveying. *It's all right. I'm all right.*

Then he turns, heads for the door, and vanishes, just like all the others. He exits our lives the way he came into them: full of light and with a smile upon his face.

30

Mr. McLachlan greets us on the path leading back to the dorms, and the relief upon his face is palpable as he rushes over.

"I thought I heard gunfire. Is everyone all right?"

He brings one hand to Mr. Hart's shoulder and another to William's as he scans the three of us for serious injury. William's burned hand needs tending to, and my own back does not look good, judging by the expressions on William's and Mr. Hart's faces when they examined it. Fair enough. Doesn't feel great, either.

More than anything, I'm exhausted. Physically, emotionally. We've won, even if I feel King got off easy. Death was a kindness compared to spending the rest of his years locked away.

"We're all right." Mr. Hart rests a hand over his friend's with a reassuring smile. I wonder if he'll tell Mr. McLachlan later that, in his pocket, he carries the letter the headmaster had of Oscar's. Before leaving King's office, I made it a point to root through his desk to find it, wanting to ensure no one else came across it. In the end, as much as I would have preferred to keep it myself, it belongs with the person it was meant for. It's what Oscar would have wanted.

When he reads it, I wonder what he'll think, how he'll feel. Guilt? Regret? Will it be something he thinks often? Because whether Oscar forgives me or not, I will think of him and all the ways I've let him down every day for the rest of my life.

Mr. McLachlan keeps close to Mr. Hart's side as he ushers us back to the dorms. He doesn't tell us anything that occurred on their end, for which I'm grateful, because I'm not certain I would remember any of it later anyway. So long as everyone is safe, that's all that matters.

Inside the second-floor common room, our companions appear unscathed. Rattled, covered in mud, and soaked to the bone, but safe. Virgil wastes no time in sitting William and me down to assess our injuries. It requires Mr. McLachlan taking a trip back to the main building to fetch some supplies, and to rouse the servants and send someone to town so the police can be summoned.

When he returns with medical supplies, Virgil orders us to my room so that I can let him strip my shirt—the back of which is shredded to ribbons and blood-soaked—and have me lie face-down in bed while he tends to me.

The pain radiates through every inch of my body, but it becomes a familiar ache, and despite it I almost doze off a few times as he cleans my wounds and stitches shut the worst of them. William is across the room, still cradling his hand, and by the look upon his face, I can tell he's in a similar state of hurting and being too exhausted to care.

"Afraid these are going to leave some nasty scars," Virgil murmurs.

I sigh. "I'm not needing to have a bullet pulled out of me, so I'll consider this a victory."

"Fair enough."

"What about all of you?"

"Not needing bullets removed, either."

"You know what I mean."

Virgil chuckles, which is an odd sound coming from him because I don't think I've ever heard him laugh. Or smile. Or do much more than scowl. "We're fine. However, let it be known none of us wish to ever become gravediggers and I feel those in the profession are severely underpaid."

I start to laugh, and the movement sets the worst of the pain alight again and makes me wince. "And the body?"

"We were lucky. About three feet deep, little left of it, really. We bundled it up, brought it to the common room, and threw it in the fireplace."

Lucky, indeed. Had the grave been even a foot deeper, I'm not certain I would be here having this conversation with him right now.

He draws back finally and turns his attention to William. As much as I struggle to keep my eyes open to listen and watch, I find myself swiftly drifting off. I'm only vaguely aware of being disturbed when William joins me in bed sometime later; he kisses my forehead and whispers that he loves me.

The best words one can fall asleep to.

31

Morning comes far earlier than I would like by someone knocking insistently upon my door. I've slept on my stomach all night, which has resulted in a most painful crick in my neck. Moving is a chore. Every muscle aches something fierce, and I can feel where my stitches are pulling. Were someone to walk in and see William and I in bed together, it wouldn't look the greatest. I cannot bring myself to give a damn right now.

William appears far more alert than I, although he lets out a groan in protest as he slowly drags himself out of bed. Unlike me, he got changed last night, and he shuffles stiffly for the door to pull it open and greet whoever is on the other side.

"How is he?" Preston whispers.

"Awake, so you needn't whisper," I call out tiredly.

Preston peers past William to me. "In that case, both of you are being asked for."

"By who?"

"The police." Preston glances down the hall and wedges his way inside past William. "Surely you didn't think they'd find a dead headmaster with a door to his hidden chambers wide open without them having some questions?"

A bitter laugh escapes my throat and I close my eyes. Far too early. "Mm. I wonder how poorly this will go over."

"They've already gotten statements from the rest of us, Mr. Hart and Mr. McLachlan included."

Ah. Hell. "How much of the story did you leave out?"

Preston crouches at my bedside to peer into my face when I open my eyes. He smiles a little. "Maxwell King, were he still alive, would be going to jail for the death of Oscar Frances right about now. Charles Simmons and Doctor Albert Mitchell are to be charged as accessories to murder. They have reason to believe Simmons assisted with disposing of the body, and that Doctor Mitchell has helped to cover up past student deaths and disappearances."

It's really, really too early for this. I swallow back the taste of bile creeping up my throat. I should have knocked Charles' teeth out when I had the chance. I wonder if Preston knows how Oscar died. If the police have given us that much information. I wonder if it's something I should even ask about, or if such knowledge will only serve to torment me. "And?"

"And Mr. Hart and Mr. McLachlan's testimonies reveal you and William were taken prisoner after discovering the truth, and you were able to get free."

"No ghosts, then."

"No ghosts."

I take a deep breath and turn my face to bury it into the pillow. It smells of rain and sweat, but also a little like William, which is pleasant. "Give us a bit to make ourselves presentable and we'll be down."

Preston takes his leave. William assists me in sitting up. Rather than stand, I perch on the edge of the mattress and draw my arms around his middle, leaning in to rest my head against his stomach. He coaxes his fingers—at least, the ones that aren't bandaged—through my hair. When I open my eyes and spot our reflection in the mirror across the room, I almost laugh.

"We both look absolutely frightful."

"Justifiable, I should think." William smiles though, faintly. "How do you feel?"

"Sore. Here's hoping Doctor Mitchell's supplies contain something for the pain."

"I imagine so, but I didn't necessarily mean physically."

"Frustrated, I suppose. I feel as though we're still lacking a great many answers. Why did Mordaunt do what he did, for instance? Why did King follow in his footsteps? Why couldn't the spirits just tell us what to do or how to help them from the very beginning?"

"Perhaps," William says solemnly, "those are questions we will never know the answer to. We might have to make peace with that."

I suppose he's right. I'll never know what started Mordaunt down the path he took, how he was caught, who was responsible for putting an end to him, or what granted him the ability to come back and torment others from beyond the grave. I will never know exactly how Oscar spent his last days, how afraid he must have been, or if there was anything I could have done to prevent what happened to him.

I suppose none of it matters in the grand scheme of things. Oscar and the other boys of Whisperwood are free. I helped him find justice and peace. I did what I set out to do.

I tip my head back to peer up at William. "Then all of that aside, I think...I am both sad and happy at once, and wondering how to reconcile the two."

William's mouth curves up into a patient smile and he brings his hands to my face. "With time, darling. With time. And I will be there with you every step of the way."

14 MONTHS LATER

"Keep them closed, dear William. Wait until we're inside."
I heave a suffering sigh, but do as instructed, permitting James to guide me by the hand out of the carriage, along some sort of stone walkway, and across a threshold into wherever it is he's brought me. As though I'm not covering my eyes well enough, he slips behind me and puts his palms over them, draws me to a stop, and says, "Are you ready?"

"Ready to break those hands if you don't move them," I reply with far more patience than my harsh words suggest.

James releases me, allowing me to take in the room around us.

The first things I notice are the high ceilings and a narrow staircase leading to the first floor. James appears to be giving me free rein to wander now, and I do so, moving through the foyer and into the adjoining rooms.

The second, but more important thing, is how wonderfully bright and airy it is. The windows are tall and wide, cracked open to allow in a cool breeze. There's space for a parlour, complete with shelves itching to be filled, a modest kitchen, and two rooms on the first floor, both with lovely views of the countryside stretching in every direction.

The word *quaint* comes to mind. Certainly, it's a small home compared to those James and I grew up in, but that's the trade-off. Either you live in the city and have a bigger home for less and deal with the poor air quality and the stench, or you pay for something much smaller but more expensive out here in the middle of nowhere.

As I find myself admiring the view from the larger of the two bedrooms, taking in the fields of flowers that seem to go on for miles, James slips up behind me, fingers splayed against the small of my back.

"It's quite cosy," he says against my ear. "Isolated, too. We'd not have to worry about being bothered. Room enough for the both of us, perhaps even a servant, if we wish. Though I suppose we could manage on our own, as well."

I could laugh at that, imagining James or myself attempting to handle laundry or cooking. We're hardly well-versed in such things. "It *is* lovely," I admit.

James watches me intently. "But...?"

I sigh. "How do you suppose we're going to afford it?" Neither of us is currently employed, after all. Newly graduated, no university education. James received nothing from his family after refusing to make amends with his uncle, and what I received from mine is…well, likely enough to pay for the house itself. But what of the cost of upkeep, and keeping food in our bellies?

A slow, sweet smile crosses James' face and he rocks back on his heels. It's a gesture that comes across as more nervous and hopeful than anything and does not bode well.

He reaches into his pocket and removes from it a letter, folded in quarters, and offers it out to me. Already, I feel my face pulling into a most unimpressed look. "What is that?"

"Read it and find out."

"I don't think I want to." Yet I take it, slipping it open with a sigh.

The writing is elegant but unfamiliar. It's addressed to James and myself, and implies that it is a response to a letter written, although I'm positive I've not sent letters to anyone in recent memory.

> *I would be pleased to accept your offer to become my pupils, as I am frequently turning down work I haven't the time for, and the added assistance would be most welcome.*

I frown, skimming over the remainder of the text. An address, an invitation to visit to speak more, and signed by one Eleanor Bennett. "I'm afraid I don't understand. Who is this?"

James presses his palms together and touches his fingers to his chin, eyebrows lifting and a nervous smile tugging at his mouth. "Mrs. Bennett is Preston's aunt."

"All right." I pause, mulling that over, trying to place the significance of it, before— "Wait. His aunt, the *medium?*"

"That would be the one."

"You want us to go work alongside a medium, purposely seeking out ghosts? Have you *completely* lost your mind?"

"Oh, don't be like that." He swiftly gathers me up into his arms, quite possibly so I don't throw the letter in his face. "We'd be quite wonderful, wouldn't we? We have the first-hand experience, and she could bestow her knowledge upon us. Between my tenacity and your brilliance, we could become the best in all of England. The spirits are particularly drawn to you, after all. Think of all the people we could help!"

I stare at him as though he's grown two heads, and I suspect that he might at any moment. After what happened at Whisperwood over a year ago, I would have thought he'd be too terrified to ever put us in such a situation again.

And yet, he has a point. Neither of us would be happy with whatever meagre, monotonous work we might find, crammed in some miserable and dusty old home in the city, where our personal affairs would surely be the talk of the town. After everything we've been through together, after having survived our fourth year of school while hiding our relationship, I've no desire to be persecuted for it now.

Besides, James' handsome face is so hopeful and eager that I cannot seem to pull together any real reason to tell him no. At least not yet.

I sigh. "You're impossible and I hate you."

"And?"

"And I suppose it wouldn't hurt to have a meeting with Mrs. Bennett, just to hear her out."

James grins and kisses me so solidly upon the mouth that it serves to soothe my frazzled nerves a bit. He has that effect on me. Damn him. He holds me to his chest, and together we look out over the fields of flowers.

"This could be ours, dear William. We could make it work. Would a poem further convince you?"

"Maybe, maybe not, but I would enjoy seeing you try."

He chuckles, bows his head to my ear, and he murmurs to me like a hymn that sends a shiver down my spine:

"*Come.*

Home."

Two simple words, and I should think it ridiculous a poem exists such as that, and yet I don't question him on it. Two simple words, and I close my eyes with a smile.

"Darling, I *am* home."

FROM THE AUTHORS

very book brings about its own set of unique challenges, and this one was no exception. Tackling a historical setting for the first time was a daunting enough task, but adding on the extra layers of addressing certain societal issues in that setting? It was pretty scary.

One of the challenges was addressing William's addiction in an era where "addiction" was seen as more of an inherent character flaw than something that needed fixing. We wanted to write it in a way that was both realistic to the period while remaining sensitive to the issue. We faced a similar dilemma with James and his trauma. Yet again, we're talking about a time where sexual assault was largely ignored, and victim-blaming was even more rampant than it is today. Of course, William and James aren't done facing these demons. Especially without much in the way of mental health care in the late 19th century, you're going to see the effects of these things, and the struggles they face to overcome them, for a long while.

A more technical challenge is maintaining a sense of historical realism while making it easy enough to read and follow for readers of today. This meant walking a line between overdoing the popular British slang of the era, especially for posh schoolboys, and not wanting things to sound *too* American.

The amount of research, time, and love that went into this book was totally worth it. We put a piece of ourselves into everything we write, but James and William's story is one of my favorites. We love their characters, their flaws, their big hearts, and who they are together—now and in the future. We like to think we've created a dynamic that's going to be really special in the stories to come.

We owe a ton of thanks for those who lent a hand in this journey. Natalie, Lacy, Beedoo!, Jamie, Jada, and Jon, who edited, beta-read, and fact-checked, and caught all the most ridiculous and embarrassing typos and Kelley's insane overuse of ellipses. (They're fun, okay!) They really were a dream team and we couldn't have asked for better. And, of course, a thank you to Melissa at *The Illustrated Author* for her gorgeous work on formatting. The moment we saw her portfolio, we both knew we wanted her for this book.

I hope our readers enjoy this story as much as we enjoyed writing it. William, James, and some of their friends will see you again soon.

Kelley and Rowan

Printed in Great Britain
by Amazon

86524376R00196